LOST ILLUSIONS:
*Latin America's Struggle
for Democracy, as
Recounted by its Leaders*

LOST ILLUSIONS

Latin America's Struggle
for Democracy, as
Recounted by its Leaders

BY

Paul H. Boeker

Institute of
the Americas,
La Jolla

Markus Wiener
Publishing,
New York

For information write to:

Institute of the Americas
10111 North Torrey Pines Road
La Jolla, CA 92037

or

Markus Wiener Publishing, Inc.
225 Lafayette Street
New York, NY 10012

Library of Congress Cataloging-in-Publication Data

Lost illusions : Latin America's struggle for democracy, as recounted by its leaders / by Paul H. Boeker.
    Includes bibliographical references.
    ISBN 1-55876-023-7—ISBN 1-55876-024-5 (pbk.)
    1. Latin America—Politics and government—1980-
2. Representative government and representation—Latin America—History—20th century. 3. Statesmen—Latin America—Interviews.
1. Boeker, Paul H.
F1414.2L67 1989
320.98—dc20   89-27993
                                                CIP

Cover Photo: Santiago, Chile; October 6, 1988—Chileans pass by policemen as they celebrate in downtown Santiago the triumph of the "NO" vote in the plebiscite with which Chile's military dictator Augusto Pinochet sought in vain to extend his 15-year rule for eight more years. (Courtesy: Reuters/Bettmann Newsphotos)

Book Design by Cheryl Mirkin

Copy Editing by Daniel Marcus

This book is printed on acid-free paper.

Printed in the United States of America

320.98
L881
1990

FOREWORD

As a graduate student at Oxford in Latin American studies, I learned an invaluable lesson which this collection of interviews by Paul Boeker clearly validates. I was writing an essay on Joaquín Balaguer's first presidential term in the Dominican Republic, naively trying to analyze him according to the dogma then prevalent in academia. The don reviewing my work made a signal suggestion: "The only way you will ever understand Balaguer and his potential will be to talk to him directly. Any other approach to him or any other Latin leader is of limited use." I promptly got on a plane, flew to Santo Domingo, and returned with a prized essay.

When the Board of the Institute of the Americas was recruiting Paul Boeker in late 1987 for the presidency, he made a suggestion which had significant appeal. Latin America was undergoing a democratic revolution. The purpose of the Institute of the Americas is to facilitate the democratic dialogue. Why not inaugurate the new president's tenure with a series of meetings wherein he, as representative of our Institute, could hear directly the Latin side of the story?

When Paul joined the Institute as President, the Board promptly took up his suggestion. We arranged two whirlwind tours in the summer of 1988 for him to meet nine existing heads of government, ten former presidents, and six opposition leaders (one of whom has since been elected president). This book is a product of those meetings. No other individual has had the opportunity to meet and discuss the democratic challenge with the main actors on the Latin American stage. Paul Boeker's interviews, conducted with a skillful diplomacy and recorded without editorial manipulation, provide an invaluable resource to policy makers and academics throughout the hemisphere. We publish it proudly with the hope that others will use it and the other resources of the Institute in achieving a better understanding of the realities of the democratic transition in Latin America.

Richard W. Fisher
Chairman
Board of Directors

Contents

Democracy Without Illusions

Profiles and Interviews

The United States and Latin American Democracy

Democracy Without Illusions

Democracy is the worst form of government, except all those other forms that have been tried from time to time.
                    Winston Churchill, November 11, 1947

As Winston Churchill said, 'democracy is the least bad system of government,' so in the end I voted 'no' to Pinochet.
                    Santiago, Chile taxi driver, October 8, 1988

A quiet revolution has swept Latin America in the last decade, a revolution not of dreamers but of jaded realists. After repeated disappointment with flamboyant leaders of varied political coloration, people are looking to a system, not a personality, to protect their rights. In Latin America today, the system in which people are putting their trust is democracy, combined with private initiative in a free market. Over ninety percent of the people of Latin America now live under democratically elected governments, whereas a dozen years ago military dictatorship was the norm. The deep economic stagnation in which past free-spending policies have now left much of Latin America mired have also spawned a widespread indictment of big government and a broad, if still incomplete, turn to local control and private enterprise.

In this quiet revolution, the political force, people's demand to control their own governance, is the dominant one—as General Pinochet discovered in Chile to his own surprise. He may have been more successful than other Latin leaders in producing prosperity by unleashing the wonders of the market, but that alone could not get him extended in power in a plebiscite. On October 5, 1988, Chileans rejected Pinochet's bid to stay in power and chose the right to pick their own leader in open elections in December 1989.

Winston Churchill's dictum is the most quoted and misquoted commentary on democracy in Latin America today. Not only

1

the Santiago taxi driver but also several chiefs of state used Churchill's adage in describing to me the spirit of Latin America's unromantic embrace of democracy today: a democracy without illusions.

The story of Latin America's democratic revival is one best told by the Latin Americans themselves who have guided it and lived through it. It is a heartening story, with many examples of courage and personal sacrifice as well as great political skill. It is one Americans should understand if they are to deal effectively with four hundred million people to the south who are undergoing a philosophical revolution which puts them closer to the United States than the U.S. yet recognizes. That is the point of this book, which introduces twenty-six of the key figures of Latin America's democracy today through personal interviews in which they give their story and perspective on the passage to democracy in their country and the threats their struggling democracies still face.

It is a story in which the United States plays a part. Most of these Latin Americans give the United States some credit for encouraging their country's passage to democracy. But they also fault the U.S. for a lack of understanding and attention to the main threat to Latin America's re-won democracy today: persistent economic stagnation and declining standards of living; the economies of most of Latin America have been stuck in neutral since the recession of 1982–83.

The corrosive effect of economic stagnation and inflation on the political popularity of many current governments raises a key question for Latin America and for U.S. interests. How durable is Latin America's democratic revival? Many Latin American countries have suffered repeated cycles of civilian government gone sour followed by military coups. Is the striking prevalence of elected civilian government in Latin America today just one more phase of that historic cycle or has a new trend been set? And, if a new trend appears under way, what has changed that would make it a durable one?

Argentina and Chile may be the first places to look for what has changed. Argentina's passage to democracy, and the one now under way in Chile, present some sharp breaks with the past which have reverberated throughout Latin America. In the past military officers have been largely immune for their political actions, whether overthrowing a constitutional government or killing people outside the law while in government. In October of

1979, for example, a frustrated and unstable Bolivian colonel took over the palace in La Paz and deposed a constitutionally elected president. The colonel ordered troops loyal to him to try to disperse unarmed demonstrators against his coup by indiscriminate automatic weapons' fire into crowds. Several hundred people were killed in twelve days before the colonel recognized his coup would not be consolidated and retired to his farm, inviting the Bolivian congress to meet and form a civilian government. No investigation of several hundred unnecessary deaths was launched, and no judicial action was initiated against the colonel.

As American ambassador I had helped the Bolivians turn back this brutal coup by cutting off all U.S. aid to the government and refusing to recognize or deal with the colonel. As the colonel walked away scot-free, I, in disbelief, confronted my Bolivian friends with two questions. How can you let a military officer get away with this? How can you ever stop the next colonel from doing the same thing if you do not make this one pay? The reply was: they have the guns and we have only the law.

In Argentina since 1984 the law has been used against the guns. Everywhere in Latin America military officers have followed the trials of their former Argentine colleagues with a concealed fascination and shocked sense that something fundamental has changed. Between 1978 and 1982 eleven thousand people "disappeared" in military jails, never to emerge, as the Argentine military waged a dirty war against guerrillas and their presumed sympathizers. This time the mothers of the disappeared would not forgive or forget and defiantly plastered the walls of Buenos Aires with photographs of those taken from their homes and gone without trace or accounting. When the disastrous defeat of Argentina in the war over the Falklands/Malvinas Islands precipitated the rapid collapse of military government under the weight of its own incompetence, an accounting was finally possible. But it took political courage to get it.

A brave country lawyer, Raúl Alfonsín, (p. 55), ran for president on a platform demanding that the military officers responsible for the disappeared be brought to justice. He could have concluded, as his opponent did, that the risk of provoking the military into a new coup and cancellation of elections was too great to permit a call for justice (the classic Latin calculation). But Alfonsín took the risk and won. Senior military officers, including a former president, were tried, convicted, and incarcerated. Three times during Alfonsín's term military units revolted

to try to bring a halt to the trials and win amnesty for the convicted, but the judicial process was sustained and a fateful message delivered.[1]

The repercussions have been felt elsewhere. In Uruguay over
600,000 signatures on a popular petition forced a national referendum on an amnesty law which held Uruguay's ex-military rulers
immune from prosecution. In Chile key leaders of the opposition
to Pinochet, such as Christian Democrat Gabriel Valdés (p. 21),
insist there must be a reckoning for those responsible for Chile's
"disappeared."

The Chilean opposition's stunning defeat of General Pinochet
in the October 1988 plebiscite reflects two other breaks with the
past. Latin America has witnessed many transitions from military
to civilian government in which enlightened military officers, for
their own reasons, have negotiated a graceful exit with some enlightened civilians. Such transitions tend to leave an uncontrite
military in the wings, ready to come back when called, even if
they place the call themselves. In Chile in 1988, and Argentina
in 1983, military government was rejected resoundingly by the
populace, with a sense it was being sent not into opposition, but
into exile and maybe into history. Venezuela's new president,
Carlos Andrés Pérez (p. 130), bases his confidence in the future
of democracy in South America largely on this phenomenon;
as he says, "the important examples of recent transition to democracy were not a result of pacts between some military and
some civilians, but rather the result of a resounding triumph on
the part of the whole civilian society which withdrew all support
from the military dictatorships."

The Chilean plebiscite also re-wrote the book on military government and economic policy in Latin America. Conservative
business interests in Chile and other Latin American countries
actually expected Pinochet to win the plebiscite because his stern
policies had produced three years of more rapid economic growth
and moderate inflation than elsewhere in Latin America. The
chamber-of-commerce wisdom was that forceful government
which could bang heads together, mainly union heads, was
needed to get Latin America out of its economic stagnation. The
Chilean people sent a message to the chambers of commerce that

---

[1]In October 1989, Alfonsín's successor Carlos Menem pardoned those officers
still awaiting trial. He left standing the sentences of those officers, including a
former president, already convicted for human rights abuses under the military
government.

their conservative wisdom addresses the wrong question. The Chilean people, like people in virtually the rest of Latin America, have made a basic choice for democratic government; the economic question is thus how to produce growth and low inflation within a democracy.

The driving force in the renaissance of democracy in Latin America has been broad popular demand for individual rights and a conviction that dictatorship in any form cannot consistently respect and guarantee those rights. It is a modern Jeffersonianism which some American historians say has little place in Hispanic tradition. But the drive to have a voice in one's own fate has a lot to do with human nature, which seems more important. Latin America today talks of universal rights and of the political philosophy which unites, not divides, the hemisphere. Gabriel Valdés (p. 32) puts it eloquently:

> Whatever common foundation there may be for relations among the United States, Canada and Latin America, it is not related to our external defense, anti-communism or other such circumstantial things, but rather more profound ones. The foundation is a shared concept of the liberties to which every individual has a right, including freedom of expression, freedom of association, freedom of thought, freedom to write; the right to a free press and to establish political parties; respect for minority views and the concept that the state serves the people. The idea of private ownership flows from this concept, as well as the right of labor to organize and the right to practice one's religious beliefs.
>
> The defense of human rights is to me a modern process of the last twenty years, propagated in particular by the United Nations and other organizations which defend democracy. It has a moral basis in the early history of the American continent. . . . Civil liberties should have priority over everything else a state may wish to do. . . . A dictatorship is a foreign body which arises by virtue of violating certain rights. . . . No dictatorship can ever respect human rights.

The widespread demand in Latin America for respect for human rights, cheered on from the sidelines by U.S. policy under Carter and Reagan, has led inevitably to Valdés' Jeffersonian conclusion: only democracy can consistently provide people the means to protect their own rights. The drive for human rights has in turn broadened Latin Americans' concept of democracy far beyond the generals' narrow one of elections and civilian rulers. In line with Valdés' fuller concept, Latin Americans tend to view democracy through the prism of rights, political freedoms, and constitutional guarantees. Regular free elections at all levels of government are seen as part of the means to protect those rights and freedoms, not as the end in themselves.

Collapse or popular rejection of military government are not the whole story of Latin America's passage to democracy. The progressive military officer on the other side of the table has played an important part in several negotiated transitions. Their side of the story is told here by four officers who themselves, as heads of military governments, launched transitions to elected civilian government.

General Hugo Medina (p. 77) in Uruguay had to recalculate the price at which the military was willing to give up power after the Uruguayan people stunned them in a 1980 referendum with an unexpected rejection of the military's offer of a "controlled" half-democracy. "No thanks; we'll take the whole thing," was the Uruguayans' response. It still took five years of negotiation to bring the military to accept full democracy. General Medina himself is refreshingly blunt in his sage conclusion that Uruguay's military is unsuited for governing and ought to stay out of it. General Ernesto Geisel (p. 265) in Brazil launched a protracted transition, still incomplete, which tries to solve the problem of the military's lack of confidence in politicians by dealing the generals into a continuing role in a civilian government, with what success still an open question.

General Francisco Morales Bermúdez (p. 155) in Peru and Admiral Alfredo Poveda (p. 237) in Ecuador represent the more traditional cases of progressive military presidents negotiating a graceful exit for military, institutional reasons and taking an unrepentant military into reserve, if not opposition. Neither in the nature of this kind of transition nor in the views of Peru's and Ecuador's military as reflected by these two progressive officers, does one find any basis to close the book on military government in these two Andean countries. In fact Morales Bermúdez predicts a coup in Peru if the Marxist-led United Left wins the 1990 elections.

The main line of this story, however, concerns the civilian leaders of Latin America's democratic realism. They are a remarkably different breed from the screeching Latin populists of a generation ago, who seemed to live on a political diet of denouncing Yankee imperialism and foreign investors and pursued an economic program of nationalizing almost anything that worked. Few Latin Americans today are impressed by such grandstanding, "balcony politics" as some of the Latins call it. The one Latin leader who has tried this old demagoguery, Alan García in Peru, has been a political flop in the reviews of his own people. Even politicians from left of center go to pains to distance themselves from the approach of Alan García, as Ecuador's president Rodrigo Borja does (p. 261).

Latin electorates today are focused on the performance of their leaders in terms of democratic reforms, jobs, and price stability. Latin Americans do not believe that either demagoguery, magical recipes, or bearding foreign devils will get them what they want from their leaders. The former Argentine publisher and political prisoner, Jacobo Timmerman, captures this point in his characterization of the candidates for president in Argentina's May 1989 elections.

> The charismatic magicians who were a recurrent presence in Argentine politics, with their posture as irreplaceable proclaimers of wealth and happiness, have been replaced by one of the keys to democratic life: Politics is not an essential activity nor can it correct years of economic stagnation and lack of organization. Argentines finally are obliged to practice politics without hope of a miracle. The three candidates are gray, their histories are unexciting and no one believes anymore that a presidential election can turn into a magical act that will resolve the nation's problems.[2]

Peru's former President Fernando Belaúnde Terry (p. 176) reflects the same jaded realism in talking about Peru's coming choice of political leaders. "I don't believe in genies. Here (in Peru) we have a profound structural problem. The solution is to be found not in one political alternative or another but in a plan and a lot of hard work over many years."

The political leaders demanded by electorates' realistic frame of mind are pragmatic seekers of technical solutions and tireless deal makers and consensus builders. Oscar Arias, Costa Rica's young president (p. 105), describes just such politicians when he cites the essence of democracy as "negotiation, deal making, knowing how to be flexible, being tolerant, rejecting absolute

---

[2]"Peronism, Without Violence," Jacobo Timmerman, *The New York Times*, July 1988.

truths and searching for consensus." In his regional diplomacy Arias has been just such a tireless pursuer of the possible deal.

The most successful of Latin America's politicians domestically have also been such patient, pragmatic dealers. Julio Sanguinetti succeeded as president of Uruguay by pursuing the substance and atmosphere of continual deal-making. He patiently negotiated with the military over five years to achieve a transition which left the military as committed as the political parties to its success. As president he carefully kept in continual dialogue with all major opposition parties, giving them a visibility and respect which was reflected in the constraint of their opposition.

Julio Sanguinetti is more typical of Latin America's successful politicians than Oscar Arias. For the primary focus of Latin America's politicians is inward, on resolving their countries' own economic stagnation. This concentration of political energies on the domestic economic task is one of the few favorable effects of Latin America's pervasive economic crisis. And it too is a break with the past. As Julio Sanguinetti notes (p. 98), Latin Americans' "personal inclinations and our romantic tendency sometimes prevent us from pragmatically facing economic realities." And campaign speeches, as former Ecuadoran President Osvaldo Hurtado says (p. 247), tended to be "rhetorical and literary, only alluding to specific economic and social problems;" but politicians competing for election today are forced to "rational debate of economic problems," because that is the core of people's concerns.

Virtually every one of the nine current Latin American presidents speaking through this book sees economic growth and price stability as his major challenge and economic stagnation and inflation as the main threats to his government and democracy in his country. Despite his historic political achievements, Raúl Alfonsín ended his term with broad popular rejection of his party because of his failure to stem Argentina's hyperinflation. The one current leader who has spent much of his effort on foreign policy, Oscar Arias, finds himself under relentless congressional pressure to redirect his energies to domestic problems—to the extreme that the Costa Rican Congress frequently denied him its authorization to travel abroad, including a trip to the inauguration of Mexico's president in December 1988.

As Latin Americans and their leaders look inward to confront their economic crisis, classical populism, which former Venezuelan president Rafael Caldera has aptly called "a drive for quick

fixes," has not seemed to offer the responses consonant with the
wary, skeptical mood of most of Latin America today. Latin
America's populists have historically offered an illusion of prosperity through quick strokes by government: mandated wage increases, subsidized food, nationalizatiòn of the holdings of carefully selected scapegoats. But most Latins no longer believe
reshuffling of shares in a stagnant economy will solve their real
problems, nor do they automatically look to government as the
instrument of their salvation. Even Carlos Menem, whose campaign slogans drew on populist themes, rode to power more on
the basis of the Radical government's failure than any popular
confidence in Menem's vague policy line in the campaign.

In response to the recognized failure of big government to lead
Latin America out of its economic stagnation, there has been a
striking shift in the philosophical approach of Latin America's
leaders to the government's role in society and the economy. Big
government, nationalized industries, regulation, price controls,
and import barriers are in decline. Budget cutting, selling state
enterprises to private investors, deregulation and open markets
are on the rise. Even Argentina, where successive administrations over the last fifty years have extended the pervasive government role in the economy, is awakening to the costs of this failed
approach. Both major parties' candidates for president in Argentina's 1989 elections advocated further "privatization" of government enterprises and the winner, Carlos Menem, began his administration with a bold announcement of his plans to privatize
one of the largest state enterprises, the national telephone
company.

In Peru, presidential candidate Mario Vargas Llosa (p. 181) got
his start in politics by mobilizing massive popular rallies to block
nationalization of Peru's banks. He calls Peru's government, "an
immense inefficiency," "a source of great ineptitude and corruption," and says that "the less aid that passes through the hands
of the state, the better." His message sounds more like Ronald
Reagan in 1980 than traditional Latin politics. Vargas Llosa and
a former colleague, Hernando de Soto, founded one of Peru's
most dynamic private institutions today, the Movement for Liberty and Democracy. The movement devotes itself to exposing
the tangle of Peru's bureaucracy, law, and regulation which have
forced much of its poorer people to seek their livelihood outside
the legal economy.

In much of Latin America there is also a strong drive to turn central government functions and resources over to state and local governments and to make the latter more representative and responsive to local concerns: bringing government closer to the people, in Reagan's terms. This "new federalism" is a marked change for Latin America, where the central government has traditionally controlled most tax resources and appointed the local officials to spend them. In 1988, Colombia for the first time elected thousands of mayors nationwide, with such success that both major candidates in Venezuela's presidential election next door found themselves pressed to support election of mayors there, which has now been legislated. Devolution of authority and resources to local government is now under way in Latin America's two largest countries. Both President Sarney of Brazil (p. 275) and President Salinas of Mexico (p. 115) launched ambitious programs to put more resources in the hands of regional and local government.

Latin Americans have in general awakened to their political rights and demanded more voice in their own governance at all levels. They have lost some of their traditional cynicism over "the system" and their inability to change it. They recognize that their vote can count and increasingly insist that it does. Pinochet counted on high registration fees and voter apathy to limit the turnout in his October 1988 plebiscite. But over ninety percent of those eligible to register did so, and ninety-seven percent of these actually voted—most of them against Pinochet.

Even in Mexico, where cynicism about the individual's impotence in the face of the system has been endemic, a powerful shift in political consciousness has occurred. Mexicans now sense that their vote can count and insist that it be counted correctly. Carlos Salinas de Gortari was elected president of Mexico in 1988 in elections which involved a smaller amount of vote tampering than in a long series of previous elections. But even a reduced number of questionable returns tainted his victory and legitimacy more than in the case of his predecessors. He thus has to start his presidency with a broad commitment (p. 119) to prevent vote tampering in subsequent regional and local elections, knowing he will be held accountable to this pledge as no previous president of Mexico has been.

Latin Americans are also increasingly insisting on more representative processes for candidate selection. In Venezuela in 1988, the Democratic Action Party leadership anointed one candidate for president, but another, Carlos Andrés Pérez (p. 127), won in the open primary. The Peronist Party in Argentina used to have its candidates picked by the boss, Juan Perón, and after his exile by a coterie of union bosses. But in 1988, the Peronist Party selected its presidential candidate for the first time in a nationwide primary election.

The party system, still a major weakness of Latin democracy, has been strengthened in several key countries. Argentina now has a functioning system of two major, internally democratic parties for the first time in fifty years. Thus, in 1989 elections when the ravages of soaring inflation prompted the electorate to seek a change, a democratic alternative was available at the polls. There was no talk of turning to the military as "the only alternative."

Democratic leaders are not irreplaceable, and the laurel of dispensability is one of the achievements of Latin America's gray pragmatists today. The caudillo, the flashy personal leader who builds an aura of uniqueness and impossible succession of lesser beings, is gone. One of the last of them, the Dominican Republic's Joaquín Balaguer (p. 293), has re-emerged as an elected, democratic politician. Other democratic politicians, such as opposition leader José Francisco Peña Gómez (p. 305), are confident that when Balaguer leaves the scene there will be others to replace him.

Traditionally one of the weaknesses of political parties in Latin America has been the failure of opposition parties to respect the limits of competition in a democracy. Some have even connived with the military to seek the removal of their rival party from power, a phenomenon which ex-president Osvaldo Hurtado laments in Ecuador's past. Such bitter experience has helped engender in much of South America an "ethic of solidarity which transcends and limits competition" in President Alfonsín's words. One senses this ethic in the respectful terms in which Raúl Alfonsín talks of this Peronist opposition (p. 58)—and in Peronist leader Carlos Menem's emphasis on his party's constructive opposition during Alfonsín's years and avoidance of the altercations, even violence, which have traditionally characterized Peronist labor rallies and demonstrations.

Even in Ecuador, where political campaigns still can look like barroom shouting matches, Osvaldo Hurtado takes credit for his party's effort "to put behind us the relentless logic of 'friend or foe' which has characterized Ecuadorian politics, and to replace it with the logic of democracy. That logic considers the opposition as both adversaries and potential allies whom one needs to work with, listen to, and consult." (p. 247) President Julio Sanguinetti in Uruguay is the master of this American brand of inter-party politics, continually consulting his opposition, and including their leaders in his diplomatic events, so that they are brought along at least part way on many of his proposals.

All of the leaders speaking through this book talk of the daunting problems their countries face in consolidating their democracy. Virtually all believe that Latin America's economic crisis poses the greatest threat to its democracy. (A prominent exception is President Virgilio Barco (p. 203) who sees drugs as the most dangerous threat to Colombia's democracy.) A cumulation of structural problems has left most of Latin America stuck in the recession of 1982–83 from which the rest of the world emerged in 1984 and 1985. Most of Latin America, therefore, including all of the larger countries, has suffered a long period of stagnation over which the standard of living has fallen year after year. Such an economic catastrophe puts great pressure on any political system and it has in Latin America. The frustrations of families struggling to live on less produced an explosion of rioting and looting in Venezuela in February 1989 and in Argentina in May of the same year. These same frustrations produced a general defeat in 1989 of those governing parties, such as Alfonsín's in Argentina, which had failed to control inflation. Yet a turn to the opposition is not a crisis for democracy when democratic opposition parties and their leadership are there to take over.

As the realistic leaders speaking through this book correctly recognize, Latin America's foreign debt burden did not cause its current stagnation. They are thus generally directing their energies to the painful internal, structural reforms needed to make their economies more efficient. The pace of those reforms is agonizingly slow in some of the larger countries. The burden of servicing foreign debt, however, does make economic recovery more difficult, both by using resources needed for domestic investment and by fueling inflation. Strapped governments have generally "borrowed" some of the local money for debt payments from their central banks (in a word, "printed" it) instead of taxing their people more or draining all of the funds from local credit markets. Thus, the pragmatic politicians speaking here are unanimous in seeing debt relief as necessary for early recovery in Latin America, even if debt relief alone will not do the job.

Latin leaders' attitudes on the debt tangle is a striking break with the politics of the past, when foreign devils and foreign saviors were often seen to hold the keys to local problems. None of the politicians speaking here blames their economic problems on the foreigners and their banks nor maintains that debt relief alone can save them; nor has the debt problem been used as an excuse for avoiding domestic reforms. The terrible test of Latin America's economic crisis, including the debt problem, has yielded a more realistic perspective of Latin leaders over their countries' problems.

When the economic crisis is combined with still weak political systems, the combination can produce serious setbacks. In some countries one of the basic building blocks of democracy, strong political parties, is still weak. Brazil's political parties have long been only loose electoral coalitions. Protracted military rule reduced their function for over a generation, further stunting the parties' development. The leader of Brazil's Constituent Assembly, Ulysses Guimarães (p. 287), sees the continuing fragmentation of Brazil's political parties and the failure of a small number of large parties to consolidate their position as one of the most worrying factors in Brazil's still incomplete passage to a working democracy. The political fortunes of Peru's oldest and best organized party were unnecessarily sent into steep decline by the capricious rule of Alan García, possibly opening the electoral road to power for the Marxist-led United Left coalition.

Mexico is a case apart, one of a single-party system in transit to a multi-party one. The stunning showing of the opposition groups in the 1988 elections, garnering about half the votes in the official count, has forced the governing Institutional Revolutionary Party to face the twin challenges of cleaning up the electoral system and making itself a more democratic party internally, so it has a chance of running successfully in untainted elections. Neither the loose left coalition which supported Cuauhtémoc Cárdenas in 1988 nor the older National Action Party on the right has yet the cohesion and national base to mount a long-term challenge to the ruling party. One of the two opposition groups may grow into this role over coming years. Without the pressure of an opposition which could win the plurality in Mexico's national elections, the ruling party's "Dinosaurs" (as Mexicans call its machine politicians) will tenaciously resist Salinas' plans for reform of a one-party state into a multi-party democracy.

For at least half a dozen Latin American countries the financial and political power of drug traffickers poses a deadly threat to democracy. Colombian President Virgilio Barco (p. 203) says that "the worst threat that confronts Colombian democracy is the drug trade." Through open warfare Colombia's drug traffickers have virtually destroyed the capability of the country's judicial system to prosecute major drug traffickers. As Barco points out, Colombia has suffered the assassination of a Chief Justice, an Attorney General, over half its Supreme Court at one time, and a large number of judges and public prosecutors, with the drug trade directly or indirectly implicated in most of these murders. Frequently, massive bribes have been combined with all too credible death threats to paralyze the key judges and prosecutors of major drug kingpins. Ex-president Carlos Lleras Restrepo (p. 231) laments that this brutal intimidation and corruption of judicial officials has destroyed the probability of punishment, without which the judicial system cannot play its role in deterring drug traffic.

In Peru drug production is increasingly providing the financial resources for "Shining Path" guerrillas who control whole areas of the countryside. In Bolivia, a military clique deeply involved in the drug trade actually took over the government by force in 1980 and ran it for a year and a half as the protector of their own drug business. Fortunately the Bolivians were able to recover control of their government and send the key figures of that military government into exile. Drug traffic played a role in aborting Panama's passage to democracy and has enough influence in some of the other Central American countries to pose a potential threat. The insidious power of drug money is a force Latin America cannot blunt on its own.

Extreme disparities in the division of income and provision of public services can turn the poor against "the system," whatever it is perceived to be. Brazil and Peru face severe problems of this nature which make their governance extremely difficult. In the case of Peru deep income disparities and social and racial tensions are part of a daunting complex of problems which make democracy very fragile. Deep social problems and war leave elected civilian governments in Guatemala, Honduras, and El Salvador a thin veneer on what Oscar Arias here calls "garrison states." For these Central American countries, lapses into military rule are quite possible so long as the Central American wars continue and for some time thereafter.

So where does one draw the balance between the new sources of strength in Latin America's maturing democracies and the old, unresolved problems, slowly corroding some of the supports of these democracies? Does the prevalence of democratic government in Latin America today represent only a high point in an old cycle or the shape of a new trend? Latin American leaders are themselves clear in their answer to this question. They believe democracy has reached a new plateau and that return to de facto, military governments, outside Central America, is unlikely except in a very few cases.

In some cases, such as Argentina, where until 1989 an elected president had not handed over power to an elected successor for sixty years, this conclusion of Latin American leaders is striking, equivalent to announcing that today is the first day of a future different from the last century. Julio Sanguinetti addresses this point specifically, with an analogy to the sudden and unexpected dawn of stable democracy after the 1958 overthrow of the dictator Pérez Jiménez in Venezuela—up to then one of South America's most unstable countries. "...In Venezuela thirty years ago," Sanguinetti argues, "people did not realize the significance of the event, yet it marked the end of Venezuela's endemic propensity to coups d'etat. Something similar is happening in Argentina." (p. 97) And in Argentina President Alfonsín confidently says, "...no one is thinking anymore in terms of coups except, of course, some absurd minorities. Argentina is clearly at the beginning of a very long succession of democratic governments." (p. 58)

Venezuela's President Carlos Andrés Pérez boldly concludes that "we are now living through...the culmination of Latin Americans' long struggle to achieve democracy and liberty." (p. 131)

One finds the same confidence in Colombia, a truly beleaguered democracy. Colombia's persistent guerrilla and criminal violence and the inroads of drug money into its economy are awesome challenges which raise potential scenarios of a breakdown of democratic governance. One might imagine either a "dirty war" in which security forces go outside the law to try to wipe out their enemies and their perceived backers, or a progressive loss of control by the government over sections of the countryside to regional warlords or drug kingpins, similar to Lebanon's national disintegration. But the Colombian president and former presidents speaking in this book are uniformly clear that Colombia's democracy will be preserved while the country slowly masters its problems under that system. President Virgilio Barco (p. 201) says:

There is no reason why we should not expect to defeat domestic actors which persist in using violence and spreading terror. Other western democracies have faced similar threats, such as terrorism, guerrilla warfare or organized crime, and they were able to overcome these difficulties without giving up either their civil liberties or their economic development. . . . It is not something that can be done overnight. But we are fighting a battle, which we will eventually win, although paying high immediate costs. . . . We are fighting terrorists and drug traffickers with some degree of success, which would be greater if we had more cooperation from the international community. . . . We will succeed.

Former President Misael Pastrana, the leader of Colombia's Social Conservative Party, is equally clear.

. . . Dictatorship is a plant that does not 'take' in Colombian soil, as history shows. We have had only two brief dictatorships in this century. . . . I do not believe we will again have that type of government; there would be too much resistance. It would almost be like being under foreign occupation. . . . Colombia has proved that in time of great difficulty, when the country appears about to dissolve and there seems to be no way out, the country pulls together to save itself at the last moment, as is happening now. . . . The winds of democracy are the prevailing ones, and the right ones for Colombia. I do not foresee any circumstances under which the constitutional institutions would break down. . . . I don't believe that the country is headed toward either military rule or anarchy. (p. 209)

Despite this confidence on the part of many leaders in South America, setbacks to Latin American democracy are likely, particularly in Central America and perhaps in one or two of the Andean countries where the military is still not resigned to a role outside of government and political parties remain weak. Peruvians are in fact deeply pessimistic about their country's future, including its democracy, and with good reason. Peru's first two democratic governments after the1982 transition failed utterly to launch serious attacks on any of the deadly threats to Peru's stability—the ascendent Shining Path guerrillas, the drug trade which the guerrillas milk to finance their drive toward power, and economic chaos slipping toward famine. Failed leadership leaves Peru's democratic center at peril of being crushed between the Marxist left and a military which may see itself as the last bastion against a Marxist takeover.

The extent of change in political attitudes and practice in most of Latin America, however, makes it unlikely that Latin America will suffer a widespread degeneration of civilian government and military coups, as occurred in the late Sixties and early Seventies. To this degree a new plateau in progress of democratic government has been achieved. Yet Latin Americans are not euphoric in their qualified confidence in the further consolidation of democratic government. The maturing evolution of political attitudes of Latin America's voters and leaders is perhaps best encapsuled in the oft-cited judgment that democracy is the least bad alternative. It is the tempered realism of a democracy of lost illusions.

Individual democratic leaders are replaceable, but the quality of leadership is itself an important part of the prospects for Latin democracy and a reflection of its maturity. The twenty-six political leaders represented in this book are a significant segment of Latin America's leaders. Nine of them were in 1989 current heads of government. Eleven are former presidents. Five are leaders of major opposition parties. In general they are impressive men, erudite and eloquent, but down-to-earth and level-headed. Having spent some time with all of them, I am impressed as well with their informality and directness. They are for the most part modern politicians who use informal and direct methods of getting business done, including picking up the phone frequently to talk to each other, as Alfonsín did with Sarney, or Sanguinetti with both of them, much as Ronald Reagan and Margaret Thatcher did.

Latin America today is producing skillful democratic leaders who should be better known and recognized in the United States and the rest of the world. The progress of democracy in Latin America is their story and I will let them tell it in their own words, confining myself to introducing them briefly as I have gotten to know them.

I will return at the end of this book to pull together the central themes and lessons in these Latin leaders' thoughts on the role of the United States in the revival of Latin American democracy and the possibilities for U.S. help in confronting threats to the survival and growth of that democracy.

CHILE

GABRIEL VALDES

Gabriel Valdés[3] was for six years foreign minister of Chile's last Christian Democratic government under Eduardo Frei, 1964–70. At sixty-nine, Valdés' hair is now silver, but he is tanned and handsome, still the urbane man-of-the-world. He is a passionate advocate of the rights of man, more in terms reminiscent of Tom Paine's fire of liberty in the belly than Jefferson's cool idealism. Valdés today is as full of energy and optimism as ever—even after two stints in Pinochet's jails. When I met with Valdés in his office just off Santiago's Plaza de Armas, he wore a tweedy, brown sports coat and slacks. He had just come from Capuchino Prison where he visited Socialist Party leader Clodomiro Almeyda, who was imprisoned under the article of Pinochet's constitution banning the advocacy of Marxism.

Our meeting took place just thirty-six hours after the announcement of the opposition's impressive defeat of Pinochet in the October 1988 plebiscite. But all the shouting and celebrating were elsewhere—in the streets, at labor union headquarters, and across town at the headquarters of the Christian Democratic Party, which Valdés headed until June 1987. For at that critical point in its long, continuing fight to end Pinochet's rule, the Christian Democrats, and later the sixteen-party Coalition for the "No" vote in the plebiscite, turned to a different leadership and a different strategy.

Yet it was Gabriel Valdés who led the Christian Democrats from 1982 to 1987, and formed the first broad alliance of political parties against Pinochet in the early phases of the struggle when nothing seemed capable of loosening Pinochet's grip on power.

---

[3]The story of Chile's transition is related here by Gabriel Valdés and two other leaders of the centrist Christian Democratic Party. This is not intended to neglect the role of other parties, including the Socialists and their scion, the Party for Democracy, whose leader, Ricardo Lagos, I was to meet in Santiago until mutual schedule conflicts frustrated our efforts to get together.

Valdés had earlier tried to rally some forces to oppose Pinochet's 1980 constitution, but to no avail. Four years later he led the opposition parties which accepted the invitation to "dialogue" tendered by Pinochet's minister of the Interior Sergio Onofre Jarpa in the wake of bloody anti-Pinochet demonstrations. The dialogue came to naught because Pinochet would not let Jarpa offer even modest concessions and finally fired his would-be peacemaker with the opposition. Valdés, in frustration, called for Pinochet's resignation. In 1985, Valdés and the Cardinal of Santiago sponsored the "National Accord for the Transition to Democracy" which brought together thirteen opposition parties to call for free elections, without demanding Pinochet's prior resignation. The parties in the accord also agreed to take advantage of Pinochet's "Law for Political Parties" to get the opposition registered and legalized.

Valdés tried to keep as much of the opposition together as possible, including the socialist and communist parties. He also joined in the strategy of "social mobilization" for street demonstrations, which encountered increasingly violent responses from Pinochet's police. Chile's sharp, steep recession of 1982–83 had swelled the opposition's protests with growing numbers of economically pressed members of Santiago's middle class, including housewives banging pots and pans in street marches. But as the Chilean economic miracle from 1984 on produced steady, impressive growth, middle class support for the protests waned, and the opposition's drive against Pinochet lost its force. By 1988 Pinochet felt confident enough to enter the year of the plebiscite with the intention of using it to get himself extended in power for another eight years. In July 1987, the Christian Democrats elected a new leader, Patricio Aylwin, and started a new tack—to beat Pinochet at his own electoral game.

Gabriel Valdés continues in the struggle as probably the most eloquent spokesman of the Christian Democrats and a key figure in the opposition. Valdés is, many believe, one of the most brilliant minds in Chile, and his elegant, passionate presentation of the case for democracy in Chile is both eloquent and from the heart. In Gabriel Valdés, the zest to lead is also manifest, more strongly than in Patricio Aylwin. But Valdés was frustrated in his desire to lead the Christian Democrats and the opposition in the December 1989 election against the government's candidate. Valdés' long-standing efforts to extend the opposition to the Marxist left made the democratic right suspicious of his leadership. His earlier strident demands for Pinochet's resignation also leave Chile's military resentful of this forceful representative of the center-left.

Whatever his future role, Gabriel Valdés' contribution to energizing the opposition to Pinochet in its most frustrating years was an enormous one. These efforts, particularly the National Accord of 1985, created the incipient coalition of democratic parties which on October 5, 1988, produced a solid majority against Pinochet and against dictatorship, opening a new phase in Chile's long struggle back to democracy.

In this interview one of Chile's most forceful opposition spokesmen reveals the passionate commitment to democracy and human rights which helped rally a dispirited and compromised democratic opposition to Pinochet when it had little grounds for hope.

*   *   *   *   *

BOEKER: How was it that the political parties and labor unions forming the Coalition for the "No" decided to play by Pinochet's rules and try to beat him at his own game—the October 1988 Plebiscite?

VALDES: You have to go back a bit to find the answer. At the time of Salvador Allende's Popular Union government, from 1970 to 1973, there was a deep rift dividing Chile's political parties because of exaggerated ideological positions which were frozen by the 1973 military coup. The military regime severely punished all political parties, declared them illegal, and confiscated all their property including newspapers and radio stations. We all suffered; many were killed, others exiled, persecuted or imprisoned. The leftist parties such as the communists and the socialists were dealt with much more harshly than anyone else. I personally was imprisoned twice. The military junta issued a decree-law which made any political activity a criminal offense—public speeches, meetings, anything. At the same time union leaders and heads of commercial and professional associations lost their privileges, dismantling the Chilean social and political structure. These shocks produced political passivity.

In 1982 I began to revive the Christian Democratic Party, the only one which had not splintered. We began to hold underground meetings and by the end of that year we had made contact with other democratic parties. Thus, in March of 1983, the Radical

Party, one branch of the Socialist Party, and the Social Democrats could join us in signing the first Democratic Manifesto since the 1973 coup. It was not published anywhere but it got distributed hand to hand. By the end of 1983 the same parties forged the Democratic Alliance, which quietly came to life at the local level throughout the country.

At that time, 1983, labor was better organized than the political parties, particularly the copper miners who had kept their unions alive under the leadership of a great Chilean, Rodolfo Seguel, now out of the country. With them we called for the first protest on May 11, 1983, when the people went to the streets for the first time banging pots and pans and closed down the city. We continued the protests through September of that year creating very serious difficulties for the government. During the last protest in September, Pinochet occupied Santiago with sixteen thousand soldiers and twenty thousand police, killing one hundred and thirty-six demonstrators.

This produced a shock, the Church intervened and Pinochet had to change the Cabinet. He appointed Sergio Onofre Jarpa minister of the interior, who called the Cardinal of Santiago to request a dialogue with us. At that time I was president of the Democratic Alliance. In the course of that dialogue we realized that we had fallen into a trap because as Pinochet himself later admitted the dialogue had no objective for Pinochet beyond cooling tensions. Once the protests stopped the dialogue was broken off by Pinochet claiming that we were not the legitimate representatives of the opposition. After all the killings and disorders people were anxious to reach some kind of agreement, but we were deceived. After aborting the dialogue, Pinochet declared a very harsh state of siege, but we were at least much better organized than we had been before.

During 1984 and 1985 we continued working, mostly clandestinely, to build up the parties' structure. At the initiative of Cardinal Fresno, the parties got together for another meeting. All parties were included, right, left, and center; only the communists were left out. The result was the National Accord, a milestone in our history of internal struggle against the dictatorship. The accord broadened the opposition coalition to include on the right those that form today the Party of National Renovation, and on the left representatives of the Socialist Party. We thus spanned a wide spectrum. In this National Accord the bases for a democracy were set not only in political terms but also in social and economic terms. The accord declared it essential to hold free and open elections, not the plebiscite that Pinochet had provided for in his 1980 constitution.

In the meantime that constitution had been put into effect after having been voted on without electoral registration, with no representatives from the parties to monitor the polling places, with political parties in fact banned and without any opportunity to advocate their position. It was thus easy for Pinochet to win that plebiscite and impose a constitution which all of us, joined by the Catholic Church, have declared illegitimate.

In 1986 Pinochet dictated the Law for Political Parties, a very restrictive law under which the parties are subject to military authority and are thus not fully instruments of the people. After long discussions we decided to accept it with the sole objective of being able to participate in the plebiscite that took place last October 5, 1988.

We had launched a whole movement for free elections, traveling throughout the country with our committee, but Pinochet insisted on his plebiscite. He finally called upon the commanders of the military services, including himself, to name a candidate, and they voted for him. Thus we arrived at the plebiscite.

The plebiscite campaign was very hard for us because we had access to television for the first time just thirty days before the voting and then only for fifteen minutes in the evening. In the campaign Pinochet spent three million dollars a day on television time and newspaper advertisements. It is unbelievable what he spent. He appeared continually on all the networks while we had just fifteen minutes in the evening and no permission and no resources for more. We can truly say that with fifteen minutes we conquered fifteen years.

At this juncture the three political parties which were able to register had done so: the Christian Democrats, the Humanists, and the Party for Democracy, a branch of the Socialist Party, but with different membership, and headed by Ricardo Lagos. The socialists themselves were excluded, with their leader in prison for being a Marxist. We registered to have some kind of control in the plebiscite process. We worked throughout the whole country to register everyone and recruit representatives to monitor the polling and vote counting.

Initially, people did not want to register. It was not compulsory, it was too expensive. The cost to register, including a photo, was approximately three U.S. dollars. The government did not pro-

mote registration because it preferred a low turnout. Nevertheless, we launched an enormous registration campaign and so did
the Catholic Church. The National Endowment for Democracy
of the United States provided resources to us for the registration
drive. We got a lot of young people to help in the drive, people
from that forty percent of Chile's population which is under thirty
years of age and thus had never experienced democracy. When
the campaign was over we had registered ninety-two percent of
the eligible citizens, and we had recruited forty thousand representatives to monitor polling places.

The government for its part went flat out, and I must admit that
this triumph is so beautiful because it was achieved under the
most precarious and difficult of circumstances. Here Pinochet appoints the governors, (whom we call intendents), delegates, and
mayors, and all those officials who are directly responsible to him
became his electoral agents. The minister of the interior was in
charge of the campaign and mobilized all the bureaucracy. This
is not the tradition in Chile where we have never had the same
president for two consecutive terms and our earlier constitution
prohibited that.

We have no congress here and no protection from any other
authority. The commanders of the navy, army, air force, and the
police, who are nominally a legislative authority, are part and par-
cel of the military government. All the local authorities were extremely abusive. The press was tightly controlled and thirty-two
journalists were indicted for denouncing these abuses, but there
was no one to appeal to. The people in the countryside, the poor,
civil servants, and workers were all pressured. At the same time
the government gave away homes, bicycles and money. The municipalities have had large amounts of money to distribute to
teachers and doctors, who are government employees in Chile.
We found ourselves in extremely difficult circumstances, but despite all that we won the plebiscite.

Why did we win the plebiscite? In the first place because once
we had come together in processes like the National Accord,
which was officially rejected by Pinochet in 1985, we began to
organize for elections. On February 2, 1988, sixteen parties
united in the Coalition for the "No" vote. That coalition took two
to three months of work and required a change of heart by both
those who wanted free elections and by those who wanted a win
for the "No." I speak from experience because I was the first to
declare in November 1987 for the "No" vote in Chile.

There were those who thought it necessary to announce a candidate against Pinochet, but it was very difficult to find one who could bridge such a broad span. If Pinochet were to be the official candidate it would be better to unite simply in a "No" vote to Pinochet. The "No" summed up a myriad of reasons for being against Pinochet: exile, poverty, politics, ideology. This strategy resulted in a solemn commitment signed in Santiago to act together: to form a coalition to mobilize for a victory for the "No;" to maximize registrations; and to organize a system of party representatives and monitors for the voting.

This Coalition for the "No" vote was remarkable because it was formed by parties which had been divided since 1970. The only party which did not participate was the Communist Party because it was not registered and only at the last minute decided for the "No" vote. Furthermore, the Communist Party has been ambivalent as to whether it prefers electoral means or violence. They dreamed of mobilizing the masses. They were influenced by Nicaragua in the sense that they did not believe that the electoral path was a viable one against Pinochet. They thought that Pinochet, like Somoza, would not leave via the electoral process.

With this large number of parties we created an Executive Secretariat, a command of five executives, and a council of all the parties. We won by an admirable margin and the Coalition for the "No" continues beyond the plebiscite victory. It is obvious that the plebiscite result was a surprise for Pinochet. In the days before the voting there were indications that the results of the last opinion polls caught him by surprise. There were people close to him who advised that he either cancel or postpone the plebiscite. At that juncture the U.S. Department of State made a statement to the effect that there were some worrisome rumors about the Chilean plebiscite which were a cause of concern to the U.S. government. That was a timely and effective declaration because there was a risk of canceling the plebiscite and of launching another coup. The plebiscite took place, and we were expecting Pinochet to change the cabinet or make some kind of response. He finally appeared on television in his military uniform. He had campaigned in civilian clothing trying to look like Grandpa instead of a dictator. Now we have a very serious problem. It is unthinkable that Pinochet will continue until March 1990 with the same system and the same powers he had before the plebiscite. This would be tantamount to ignoring the results of the plebiscite.

The result of the vote demonstrated that Pinochet truly does not have a large following. He won forty-four percent of the vote because many are scared of change, or because they like the economic model, but the opinion polls indicate that his personal support is no more than nineteen or twenty percent. A large majority of those who voted for Pinochet would have preferred a different candidate because they realize that he is a man of war and confrontation. He is working on the basis that he had forty percent of the vote.

The people definitely want a new cabinet, a political opening, constitutional reforms, and some concrete steps which demonstrate change: free access to television; no internal exile of labor union leaders; freedom for Clodomiro Almeyda; all those things that would indicate that here in Chile there is compromise and not persecution.

I dare say that not even the officers and commanders of the armed forces want Pinochet to stay on indefinitely, or even until 1990 as head of the army, because it would compromise the armed forces. Chile is going through a very dangerous period, but I cannot conceive of a military coup such as we had in 1973, because Pinochet no longer has the strength he would need. He is a defeated general. Things could certainly happen but forces inside and outside the country will ultimately lead the armed forces to demand that Pinochet begin a process of negotiation.

BOEKER: Do you believe that there will now emerge a series of divisions and disagreements between the armed forces and Pinochet?

VALDES: That's possible. The armed forces want to maintain certain principles in the constitution, but they do not want to continue to participate in a regime which is so personalized. Their behavior during the plebiscite, as well as their statements the evening of the voting, indicate that at least the air force and the police want a political opening.

---

[4]The armed forces did indeed induce Pinochet to compromise, beginning with his own constitution, which he had intended to be virtually impossible to amend. In May 1989, the opposition parties achieved agreement with the government of the armed forces on major amendments in Pinochet's constitution which were approved in July by a national referendum. While these amendments did not meet all of the opposition's demands, they included significant easing of the requirements for future, further amendments.

BOEKER: What will Pinochet's role be in coming years?

VALDES: That is a very difficult question to answer because such men are unpredictable. I have never known a forty percent dictator; they are one hundred percent types. By definition a dictator is someone who puts himself above the law. But a dictator who falls in a trap of his own making has lost his prestige, and his room for maneuver becomes very limited. His time to leave is fixed and he is a lame duck.

What will become of him? My impression of Chile, a country I know very well, is that its taste for vengeance is not very strong. But there is a sense that there must be justice, that those who have committed crimes have to pay for them, and above all that the truth must be known. For example, Pinochet has covered up what happened in the murder of Orlando Letelier in Washington. He knows the truth. Those who traveled on the passports, with the money to hire assassins, were actually sent by the National Information Center, which at that time was called DINA, the clandestine service of the government. The head of DINA, General Contreras, worked side by side with Pinochet. It is not possible that Pinochet did not know all about Letelier, or who was responsible for the murders of General Prat and his wife in Buenos Aires, and who shot Bernardo Leighton. There have been crimes inside and outside the country that will not be easily forgotten even after Pinochet leaves. He really ought to tell the truth.

I believe that what Chileans want is for Pinochet to disappear. There is no desire to punish him physically. People just want him to go, because he symbolizes years of extreme cruelty.

Here our first fight was to prevent Pinochet from being elected president until 1997. That's crazy! By that time he would have been president for twenty-four years!

Our second problem is that we have his constitution which is "carved in stone" as international jurists say. According to his constitution he would be senator for life, and commander-in-chief of the army for eight years.

There is another provision which is unacceptable from the democratic point of view: the 1980 constitution provides for a National Security Council with a self-perpetuating majority of military officers, who would chose their own replacements. According to the constitution, this National Security Council has the power to veto any action of the executive, the legislature, the judiciary, or any other Chilean authority. This requires fundamental change.[5]

BOEKER: Do you believe it will be possible to reach an agreement with the armed forces?

VALDES: I believe there will not be a big problem with most of the changes in the constitution, including the National Security Council. I think they are going to follow along the lines of the Brazilians and seek a voice in the more important political decisions. We have never had anything like that in Chile. There was total separation, Prussian style. There was a National Security Council but it dealt only with border issues or foreign affairs. We have told them that we should follow the U.S. model or something similar which would be totally compatible with democracy: a steady and fluid relationship between the armed forces and the executive. The law can reasonably provide a channel for the military to present its problems, express opinions and make its needs known. I think that this can be resolved.

We are going to have a problem with the position of the armed forces toward the Communist Party for three reasons. Anticommunism is very strong in the Chilean armed forces. Between four and five thousand Chilean officers went to school in Panama at the U.S. Southern Command where they were instructed in guerrilla warfare and anti-communism. Pinochet's coup d'état was also based on the premise that Salvador Allende was taking the country toward communism. Pinochet sees himself as the world's foremost anti-communist hero. He has often said that he will not give up this fight and has accused the United States of having lost the wars against communism. In his speeches he has stated that the United States really lost the First World War because it allowed the Russian Revolution to happen, lost the wars against communism in Vietnam, Korea and Cuba. Pinochet is adamant that the same will not happen to him.

Because of the plebiscite he had to allow all those in exile to return, but he was not acting in good faith. He thought that bringing the communists and the socialists back would frighten people. It did not.

---

[5]The constitutional changes approved in July 1989 eliminated the national security council's veto powers and increased the civilian members of a council whose powers are now largely advisory.

The Communist Party has been in existence here since 1922; it has had senators and representatives and was in the government in 1938 and 1946. It is obvious that it is now a much smaller party, and it would not win more than eight or ten percent of the vote if there were elections today. It is a party that is suffering all the crises of international communism caused by perestroika and internal divisions. We don't think it will survive here, as it did not survive in Argentina or in Uruguay where it is almost nonexistent. In Chile we think that with democracy the Communist Party is going to disappear, because it no longer has ideological force.

It is very difficult for the armed forces, however, to accept that the communists are alive. That is why Admiral Merino, spokesman for the government, defined the plebiscite as a referendum of those for Satan against those for God. It is a simplistic concept of black-and-white, good-and-bad, which reflects some of how the military think.

We want to be very pragmatic and demand that no one be excluded because of his beliefs. By the same token we also demand that those who preach democracy act accordingly. This is a subject we are going to treat with extreme caution.

BOEKER: Do you believe that international pressure to shorten military rule had any significant effect, when compared to the pressure exerted by Chileans themselves?

VALDES: I think it has been important and positive because it has been constant in its demands for accountability on subjects of concern to us, such as human rights. Though our country is very jealous of its sovereignty, it is also very sensitive to world opinion.

Chile has been a country very concerned with international issues and very active in foreign affairs. It was one of the initiators of the Pan American Union which was later replaced by the Organization of American States, and of the Inter-American Development Bank through the efforts of Felipe Herrera. Through the Andean Pact, Chile has led Latin American integration and has always advocated international cooperation. In this area our experience is rich. We have always been proud of the trips our presidents have taken abroad and of how well they have been received throughout the world.

The international role and the concern of the United States as expressed through Ambassador Harry Barnes has been very good. The situation was different at the time of the previous ambassador, who was a Pinochet sympathizer. At that time Pinochet's economic successes were more important than human rights. With the arrival of Ambassador Barnes the U.S. Embassy became a center for meetings and for exploring political openings. Ambassador Barnes has made great efforts, has risked his prestige and his personal safety. Pinochet detests him but Barnes has the affection of the people which is unusual here in Latin America. Even in the most remote village, Barnes was greeted with applause.

I believe that the Chilean experience has proved one thing: foreign intervention generally does not work, and economic boycotts do not produce the expected result, but rather the contrary one, unity against foreign intervention. At the same time we are seeing how in the Chilean case the universalization of the concept of human rights, not just in the sense of torture but of liberty, is something that the country has accepted and needs and that we have greeted with much enthusiasm. Amnesty International, for instance, has been very helpful as well as other concerned institutions which have had enormous influence with local groups fighting for civil liberties, such as those formed by academic and professional personalities, labor and church leaders.

I believe that the concept of human rights is precisely the foundation of a hemispheric system. Whatever common foundation there may be for relations among the United States, Canada, and Latin America it is not related to our external defense, anticommunism or other such circumstantial things, but rather more profound ones. The foundation is a shared concept of the liberties to which every individual has a right, including freedom of expression, freedom of association, freedom of thought, freedom to write; the right to a free press and to establish political parties; respect for minority views and the concept that the state serves the people. The idea of private ownership flows from this concept, as well as the right of labor to organize and the right to practice one's religious beliefs.

The defense of human rights is to me a modern process of the last twenty years, propagated in particular by the United Nations and other organizations which defend democracy. It has a moral basis in the early history of the American continent. The inhabitants of the United States fled persecution in Europe and came looking for dignity, liberty and respect for the rights of the individual. This is a basic principle which we share and the one upon which we should build the relationship between the United States and Latin America. If we had an institution based on this concept we would not need the OAS (Organization of American States), which is defective, except for its Human Rights Commission. The OAS treats equally dictators like Pinochet and democratic leaders like Alfonsín or Arias. That just can't be.

I agree that countries are sovereign in their acts within the international order and framework of law. The right of self-determination is extremely important, but even more important is the concept of human rights. Civil liberties should have priority over everything else a state may wish to do. So when it comes to human rights, intervention is not only acceptable, it is necessary.

This has already been accepted in Europe. There are courts available to all citizens, and there are no violations of human rights. The Greek colonels did not participate in the European Economic Community and neither did Franco. The EEC is defined in terms of human rights. Here in the Americas we still need to consecrate the principle of human rights as the basis for our relations. Once this concept is promulgated the conclusion follows that the hemisphere is an association of democracies and that a dictatorship is a foreign body which arises by virtue of violating certain rights.

No dictatorship can ever respect human rights. From the philosophic principle of human rights a new concept of hemispheric life could emerge which could result in an association of nations which—regardless of how their interests might differ in other matters—will be linked through their common belief in human rights not only for themselves but for the whole world. By sharpening our focus on the principles we share, we will reduce the areas of conflict. A relationship based on human rights can have very positive results. I don't have any problem with five American congressmen arriving suddenly, or seven lawyers as happened the other day, to observe the human rights situation, nor do I have any problem with a delegation from Chile going to the United States to investigate whether the rights of the Chicanos in the South are being respected. These are basic rights to which every human being is entitled, most particularly in the Americas. If this hemisphere has a raison d'etre it is as a collection of free nations.

BOEKER: It seems to me that one of the things you are saying is that we need to go back and review the concept of the OAS?

VALDES: Absolutely! For instance, here labor unions are suppressed, their leaders are imprisoned because of some strike or some demand, which is what happened to Manuel Bustos, president of the Central Union of Chilean Workers. He went with his council to present a letter to Pinochet and the police arrested him. He was sentenced to internal exile for eighteen months. I am convinced that a labor union such as this, which legitimately represents the interests of the Chilean workers, should have some place it can turn to. I am not just talking about the International Labor Organization in Geneva, but about establishing a body here in America where Chilean workers, for example, could bring their complaint and the Chilean ambassador would have to give an explanation. One of the advantages of having the freedom to unionize is that it provides an avenue for petitions. There has to be an organization to which a union leader can go and say: "Look, I expressed my opinion and was tortured."

Just before the October 1988 plebiscite a friend of mine, a great Uruguayan singer, was tortured. He is a young married man whom I know very well. I traveled with him because he is a popular idol to the people, especially the young. Using some libelous accusation, the police took him prisoner at dawn, and no one could see him. He was held for over an hour, naked, being accused and threatened so that he would sign a phony confession. He signed everything, confessing to the most atrocious crimes. We were able to get him out of the "National Center for Information" and take him before a judge who after questioning him let him go free. These incidents continue to happen and it just can't be. These things cannot and should not happen. The poor suffer this kind of abuse all the time. It does not happen to me because I can make a lot of noise and enough people know me that I am protected. The big problem we have to face in such dictatorships in developing nations is protecting the rights of the poor. I am not referring only to their money and property but to their dignity.

EDGARDO BOENINGER

Edgardo Boeninger is not a Christian Democratic Party insider, nor basically a politician. He is an academic who was rector of the University of Chile from 1970–73, beating out Allende's candidate, and more recently head of a think tank, the Center for Development Studies. But circumstances, and Boeninger's brilliance in political concepts and strategy, presented him an opportunity to contribute to the opposition's defeat of Pinochet in the October 5th plebiscite.

As a Christian Democratic Party member and advisor, Boeninger participated in the dialogue Pinochet offered the opposition in 1983 and 1984, and then cynically canceled when street demonstrations subsided. This experience convinced Edgardo Boeninger that Pinochet was so strongly entrenched that the one course left to the opposition was to take maximum advantage of the openings Pinochet himself had created in his self-serving 1980 constitution. The most alluring of these openings was the possibility to defeat Pinochet on his own ground in the October 1988 plebiscite. Boeninger also strongly believed that the strategy of "social mobilization," protests in the streets, supported by the party in the mid-Eighties, was a dead end which would cost the Christian Democrats middle class support. His concept was a campaign which would have the democratic opposition parties appear more committed to order and peaceful change than Pinochet. The strategy also involved expanding the coalition of the 1985 National Accord to the right and opening contacts with the military, to project a stance of opposition to Pinochet, the dictator, rather than animosity toward the armed forces.

The strategy was a collective effort, but Boeninger, in December 1986, drafted the initial plan which soon became the opposition's strategy. Boeninger subsequently played a role in convincing his friend Patricio Aylwin that he was needed to lead the Christian Democrats and forge the broader party coalition for the campaign to turn back Pinochet in his own plebiscite. The Christian Democrats had help, including some from Pinochet. By deciding to run in the plebiscite himself, rather than picking a rightist civilian, Pinochet gave the opposition the clearest possible target for its campaign against dictatorship and repression.

Edgardo Boeninger, 63, became a vice president of the Christian Democratic Party for his efforts and has since December 1986 been absorbed, first in the campaign for the "No," then the subsequent effort to pick a single opposition candidate, Patricio Aylwin, and finally the drive to win the December 1989 elections. But Edgardo Boeninger is still the thinker and the writer who would rather advise when called on than become a gear in the political machine which has to turn out four million votes.

I called on Boeninger at his modest one-story home in Santiago's attractive Apoquindo district on a lovely Saturday afternoon. Here Boeninger and his wife live next to the families of their grown children, an example of the closeness of the family which seems to serve in Latin America life-long functions which it has lost in the United States. Edgardo Boeninger had to hurry home from a party meeting to see me. But he was wearing a baggy sweater and slacks, which seemed to validate the appearance of a man not running for anything.

His face could be that of a retired English don. It is lean and angular, topped by an impressive high square forehead with medium length gray hair curling back over his ears. Despite his widely recognized intellect, he is a modest man who does not like to talk about himself or the small but important role he played in the campaign to beat Pinochet. Credit is due to many politicians and labor leaders and even more to the millions of Chileans who turned out to say "no" and "no more" to a dictator who still had arbitrary powers over their daily lives. In this interview, therefore, I asked Edgardo Boeninger to relate the whole story of the gestation of the political strategy which produced the dramatic victory of the previously dispirited and divided opposition parties against South America's strongest, and in some ways most successful, dictator of this generation.

* * * * *

BOEKER: How was it that parties which were so long such bitter rivals finally united in the Coalition for the "No" to Pinochet?

BOENINGER: It was a gradual process. The Pinochet regime

reached the peak of its power once the 1980 constitution was passed. His political power was solidified through the transition articles of that constitution. At that time we had also an "economic boom" with popular expectations of ever-increasing prosperity. But the boom was short-lived and by 1982 this country entered an acute crisis, with high unemployment and deep disillusionment. That hard fall generated popular protests against Pinochet's government.

The protest movement had two effects. First, it forced the government to liberalize the society. Up to that time Pinochet's dictatorship had been very stern—totally restrictive. After 1983, the government had to give space to the opposition and this allowed the political parties to re-emerge.

Second, the force and emotion of the popular protests generated a sense among the parties that the regime could not last. It came to be viewed as a struggle between the good guys and the bad guys with a sense, half emotional, half ethical, that the good guys had to win in the end. Efforts concentrated on bringing down the regime quickly, as was reflected in slogans like "this is the decisive year." But as time went by many of us began to see clearly that social upheaval would not defeat a military force which still had significant, if minority, popular support.

The historical wounds of Allende's Popular Unity government also assured a divided opposition to Pinochet, as became obvious at the time of the protests. When the communists came out to join the protests, the middle class went home. The protests waned not because politicians failed to seize the initiative, but because the middle class did not want to be seen in the streets with the communists. I believe that was our mistake.

The labor unions, particularly the transportation workers and copper miners, as well as the professional associations, had the power to virtually paralyze the country through a general strike, but they were the same ones that had contributed to the fall of Allende. Many of those groups, especially the truckers, had been against Allende's Popular Unity Government and in some way sought the military intervention. It would have been too much to ask that they get together with their former adversaries of ten years ago in order to oust the military. At that point many of us began to realize that even though popular protest had considerable support, it could not successfully be extended to a general strike, that favorite dream of the left. The only possible way to defeat the military was through the electoral route. That belief began to take root gradually. Some academics and political moderates gradually persuaded the left to support a strategy based on elections.

The key step was accommodation among politicians of the center-left, all of which had previously been adversaries. A gradual convergence among Christian Democrats, Social Democrats, and the left, actually had begun earlier, in 1977. The Christian Democrats, together with some socialists and radicals, had then formed the so called Group for Constitutional Studies. The group reached a full consensus, including the communists, on an alternative constitution to that passed in 1980. That was the beginning of a history of increasing cooperation.

We have seen here in Chile a growing closeness between the socialists and the Christian Democrats. Socialism, and the political center in general, is now undergoing an ideological reform inspired by the European experience, plus disillusionment with Cuba, and lack of attraction to the Nicaraguan experience. For its part, the Christian Democratic Party began to function more like a coalition member because by itself it could not win a confrontation with Pinochet. The non-religious center (the Radicals and the Social Democrats) was drawn into this growing coalition as well.

By 1986 a consensus had been strongly consolidated behind the movement for free elections. The majority of those who were in this movement were well aware that we would probably end up with a plebiscite, not free elections. However, this was part of a difficult process of committing everyone to the electoral game. All the parties deciding for free elections had effectively abandoned the idea of calling for Pinochet's resignation before the end of his term. With reason, the opposition saw the plebiscite as Pinochet's game, and the movement for free elections was born essentially to demand a fair game, free and competitive elections.

Coincidentally the dictatorship had created an opportunity by placing a limit on its time in power. The 1980 constitution stipulated an eight-year presidential term and then a plebiscite to decide the future. Pinochet saw the plebiscite simply as a way to legitimize his rule and extend it for another eight years. But he needed to give the plebiscite the appearance of legitimacy, and thus passed a law providing for political parties and registration of voters. I believe that initially this was seen as a mere formality so that it could be said that there were other political parties, but they were to be tightly controlled by the government.

We looked at that scenario and thought: "Here is our chance to construct the necessary guarantees for clean elections." The process of uniting the opposition thus began. All the parties, except initially the communists, accepted the requirement to register, and even they were finally pulled into the process as well.

The 1987 election of the leadership of the Christian Democratic Party was closely linked to the dilemma of whether or not the party should register. The group supporting the candidacy of Patricio Aylwin argued that it was necessary, not because we liked Pinochet's Law of Political Parties, but because we needed to be registered to be able to use that law's openings to work for guarantees of a clean electoral process. First, by becoming a legitimate party we were protected from government repression. Second, the law permitted us to demand access to the media and to carry out political campaigning. Third, it permitted us to appoint monitors for the voting. The party decided on a political strategy of striving for clean elections and thus we decided to register, despite serious internal opposition on ethical grounds. Groups within the party, such as the one headed by Gabriel Valdés, opposed this strategy because it meant playing the dictator's game, and lending him legitimacy. We considered ourselves more realistic. The decision of the Christian Democrats to register the party under Pinochet's law was at first rejected by the other parties, but later accepted.

Obviously there were not free elections because Pinochet would not change the constitution—requiring a plebiscite. But we decided that if our minimum conditions were met, we would participate in the plebiscite. Subsequently other parties reached the same decision. The more moderate socialists formed the Party for Democracy (PPD) and wanted us all to form one single party, but the Christian Democrats declined believing this would create too unwieldy an instrument.

We then had the problem of organizing a political campaign, a Coalition for the "No" in Pinochet's plebiscite. This was the culmination of the effort to bring the opposition together and unite all the parties except the communists, who luckily for us were always a few steps behind. The document itself, "The Convergence of Parties for the No" signed in February 1988, contained only the commitment to cooperate in the campaign and then to reach an agreement with the military for a quick and orderly transition toward democracy.

To be honest I believe in the end the decisive factor was the general feeling, prevalent in November and December of 1987, that Pinochet would handily win the plebiscite because deep divisions in the opposition made it look like a bag full of cats. The fear of defeat created the opportunity to unite just at the point when all believed we had little possibility of winning. From then on there was an awareness that we had to work together and that the path to victory was moderation.

Afterward, a step at a time, came the agreements that reinforced this multi-party cooperation. In May we finalized the "Economic and Social Commitment" which was really a commitment to act with economic responsibility. It harked back to the thirteen points of compromise previously included in the National Accord, which was signed even by those conservatives who later supported the "Yes" vote. The "Agreement on the Basis for Institutionalizing Democracy" was also similar to the National Accord, but had the signatures of all sixteen political parties which comprised the Coalition for the "No." This document outlined essential reforms in the 1980 constitution as well as objectives for an ideal constitution.

The next step was the appointment of a leader. The strategy of the Christian Democrats when we elected Patricio Aylwin was to have a coalition with a single program and candidate. We had a program in January which was signed by seven center parties, but it was not possible then to include the new socialist groups in a coalition because they did not want to commit themselves so early in the game. To the right, the government effectively dismantled the National Party. We finally were able to form a limited coalition with a program which was not very significant in the plebiscite campaign except as a reflection of the moderation which a future government would represent.

Unfortunately, we were not able to agree on a single opposition leader for the plebiscite because many feared that person would automatically become the presidential candidate, with negative effect on their personal ambitions. However, we took one step in that direction and appointed Patricio Aylwin spokesman for the group. We thought of this as a small step, but it proved indispensable for us to have a head. Patricio Aylwin became a visible, personal leader, especially during the last months of the plebiscite campaign. The government tried to impair that image of leadership by arguing that socialist Ricardo Lagos was leading the opposition, which was not true at all.

The successful story of the opposition's political cooperation thus began with a realistic vision imposed by a defeat born of excessive expectations and a failed effort to bring a quick end to military rule. The predominant part of that realistic vision was that the road to success went through elections.

The government's effort was based on a campaign of terror. They accused the opposition of being a new version of Allende's Popular Unity Movement, dominated by Marxists. The government allowed political exiles to return a month before the plebiscite so that it could highlight returning communist leaders on television. Despite this last-minute attempt to instill fear we were able to persuade the people that ours was a moderate opposition.

BOEKER: The opposition decided in effect to play Pinochet's game, on his field, by his rules. Where did you get the confidence to join such a game?

BOENINGER: Basically I think there were two ways of looking at the situation, one positive and one negative. On the negative side we knew that was the only way; on the positive side there was the fact that we had made important advances.

From the very moment any popular, sectoral elections were held, we consistently won—in vocational schools, universities, and unions. We thus gained a lot of ground and acquired a certain electoral capacity. If were able to get the votes from all these sectors, despite the government's opposition, there was no reason why we would not get the national vote. If we were able to liberalize the system enough to take this first step, we thought we would eventually be able to create the necessary conditions for a national victory.

This was in fact confirmed when the first institutional decisions were taken: electoral registration to prevent massive fraud, and the Law of Political Parties. When these two minimal conditions were met, we decided to play on Pinochet's court. There were risks, but it was not a reckless gamble. There was an objective element of analysis.

If we had not had the capacity to name monitors for the polling tables, we would not have participated in the plebiscite. The events of the night of October 5 proved our assessment correct, because we had to exercise maximum pressure to prove that we had won, and to make sure the government stopped its effort to distort the results. This was accomplished because our political organization worked, and because the main party of the right,

National Renovation, accepted the plebiscite results and would not support any attempt to overturn them by force.

BOEKER: If you had already named one candidate, do you think you would have gotten a higher percentage of the vote?

BOENINGER: Yes, with a single moderate candidate, we would have won by approximately sixty-five percent, but we would have needed broader political agreement than we actually had. We could not impose a leader; that would have fractured the coalition.

For the subsequent electoral campaign there has been a stronger sense of urgency on the part of all involved. We need the face, we need the candidate, because it is the only way to keep the people active and supportive. There is a consensus that we need a single candidate and that he needs to be moderate. This is the best chance to stick together.

We in the Christian Democratic Party believe that the nucleus of the first democratic government will be the political center. That is basically the coalition we have already built with other centrist parties. Our effort is to gain the confidence of the business community and expand the coalition toward the left, provided the political platform remains moderate. We need to convince all the parties of the left, center, and right, to support a single candidate and commit themselves to strengthening democracy itself. The basics are there, and right now it is a question of political will.

BOEKER: What happens to Pinochet personally?

BOENINGER: Well, I guess he is trying to rebuild his image and say nothing happened. Pinochet is still president until 1990.

According to the constitution he cannot run again, and no party on the right would be willing to support him. He still has power to block or veto the initiatives of others (i.e., constitutional reform) but can no longer dictate political solutions on his own terms.

The most sensitive problem still remaining with regard to Pinochet is the fact that under the constitution he could remain as commander-in-chief of the army. It is hard to envisage a democratic president living with such a situation. This will be a very serious issue.

PATRICIO AYLWIN

I met Patricio Aylwin, president of the Christian Democratic Party, spokesman of the Coalition for the "No" in Pinochet's plebiscite, and subsequently candidate to succeed Pinochet as president, in his office at his party headquarters. It was October 7, 1988, just two days after the "No" coalition's stunning victory had released an explosion of celebrations in the streets and a palpable spirit of personal liberation throughout Santiago. Christian Democratic headquarters was a bustle of exhilarated staff members cramming the halls and anterooms. Patricio Aylwin himself gave me an hour before he left for his next victory celebration, an evening rally in Bernardo O'Higgins Park which drew over 200,000 shouting and singing celebrants. But Patricio Aylwin, at seventy the grand old man of the Christian Democrats, was as calm as if I had come for tea on a Sunday afternoon when neither of us had anything else to do.

Patricio Aylwin's slightly puffy face is saved by some sharp accents: a rim of white hair which highlights his large forehead before turning dark and full as it combs to a point at the back of his neck; heavy eyebrows which form a pointed arch; and most prominently of all, a Nixon-like nose which curves convexly like a ski jump, with the same sense that its last thrust is up. He adds another sharp accent of his own by frequently thrusting his extended hand and lower arm forward, to emphasize points as he speaks.

Aylwin has been president of the Christian Democrats half a dozen times in his long career. He was simultaneously president of the Senate during Allende's years and negotiated with Allende, on behalf of the opposition parties, "guarantees" seeking to limit Allende's abuse of his presidential powers. Allende paid no heed to his "guarantees," a bitter blow to the democratic parties, some of whom still seem to hold this failure against Aylwin. He was still head of the party when the military overthrew Allende on

43

September 11, 1973, in a coup which many Christian Democrats initially welcomed before its repressive and long-term character became all too apparent. But Aylwin seems not to have been compromised politically by the Christian Democrats' moral muddle in the period after the military coup. After Pinochet banned political party activity, Aylwin virtually retired from politics, devoting his time to writing and to his law practice, until the party came calling more than a decade later.

When the Christian Democrats in 1987 decided on a strategy of beating Pinochet at his own game, Patricio Aylwin seemed the right leader for the Christian Democrats and the Coalition for the "No" in Pinochet's plebiscite. The strategy called for reaching out to the stability-minded middle class by playing by the rules, even when they were loaded ones written to Pinochet's advantage, and for avoiding battles in the streets. Aylwin, a respected constitutional lawyer who had sat out the era of the Christian Democrats' support for protests in the streets, fit the bill. The strategy also called for expanding the coalition of the thirteen-party National Accord toward the right. Aylwin, a low-key broker of compromises, unthreatening to the parties of the center right, again fit the bill.

Aylwin is a man less hungry for power than most politicians, and one with limited popular appeal in the past. He did not initially seek the leadership of the party. He was talked into coming out of retirement by a group, including Edgardo Boeninger, which needed a leader for their strategy to concentrate all opposition parties efforts on a coordinated effort to defeat Pinochet in his own plebiscite. Aylwin rose to the challenge, first by winning the election for president of the Christian Democrats from Gabriel Valdés in July 1987. By February 2, 1988, Aylwin succeeded in getting together the Christian Democrats and twelve other parties, later expanded by three, into the agreement creating the Coalition for the "No." In a tremendous, nation-wide effort over succeeding months the coalition got a record number of Chileans, 7.4 million, representing over ninety percent of those eligible, to register to vote. Of those registered ninety-seven percent actually voted on October 5, 1988. This was an impressive achievement of grass-roots organization. The opposition did not have access to the media until thirty days before the plebiscite and long after registrations had closed.

Aylwin himself was a solid, energetic leader who made no major mistakes and was increasingly effective and forceful in the campaign. He was also a skillful team leader who gave plenty of scope to other more charismatic opposition representatives, such as socialist Ricardo Lagos and Christian Democrat Gabriel Valdés. His skill as a peacemaker was needed by the opposition again as it engaged the armed forces in a discussion of changes in Pinochet's loaded constitution—and again as the coalition faced the tough challenge of trying to unite on a single candidate for the December 1989 presidential elections. Aylwin was many politicians' second choice for that job, which made him the logical consensus candidate of parties deeply divided over their first choice.

In his interview Patricio Aylwin is once again the low-key, understated broker of compromise and a reassuring voice of moderation and peaceful passage from Pinochet's dictatorship to the democracy Aylwin hopes to lead.

* * * * *

BOEKER: Why is it only now that the democratic parties were able to effectively unite against Pinochet? Why not years ago?

AYLWIN: It has been a process which took a long time to reach its stride. The scars of old conflicts made it difficult to reach an understanding among parties now finally united. The parties had to overcome many years of conflict. The Socialists and the Christian Democrats in particular had dug their trenches on opposite sides, not only during the regime of Salvador Allende but also during the last Christian Democratic government of Eduardo Frei, when the Socialists were totally closed to any dialogue with us.

The need to unite became more obvious every day. There was a clear tendency toward realism and moderation in contrast to the extremist ideology which prevailed fifteen or twenty years ago.

Politics have become more moderate worldwide. Parties have come closer together in franker recognition of the limits on their actions and policies imposed by reality. Today's François Mitterand in France is a different person from the Mitterand of years ago. Nobody would have thought twenty years ago that Spain could have a socialist government with the moderate characteristics of the current one. These winds of realism and moderation have reached our country. Here one talks with socialist politicians who say today: "Look, I want a different socialism now from the one I wanted at the time of Allende."

BOEKER: On the night of the vote Pinochet called an emergency meeting of the armed forces' commanders and there was talk of interrupting the vote count. There were even rumors that the meeting of the armed forces' commanders would consider "alternatives." What do we know about the facts?

AYLWIN: On the night of the plebiscite the delay by the interior ministry in announcing the official tabulation clearly foreshadowed an attempt to manipulate the count. The delay could not have been due to anything else but an attempt to alter the count. But fortunately the air force commander and the head of the police were very explicit in saying that the actual count had to be respected and, before the meeting of the armed forces commanders, they went public with the fact that the "No" had won, which had a decisive effect by creating a fait accompli.

BOEKER: After your impressive victory in the October 1988 plebiscite, are you satisfied with the vote count?

AYLWIN: Yes, the official count recognized by the government basically corresponds to our own and I believe it is correct.

BOEKER: What is your interpretation of the victory of the "No"? What motivated people to vote "No"? Was it a rejection of Pinochet, or a vote for a new democratic system?

AYLWIN: I believe that both factors had equally strong impact. People do not want Pinochet any more, not only as a person but as the symbol of a style of government that is authoritarian and unjust. Consequently we believe that the "No" vote was a rejection of both Pinochet and his style of government.

BOEKER: You were quoted in *The Wall Street Journal* as saying that the opposition had to give Pinochet a "knock-out" punch in the plebiscite and not just win on points. Do you think that the margin of your victory is sufficient to finish Pinochet?

AYLWIN: I was asked the question: "What was going to happen after the 'No' wins?" I said that it all depended on the margin of victory, whether it were 70–30, which I considered a "knockout," 60–40, or 52–47. A narrow victory would make negotiations for accelerated change much harder. A solid victory would further deteriorate the image of the government and make negotiations a lot easier. For that purpose we achieved a victory which is enough, a margin of twelve points, but it is not a "knock-out." It has not given us the leverage to tell Pinochet he must leave right now.

BOEKER: What role will Pinochet play in the years to come?

AYLWIN: He will continue to be president until March 1990. But his power has been sapped by the results of the plebiscite, and it is going to deteriorate even more, notwithstanding the high percentage of the vote, forty-four, he won. What is certain is that the armed forces and the right are blaming their defeat on the fact that Pinochet was the candidate. I think they will curtail his power but I would not venture a guess as to whether he will retain enough power to remain as commander-in-chief of the army after his presidential term ends.

BOEKER: Is there a possibility of divisions within the armed forces?

AYLWIN: I believe so. What we hear is that there have been serious disagreements, particularly in the days just before the plebiscite. Now with Pinochet defeated these can only grow.

BOEKER: You are at the beginning of a period of extremely delicate negotiatións. In his speech conceding defeat in the plebiscite, Pinochet reiterated that there would be no change in the "constitutional order"; however, you are insisting that there should be constitutional changes.

AYLWIN: If you read Pinochet's speech carefully, you will notice that he insisted twice that you cannot change the constitutional schedule for elections and that he will respect it. That would seem to leave open the possibility for amendments to the constitution by the military junta itself, which do not change the schedule in the constitution. We want to change the requirements for amending the constitution so that changes could be made by the next Congress, and to have that Congress be an elected body, with no appointed senators. From reading the text of Pinochet's speech, I conclude that these reforms are not rejected a priori. I believe that the reforms we have proposed are reasonable and should generate support. I have information to indicate we could have backing from some branches of the armed forces. The Coalition for the "No" has decided that some changes need to be sought in negotiations with the governing junta before the next presidential and congressional elections. Others can be made by the future congress and president after they are elected, as long as that congress is given the constitutional powers on which we insist.[6]

BOEKER: Will it be possible to maintain a peaceful campaign and an orderly transition over the coming years?

AYLWIN: Such a political truce could be the biggest problem we may yet face. The victory for the "No" generates among the common people, especially the young, expectations which could be frustrated if we don't come up with early solutions. Since Pinochet will undoubtedly resist all change, these sectors will press for popular demonstrations and protests. The biggest challenge that we political leaders face is controlling such pressures so that our political opportunity does not elude us.

BOEKER: Yes, I saw the night after the plebiscite that most demonstrators were young people, who surely were voting for the first time in their lives and have only the heady experience of having brought down a dictator.

AYLWIN: Yes, this phenomenon among our new generation is in this sense worrisome. Chileans under thirty-three years of age have not had any experience with democratic life, in which the rights of the minority have to be respected as well; they were all minors at the time of the coup against Allende in 1973. They have known only the logic of authoritarianism; that is, the one on top has all the power and the rest have nothing. Now they are inclined to think that the tables are turned and they ask why is it that we don't have all the power. This is an extremely serious problem.

---

[6]The subsequent negotiations in May 1989 between the military government and the opposition validated Aylwin's judgment. The opposition basically obtained the changes Aylwin cites here, except that the number of appointed senators was reduced, not eliminated.

BOEKER: At the beginning of the plebiscite campaign the parties considered naming one candidate, but could not come to agreement. Now you must decide on one candidate for the 1989 election.

AYLWIN: In reality, we are facing this decision for the first time. Before the plebiscite some parties considered the advantages of naming one candidate then, but others insisted that we did not need one. The problem was not failing to select a candidate, but of being unable to agree that we needed one before the October plebiscite.

We are now in agreement that we need one single candidate, and we will have one because there is no other way. The supporters of the present government insist that they have to hold together their forty-four percent of the vote as their only chance to win the presidency in 1989 elections. Facing that challenge it would be very irresponsible on our part to fail to field a single candidate for the entire democratic opposition.

I have observed some recognition that a socialist, whoever he may be, would have little chance of winning immediately after an authoritarian regime. Examples in the rest of the world indicate that the first democratic government after a dictatorship tends to be headed by moderates. The obstacles a socialist would have to overcome, especially with respect to the armed forces, would make it very difficult to govern. There is thus awareness that the candidate should be a moderate, someone from the center right, or a Christian Democrat.

BOEKER: Outside Chile one hears a lot about the success of Pinochet's economic policies. If you were elected president, would you continue the same economic policy or do you have some other ideas?

AYLWIN: I believe that the fundamental elements of Chile's economic policy should be maintained: that is, limiting the role of the state, expanding the private sector, strengthening market forces, encouraging foreign investment, and opening to foreign trade, but with some variations.

These variations would be related fundamentally to two aspects. A greater role for the state is needed in determining the basic direction of the economy, and in giving greater attention to

the basic necessities of health and education. We also see a need
to share more of the benefits of growth and development with
labor. Basically, we believe that the country should have a mixed,
or social market, economy as it is called in Germany. We believe
that with this policy of a mixed economy, the state must play a
more active role than it has during Pinochet's time, and we also
believe in an economic policy conditioned by the idea of social
justice.

BOEKER: Do you believe that the private sector in Chile has
been hurt by its support of Pinochet?

AYLWIN: There is no doubt they have identified too much with
the Pinochet regime, and that this may create difficulties in the
future with respect to cooperation between management and
labor.

BOEKER: Some representatives of labor are unhappy with what
they saw as their supporting role in the Coalition for the "No"
vote. They feel that they started the movement of opposition to
Pinochet, at great cost to many of their members, and that the
political parties left them behind with inadequate consultation. Is
this accurate?

AYLWIN: I believe it is an exaggeration. It is human nature to
want to play the protagonist. There is no doubt in my mind, however, that the management of the struggle in which we are now
engaged must be essentially political; it is not a labor issue.

The first confrontations took place between organized labor
and the government, but with the support of the political parties.
It started with labor because they were legal when political parties were outlawed. Because of their legal status labor unions, unlike political parties, could go on strike. In Chile labor leaders
have continually accused us of political manipulation, but I don't
think their role is any less than in developed nations.

BOEKER: What will be the impact of the Chilean plebiscite in
the rest of Latin America?

AYLWIN: I think that a victory for Pinochet would have had a
very negative impact on the emerging democracies of Latin
America. Those who came here as observers were very happy,

especially those from Argentina and Uruguay, who told us that the result of this plebiscite would have great impact on their efforts to consolidate democratic government in their own countries.

BOEKER: In Peru I heard it said that Pinochet has proven that only dictatorships can take the tough actions needed to manage an economy these days in Latin America.

AYLWIN: Yes, I have heard that, but Peru and many other countries have had dictators who have handled the economy poorly.

BOEKER: Do you think the pressure that the United States and other friendly countries exerted has played any significant role?

AYLWIN: I would say that what has been most effective is sustaining and supporting the courage of political and labor groups, that is, our political leadership in this struggle for democracy. I don't believe that foreign pressure has had much effect on the government. It is hard for me to judge the impact on the people. The more educated groups put value in U.N. condemnations of Pinochet's human rights abuses, but the government tries to deflect this by claiming Chile's autonomy is being violated by such international actions. However, I believe that the impact of foreign support on the morale of the people carrying the fight has been extremely important. I also believe that having world attention fixed on the plebiscite, and foreign observers here, were very important in dissuading any attempt at fraud.

BOEKER: If the new government in the United States is inclined to give more attention to Latin America, where would you suggest it look?

AYLWIN: Servicing our foreign debt creates a vicious circle for Chile, because dedicating four percent of our gross national product to service the debt greatly damages our capacity to invest. The same is true for other Latin American countries.

We also have the problem of the terms of trade which has never been solved. Periodically the income from export of Latin America's raw materials drops drastically. This is a subject that remains open.

The Latin American countries placed great hopes twenty-five

years ago in the Alliance for Progress. We are not trying to create another Alliance, but we must somehow raise the standard of living of the people of Latin America. The United States could help and that would be a positive step, both to prevent social and political upheaval in our continent and to improve the possibilities of mutual trade.

RAUL ALFONSIN

No aides ushered me into the presence of Argentine President Raúl Alfonsín. This unassuming man is the only chief of state I have met who came into his anteroom to greet me and take me into his small working office. There he seated himself behind a black table desk, half covered with piles of paper. Three chairs in front of the desk completed the furnishings of this unpretentious office.

Alfonsín, a man of medium height and slightly pear shape, wore a loose tweed suit with full side pockets, giving him a professorial air. The striking feature of a wonderful face is the brown eyes which turn down at the outside corners, framing a gentle arch over a brush mustache and creating an engaging, warm appearance. Alfonsín breaks easily into a melancholy smile, which recalled for me the poignant visage of King Hussein of Jordan.[7] It is the face of a gracious, decent man, but one carrying tremendous burdens which weigh on him all the time.

Alfonsín in the last year of his six-year term was a lonely man. His two closest old friends in government had died within the last two years, and a third left after a personal falling-out. President Alfonsín finished his term surrounded by younger operators who could not provide the comradeship of an old friend.

In 1983, Alfonsín's victory in Argentina's first election after seven years of brutal military dictatorship thrust this country lawyer-turned-politician into the flow of an extraordinary political passage for Argentina. In this remarkable passage, Alfonsín showed great courage in the face of some political challenges. In a bold gamble Alfonsín, unlike his opponent, ran in 1983 on a platform of refusal to recognize the military's hasty amnesty for itself on the way out the door. He thus took the risk that the military might try to prevent his taking power, but successfully turned his

---

[7]Where I was U.S. Ambassador, 1984 to 1987.

election into a mandate to bring the generals to justice. With that mandate in hand, Argentina's courts tried and convicted the military figures principally responsible for the death of thousands of the "disappeared" under the military regime. These trials were a "first" for Argentina, where the military has too facilely seen its de facto acts as above the law.

Having set in motion a process Argentina's re-awakened courts have pursued with vigor, Alfonsín the politician later smarted under criticism of his effort to bring the trials to an end after five years. Alfonsín wanted to avoid a permanent grudge against civilian government by a new generation of military officers—one which would have threatened Argentina's uneasy civilian-military relations. Three times during his term, Alfonsín had to face down revolts of military hard-liners demanding amnesty for convicted military officers. In his effort to manage these conflicting pressures, Alfonsín had to draw agonizingly a balance between principles of equal justice and his obligation to preserve a still fragile democratic system. The management of such painful trade-offs is what tempers a successful pragmatic politician in the forge of Latin American politics.

Alfonsín's six years have brought significant political accomplishments for Latin America's chronically most unfulfilled and under-performing society—relative to its own potential and self-image. Today the practice of democratic government seems surprisingly well-established among Argentinians. Yet in 1989 when Alfonsín, as one democratically elected president, handed over power to another, it was the first such transition in Argentina in sixty years. Future transitions are more secure because Argentina today has a system of two strong democratic parties. Alfonsín's 1983 and 1985 defeats of the Peronist Party at the polls—another "first" in Argentina—helped produce both strong parties, his own and the Peronists, forced into democratic reforms by the shock of unaccustomed defeat.

In the economic realm Alfonsín's approach was too slow and too timid, and he paid a terrible price for his failure to attack the basic causes of Argentina's slow growth and soaring inflation. During the first two years of his term, he wasted valuable political time trying to apply the populist social doctrine of his own party, concentrating on cutting up the pie, instead of baking a bigger one. He underwent a reluctant and partial late-life conversion to market economics. Alfonsín's first high-stakes effort to get Argentina moving, the Austral currency reform of 1986, was a failure in part because he did not accept in time the need for even more painful structural reform to sustain the dramatic initial impact of the currency reform. After an electoral setback in 1987, Alfonsín's economic policies turned more timid and inflation spun out of control in a whirlpool of government red ink.

Alfonsín finished more popular abroad than at home, where soaring inflation evaporated his political image. Spiraling to hyperinflationary levels of several thousand percent per year, inflation's devastating impact on the purchasing power of wage earners destroyed the electoral prospects of Alfonsín's Radical Party. Foreign debt also weighed heavily on Alfonsín, and perhaps more heavily on Argentina than on any other Latin American country. Alfonsín believes that Argentina must get some debt forgiveness to revive its growth. He has personally restored Argentina's political image in the world to a degree no one thought possible at the end of a bloody military era which became everyone's image of a nightmare. Yet he failed to consolidate the economic underpinnings of a stable democracy, a problem on which he and Argentina are looking for help from abroad, as this interview reveals.

*   *   *   *   *

BOEKER: Your election to the presidency in October of 1983 was very important for the maturation of Argentine democracy in several ways: one that impressed me is that you maintained during the campaign a position that the military's amnesty of itself was invalid, whereas your opponent was willing to accept the military's action. Was your position a well calculated risk? Were you ever concerned about a military reaction to your victory?

ALFONSIN: I was certain that democracy could not be built on the basis of what I would have considered a fundamental ethical failure: to go on in Argentina as though nothing had happened. However, I also knew that we could not build a democracy by only looking backwards. That is why within the framework allowed by law we proposed to consider three different categories of crime associated with repression: first, that of those who gave the order; second, that of those who followed those orders; and third, that of those who exceeded authority when carrying out such orders.

Ethical considerations had to transcend any other concerns; if we did not do it that way we would have lacked the indispensable moral integrity we needed if we were to build a democratic system in our country.

BOEKER: Mr. President, in 1989 you will reach one more milestone in Argentina's democracy and in your distinguished career when you, a democratically elected president, turn over power to another for the first time in sixty years. Are you confident that your successor will finish his term and become the second in sixty-six years?

ALFONSIN: Absolutely! Argentinian democracy has been consolidated and no one is thinking anymore in terms of coups except, of course, some absurd minorities. Argentina is clearly at the beginning of a very long succession of democratic governments.

BOEKER: The October 1983 electoral result was a sobering experience for the Peronist Party, encouraging a transition to a less class-based and more democratic political party. Do you believe that transformation will be successfully completed?

ALFONSIN: I think the Peronists have taken great steps to democratize, as demonstrated by their carrying out for the first time primary elections within the party to select a presidential candidate. In any event, I don't think they have recanted their doctrine, which is still so open-ended that it creates uncertainty as to what they would do in power.

BOEKER: Mr. President, you have said that for a democracy to work, political parties have to recognize "an ethic of solidarity which transcends and limits competition. If we are going to put a country like ours back on its feet, we must meet all the challenges and adopt the necessary policies regardless of how harsh they must be." Would you say that such ethics today characterize your party and the Peronist Party?

ALFONSIN: I believe that in general, the Argentine people are clearly in favor of all the messages which we have tried to get across. I would say that there is solidarity among Argentines. We are doing a good job of consolidating democracy under very difficult economic circumstances while attending to the poorer sectors. I would say that the Argentine people have indeed shown solidarity without regard to political affiliation.

BOEKER: You have spoken eloquently and persuasively of the need to end Argentina's economic stagnation by abandoning the semi-autarkic model and exposing a more open Argentine economy to competition from abroad. Has much progress been made in this direction?

ALFONSIN: We have made progress, but it has caused us headaches. We have to fight to make Argentina competitive in a world where protectionism prevails, making competition very difficult. Argentina has suffered quite a bit of discrimination when it comes to international trade. It is an unfair international order. However there has been some headway in our industrial goods exports through measures such as reduction of export taxes and higher exchange rates. So my answer is yes, we are working to change the model which led us to disaster and are now beginning to see the world as an opportunity.

The position of my administration is completely different from that of the military government. They talked about opening the economy, but with the result that the world took advantage of Argentina. What happened was that we were overwhelmed with superfluous imports. What Argentina needs is to export, and to import more capital goods for our development. In 1989 we will probably break our record for exports. We are also striving to do the same with imports. That is what I call growth.

BOEKER: Regarding the debt problem and creditors' failure so far to act on proposals such as your own, for reducing the interest rate below market levels, you said in New York: "I am absolutely certain that what is not accepted today will be imposed tomorrow, by the force of events." Are you still absolutely certain?

ALFONSIN: I believe that creditors' positions will be changed first. When I became president it was considered out of place to talk about the political consequences of the foreign debt. It just was not understood. If you compare newspaper articles and statements made by officials and by bankers at that time with what is being written and said now, you will see the degree to which we have reached a better understanding of the problem.

Still, the pace of increasing understanding does not match the pace of our growing crisis, but it is advancing. The U.S. government is going to have to take into account Latin America's real needs.

The United States uses a different criterion when looking south. Just as it is true that we have advanced greatly in regard to democracy—for now it is judged that hemispheric security should not be in the hands of military governments in Latin America—so it needs to be understood that the burden of the foreign debt is generating tremendous problems in our continent, stagnation, misery, drug traffic, guerrillas. We are clearly seeing people who desperately look for alternatives—still within the system for now, but who knows what can happen. There are unsettling signs. Imagine that in Bolivia the party of the president of the country, Victor Paz Estenssoro, won only ten percent of the vote (in mid-term congressional elections). The prestige of another good president, José Sarney in Brazil, has been diminished. In Ecuador, the candidate for the incumbent party didn't even make the run-off in 1988 when it was earlier thought that he might win. There was trouble in the Dominican Republic and now the governing PRI Party in Mexico is having serious problems. Something is very wrong. People are looking for alternatives, seeking change; they are desperate with things as they are.

I frequently cite what happened in Europe. After World War I, the allied countries acted with economic toughness and the result was the rise of Hitler and Mussolini. In contrast, after World War II, the Allied countries acted with creativity, imagination, and generosity—the Marshall Plan—and democracies were thus consolidated.

Today in Latin America the democracies are being reborn within an economic framework similar to the postwar era. Even though there has been no war, our economies are devastated. Yet we are being subjected to a[n economic] "Treaty of Versailles." This cannot be.

In my opinion the people of the United States just don't think of Latin America as very important in their foreign policy. While there is of course concern for the situation in countries such as Cuba, Nicaragua, or Panama, the general problems of Latin America are just not portrayed to the American people as a subject of importance.

BOEKER: Your debt proposal had some useful elements, such

as the debtor countries working out programs of structural reform with international agencies; do you think that your emphasis on a four percent interest rate might have closed ears to your whole concept?

ALFONSIN: Do you know that most of the debt was acquired at a five percent interest rate? This was at the time when economies were swamped with "petro-dollars." The banks had to place their excess cash somewhere and were making loans at five percent, but later they raised the interest as high as twenty percent.

Right now prices for our exports are doing much better, but due to the increase in the interest rate we are going to have to pay in 1989 one billion dollars more than we paid in 1988. How long can this go on? What hope is there for our people when we are forced to accept higher interest rates due to problems in other countries over which we have no control? Just when we were doing so well with our exports, interest rates rise and we are in worse shape than before. In my opinion it is a tremendous injustice!

BOEKER: Mr. President, what would you advise the new administration in Washington regarding its actions and policies toward Latin America?

ALFONSIN: To talk, to start a dialogue, and not to act with arrogance and unilaterally. If we are going to live in a developing continent, clearly defined as democratic, why the unilateral action? And why not talk about our problem? I believe that through dialogue, and by getting to know each other, we will find fruitful solutions for all the parties involved.

BOEKER: You have referred to the relationship between the United States and Argentina as "mature." What do you see as indications of that maturity?

ALFONSIN: I believe it consists fundamentally in recognizing both our mutual interests and our differences. Both the United States and Argentina have much in common, but there are also different and contradictory concerns. Recognition of this situation is what I call maturity between friends.

CARLOS SAUL MENEM

Carlos Menem, the Peronists' successful candidate for president in Argentina's May 1989 elections, is a striking man. His piercing brown eyes, set over a prominent nose, are spectacularly framed by long black hair and massive black mutton-chop sideburns, cleanly divided by a white shock of hair flaring outward from each temple. The dramatic coiffure might fit comfortably in the salon of a romantic composer of the 1830s, but one hundred and fifty years later it assures that Carlos Menem stands out. If the effect was designed to overshadow his short, slight frame, it succeeds.

Carlos Menem and I met for this interview in the library of the American Ambassador's stately residence in Buenos Aires' Palermo district. Menem, a fastidious dresser, wore a trimly tailored black suit, white silk shirt and dark blue tie with a silver stripe; a compatible blue silk handkerchief was neatly arranged in his breast pocket. He looked rather the Edwardian gentleman, at home in this elegant setting. He presents a stark contrast to the thuggish Juan Perón who over fifty years ago founded the party whose banner Menem now carries. Likewise, the modern party, now officially the Justicialist Party, presents a marked contrast to the motley band attached to Colonel Perón in the '40s.

Along with party chairman Antonio Cafiero, Menem was a founder of the "Renovador" or Renewal Movement which has transformed the Peronist Party into a broad-based democratic party. The spur to reform came from two shocks, the brutal repression of the Peronists by the military regime in power from 1976 to 1983, and the first electoral defeat ever of the Peronists, by Alfonsín's Radical Party in 1983. The Renewal Movement's objective was to broaden the Peronists' appeal beyond their traditional base in Argentina's declining industrial unions to Argentina's middle class, a group longing for a truce in Argentina's class struggle. The Renewal Movement thus cast the party in the role of responsible opposition, eschewing violent demonstra tions and emphasizing good government and pragmatic eco- nomic policies in regional governments run by Peronists. The Renewal Movement also democratized the party itself.

Carlos Menem himself was one of the first to benefit from the party's internal reforms. He took the party's presidential nomi- nation from party boss Antonio Cafiero in the Peronists' first di- rect primary election in July 1988. The unions threw their support to Menem, but he claims he is not beholden to labor and em- braces still the Renewal Movement's commitment to a broad- based party and a pragmatic governing style.

Success has not come easily or without cost to Carlos Menem, now fifty-three. He is not from the main-line European stock and tradition which dominate Argentine society. His father was a Syr- ian merchant and Carlos' wife, a Moslem, is also from Syria. De- spite his family's modest means, Carlos Menem made it through the best of Argentine law schools and practiced law until politics absorbed all his energies. Along with many other Peronist offi- cials he was arrested by the military after the 1976 coup against Isabel Perón, tortured and held for five years in various prisons, where he became friends with many labor leaders. He claims no taste for vengeance against his military captors and says the last- ing impact of his degrading treatment has been a personal com- mitment to restoring human dignity to its rightful place in his country.

Carlos Menem has a convincing way of speaking straight from the heart. He impresses one as a warm, decent man who greets his friends with a Latin embrace. Carlos Menem wants to be liked by as many people as possible. That trait leaves some wondering whether he is tough enough to shape up an over-sized govern- ment. But his popular appeal on the campaign trail or elsewhere is impressive.

Governor of one of Argentina's smallest provinces, La Rioja, until 1989, Carlos Menem has much to learn about governing a vast country in a deep economic crisis. His efforts are concen- trated on that economic crisis which he correctly considers his government's overriding challenge. He is groping for an eclectic mix of approaches to reviving Argentina's growth, but starts from some populist presumptions (the domestic market is all im- portant; purchasing power must be pumped up) as did Alfonsín, although both reject the populist label. Menem wants a "grace period" or breathing space during which Argentina would not be charged interest on its debt to foreign commercial banks. This breather would not be a "moratorium," insists Menem, because it would be negotiated with banks, not imposed. He expects banks to recognize that Argentina cannot make any net payments now, if its growth is to be revived. He has no idea how one gets commercial banks to negotiate an arrangement they consider contrary to their interests.

Carlos Menem also wants to reach out for understanding in Washington, which—as he painfully recognizes in this interview—has some lingering memories of the old Peronism Menem and his Renewal colleagues hope to leave behind.

* * * * *

BOEKER: You had the bitter experience of being a political prisoner for five years. What impact has that experience had on your way of thinking?

MENEM: Such an arbitrary, brutal, and stupid action provokes its own resentment. But my imprisonment also instilled in me greater respect for the meaning of democracy and freedom. Until one loses freedom one cannot fully comprehend and feel what it means to be free. Of course nobody thinks it could happen to him, and for five long years. I used the time in prison to reflect, to understand that hatred does not provide a foundation to build anything. I thus left jail with no desire for vengeance or confrontation with my captors. Rather my ideas and my commitment concentrate on justice, peace, and liberty, so people can build the kind of communities in which they can realize their potential. Imprisonment did not leave me with a complex of internal conflicts. On the contrary, this injustice made me realize what it means to live in liberty and democracy. This is why we defend so passionately and consistently the way of life Argentinians chose in 1983, after many years of struggle.

BOEKER: Do you think that Peronism has definitely left behind the anti-democratic part of its origin?

MENEM: Peronism was never anti-democratic, not even tangentially. That idea was part of a campaign in which a U.S. ambassador (in the Forties) actively participated. Characterizing Peronism as fascist was their way to fight Justicialism (Peronism) in the face of its broad popular support. To this day, despite all our efforts, we have not been able to rid ourselves of that label which they hung on us in 1945–46.

Justicialism has proven during all these years that if there is a democratic movement in the world, it is ours. All the senseless killings of our members by our country's tyrants, all those deaths, persecutions, tortures and disappearances, have not caused us to change our direction. We have demonstrated that direction in this year's primary elections, which were a model for the rest of the country's political organizations. We continue to consolidate the concept of dignity for communities and for individuals as the core of the philosophy of our Justicialist National Movement. Of course we have our spats; who doesn't? There are acts of violence here and there as happens elsewhere. But that does not justify our continuing to be labeled fascist.

There were even times when we were called Marxists. Nothing could be further from the truth. If Marxist thought holds no place in Argentina's politics, it is because Justicialism has built a firewall with its broad-based, national, popular, urban, and Christian movement.

BOEKER: The name of Carlos Menem was linked to the beginnings of the Renewal ("Renovador") Movement within the Justicialist Party. Do your concepts of the class base and objectives of the party still correspond to that movement's goal of a party cutting across the classes?

MENEM: My concept continues the same. What has happened is that we cannot afford the luxury of emphasizing differences within our party. Even though I am the founder of the Renewal Movement, I don't want any more talk of "renovadores," orthodox-Peronists, Cafiero followers or Menem followers, because that doesn't get us anywhere; it only creates divisiveness. I prefer to speak simply of the Justicialist Party or Movement.

All the currents of thought within the party have served a purpose. The Renewal Movement changed the methods of the party, but this phase has been completed as has that of the orthodox Peronists. What was orthodoxy? It was a total and absolute commitment to Justicialist ideology during a period of tyranny, when the party was outlawed and mercilessly persecuted. Of the roughly thirty thousand dead or disappeared, twenty-eight thousand were Justicialists,[8] plus many more who were tortured. In the face of this persecution we needed to cling to our principles and reaffirm our conviction, and orthodoxy did that. After 1983 there were those who did not understand that the right approach was not to refine the same principles further but to open up in order to enrich our thinking. Thus some colleagues and I started the Renewal Movement. That movement and the orthodox tendency have thus complemented each other and invigorated our cause.

BOEKER: Your origin is different from that of other politicians in Argentina and in Latin America. Do you think that being a member of a family of relatively new immigrants, and not from Europe but from the Middle East, affects your point of view with respect to Argentina's problems?

MENEM: Not in the least. My parents are Syrian; they come from a small corner of that country. My Arabic ancestry does not affect my views on Argentina. There are other influences which are more important, including that of the founder of our party, Juan Perón.

In government I will continue along the same general lines (as at present), trying to improve the situation left by previous administrations, especially with respect to our relations with the United States.

BOEKER: In your opinion, are relations in Argentina between civilian authorities and the military still very fragile? Is there not a possibility that a breakdown here could once again threaten the continuity of democracy in Argentina?

MENEM: No, there is no possibility that the stability of constitutional government will be compromised by the sort of temporary restlessness we have seen in the armed forces. We must not forget that the courts are now prosecuting a large number of members of the armed forces, which obviously upsets elements in the military. But they do not have the kind of strength which would endanger the constitutional order.

My government's relationship with the armed forces will be the one provided in the constitution, based fundamentally on obe-

---

[8]Menem's estimate of thirty thousand disappeared is much higher than most.

dience and discipline. The president is the commander-in-chief of
the armed forces. Just the other day a high official of the army
told me that we would have its support. My answer was: "Look,
I don't want your support, but your obedience and your total and
absolute subordination."

To put an end to this problem we need to change the mentality
of the armed forces, to make them purely professionals, with a
defined mission and the modern, technologically advanced tools
to do it. They have a vast territory to defend; Argentina has an
area of three million square kilometers; there are regions, especially in the south, which are completely unprotected. To better
protect our territory we are thinking of dispersing military installations throughout the country.

There will be no breakdown of the constitutional order by the
armed forces.

BOEKER: What then do you see as the greatest threat to Argentine democracy?

MENEM: The greatest threat to Argentine democracy is the economic problem. Unfortunately during the last few years the rate
of inflation has surged. There has been a tremendous recession;
factories continue to close down. The purchasing power of our
workers has decreased and as a result there is great social and
economic instability. These conditions are dangerous for democracy, not only in Argentina but in other Latin American countries.
Brazil already has serious problems with its rate of inflation, recession, and the inability to employ all the resources it has.
Argentina's most serious threat is economic, not political.

BOEKER: Some foreign analysts expect that you will follow a
populist economic policy. Do you consider that "populist" is an
accurate description for your economic philosophy?

MENEM: That remains to be seen. Journalists confuse populism
with demagogy, but neither term describes our political views.

We will try to start a real revolution in production and industrialization by reviving our domestic market and gaining international markets. The enormous potential of our economy must be
liberated from an economic policy based purely on monetary and
fiscal restraint, which have produced complete stagnation. It is
unthinkable that over the last eleven years a country with all our

resources has had an average rate of growth of only .7 percent while our population has grown 1.7 percent. In other words the country's productivity has been shrinking at a rate of approximately one percent annually. That is what we want to change.

We want to put an end to this speculators' paradise here in Argentina. It is easy to make money here; you get dollars, change them to local currency, and earn interest of thirty percent while in most of the world the interest rate earned on dollar deposits is eight percent or nine percent. We want to end this.

We have to bring morality to government as well. Corruption is rampant and has got to stop. It is painful for me to speak like this, because I am talking about my country and my government, which is the government of all Argentines. Corruption is one of the wounds keeping our country paralyzed in a state of complete stagnation. We read a few days ago in *El Clarin,* Argentina's largest circulation daily newspaper, that in 1987 more than three billion dollars were overpaid through fraudulent invoicing originating in government departments. When Argentina's trade balance is barely five hundred million dollars, and three billion dollars are stolen, growth won't happen. People have put their hand into the state's pocket for three billion dollars, and then taken them out of the country.

We will start the country on the road to economic recovery based on work, increased production, and industrialization. Growth and development are the two main objectives. Of course, we cannot do this from one day to the next; there is no such magic. We are going to need at least three years of steady, conscientious work to get on the right road to achieve our people's objectives: greatness for Argentina and happiness for its people.

We have to cut income taxes in half, which are now almost thirty percent. We are going to broaden the income tax base which should mean we will collect about three billion dollars more a year. Everyone should be able to understand the tax system. I pay taxes, but have no idea what it is that I am paying. We need clear, concise and fair tax legislation which will facilitate better collection. Along with the tax reform the penal code should be changed. In the United States you have a long tradition of enforcing tax laws; Al Capone went to jail for income tax evasion, not for his other crimes. What we propose to do in Argentina is exactly that; whoever doesn't pay his taxes will go to prison.

If I had to define what populism means to us, I would say that it means simply providing greater purchasing power to the working classes. That is the narrow definition which is more consonant with the ideology of the Justicialist movement.

BOEKER: Will you continue efforts to privatize some of the state-owned industries?

MENEM: We are not opposed to privatization, but property of the state is owned by the people, not the government; therefore, sale of state industries has to follow the requirements of the law. We are pragmatists but we want all these procedures to be open ones. We will ask for public bids, and the granting of contracts will be subject to congressional approval.

Privatization for the sake of privatization does not make any sense and that is what has been happening. Furthermore, we are now privatizing profit-making public enterprises, especially in the petrochemical industry. Privatization should begin with enterprises which are lagging and not important to our national defense.

BOEKER: What do you mean by your proposal to negotiate, with the approval of Congress, a five-year moratorium on payment of the interest on Argentina's foreign debt?

MENEM: I have never spoken of a moratorium. What I have said is that we must make a distinction between the principal we owe, which is now sixty billion dollars, and the payment of interest. The Congress should define the framework within which the negotiation regarding the principal would take place, under Article 67–6 of the Argentine constitution.

Regarding the interest on the debt, we have to negotiate not a moratorium, but a grace period on a basis mutually agreed between the interested parties. Many economists and many debtor countries argue that payments must be restructured so that debtor countries can pay without sacrificing their growth. Without growth and development there will be little possibility to pay.

What does it mean to talk of a moratorium on the commercial debt, if in effect not a cent has been paid on it for I don't know how many years? In reality there already is a moratorium. As for the financial debt, according to the reports I have seen, Argentina has not paid one cent since April 1988.

An agreement must be reached on the form and terms of payment. We are not refusing to pay, but we must be able to grow and develop. It should be easier in the future. As a creditor of any business I would prefer that the business grow so that eventually it could pay me; otherwise payment is impossible. Latin American countries owe four hundred and twenty billion dollars, and if we cannot pay there could be a "crack" in the international economic order.

BOEKER: What kind of policies would you like to see from Washington with respect to Latin America, and particularly with respect to Argentina?

MENEM: We need a Marshall Plan for the countries of the region, one which would have here the same effect that the Marshall Plan had on postwar Europe: it enabled those countries to recover from the terrible situation they were facing.

The United States could also exert its influence in favor of the integration of Latin American countries. A positive U.S. attitude would help us proceed with a better possibility of success in our efforts to make Latin America a full economic partner in the world.

BOEKER: The subject of Latin American economic integration has come up in almost every interview I have had. Economic integration seems to be seen as a necessary response to what is happening in the European Economic Community, the Pacific Rim, and between Canada and the United States. There seems to be a fear that Latin America is being left behind in a world of commercial superpowers. Nevertheless, aren't the necessary preconditions for a realistic plan of Latin American economic integration still lacking?

MENEM: But, what are those preconditions? Whatever they are, they were even less established in postwar Europe, and yet not only has Europe done it, but it is also now in the process of further consolidating its economic integration. In Europe you have countries with different languages and different religions who have fought devastating wars; yet they have been able to unify. Latin America has a common language and religion. It faces common problems and has not been plagued by the bloody nationalist divisions of Europe. Truthfully I don't see what further preconditions we need for our integration.

BOEKER: Besides economic integration, what would you see as the most effective way for the hemisphere's democracies to help each other?

MENEM: Well, economic integration is necessary, but political integration is indispensable as a platform for economic integration. I do not mean doing away with the nation state, but rather forming a confederation or a federation of American states, something similar to what the United States has done. It could also happen in our continent. Such a confederation would have a common legislative body, such as the European Parliament, and a common identity document for people. We also need to start working toward achieving a common currency. This is fundamental.

BOEKER: Yet the traditional inter-American institutions, such as the OAS, have fallen into such a state of disuse that the countries of the hemisphere have felt the need to create new ones, such as the Group of Eight.[9] Why has Latin America neglected the existing institutions?

MENEM: It is very important that institutions such as the OAS be strengthened. However, the goals of the OAS should be compatible with the interests of other international organizations, such as NATO, in which the U.S. is a member. It would be a good idea both to strengthen the inter-American institutions and to make the security treaties more compatible with the United States' other commitments.

The clearest example of the inability of the OAS to deal with a crisis was the conflict of the Malvinas (Falkland) Islands. The OAS was supposed to be the institution through which we would be able to put an end to the process of colonization of the islands. However, the behavior of the organization during the conflict was not in the best interests of the nations of Latin America, and certainly not of Argentina. These organizations and the related treaties have become increasingly weak because they have not fulfilled their mission. The British are still in the South Atlantic and

---

[9]The Group of Eight was formed in 1985 by the elected presidents of Mexico, Colombia, Venezuela, Panama, Brazil, Argentina, Uruguay and Peru as a consultative group of democratic leaders. After General Noriega effectively deposed President Delvalle in 1988, Panama was suspended by the remaining seven who now also refer to themselves as the "Group of Rio."

the Malvinas Islands which they took from us in 1833 when Britain invaded and occupied territories which had belonged to us for centuries.

HUGO MEDINA

General Hugo Medina was a key figure in Uruguay's return to elected, civilian government in 1985. After an aroused Uruguayan public stunned the military regime in 1980 by rejecting its plan for a permanent military role in civilian government, Medina picked up the pieces and found another way out. He negotiated over a period of years with elected representatives of political parties until he was able to conclude a deal with Colorado Party leader Julio Sanguinetti and leftist coalition leader Liber Seregni for elections on a basis Medina could sell to the military. Medina left with a deep personal regard for Sanguinetti, whom he later served as minister of defense.

In an Uruguayan military long segregated from civilian society and with few skills for governance, Medina stood out as a reflective man with both negotiating savvy and a persistent, clear view of why the military should find a graceful retreat from government once the internal security threat of the Tupamaro guerrillas had clearly passed. As minister of defense, he has prudently shrunk Uruguay's military to the modest numbers it maintained before the military government.

Medina met me in the small villa which houses the ministry of defense. There was little security in evidence, and his personal office had fewer military trappings than that of the U.S. secretary of defense in the Pentagon. Medina's office displayed only an ornate sword of an Uruguayan military hero and, on Medina's coffee table, a bronze model of the equestrian statute of Paraguayan General Solano Lopez, commissioned by a committee Medina headed. Solano Lopez, who died in 1870 leading Paraguay's forces in the disastrous war of the Triple Alliance, was, Medina poignantly explains, actually protecting Uruguay's interests, but no one understood.

Medina's empathy for Solano Lopez is manifest. For Medina

today is an unhappy, almost resentful man, who sees himself suffering a similar fate. He resents that the military's role in defeating the Tupamaros is forgotten, while the issue of torture and murders involving some military officers lingers. He resents U.S. hesitancy in helping Uruguay's army, in part because of its past human rights abuses. He resents what he sees as a dual standard behind Uruguayans' 1988–89 debate as to whether the military deserves the same kind of amnesty for its excesses as the Tupamaro guerrillas earlier received. Medina is anxious to get some of this off his chest as soon as he orders each of us a cup of coffee.

Medina is short in stature and appears slightly stocky in a gray, three-piece suit. His gray and white hair is pressed flat across the top but brushed back on the sides over large, flat ears. I was not the first to notice a remarkable facial resemblance to Chile's Augusto Pinochet, but with softer features, not to mention personality. For Hugo Medina is an unassuming man, with a penchant for working things out quietly and a frank view of why Uruguay's military is not its ruling class.

General Medina is, however, a proud man, with some creditable things of which to be proud. He takes pride in his relationship of mutual trust with President Sanguinetti and was pleased to be asked to be his defense minister. He is proud of his role in the orderly, if protracted transition from military dictatorship to elected civilian rule. He pointed out to me the rooms in the villa where, during the transition, various key negotiations took place. At the same time, Medina believes it is the military's job to restore order, and it will be there again if civilians cannot settle their disputes nonviolently. Uruguay's military may have a narrower concept than some of its Latin counterparts of the trigger for military intervention in politics, but the concept is still there, as Medina makes clear in this interview.

*   *   *   *   *

BOEKER: Uruguay has not had a history of military governments. What were the reasons for the intervention of the armed forces in 1973?

MEDINA: The government as well as the country were deteriorating. There were labor conflicts, economic disorders, and a diversion of our legislators from their true responsibilities. This created a power vacuum. The military was the only viable, organized institution which could fill the vacuum, and it made its move only after years of trying to fight sedition from outside the government.

That sedition had started years before. It had begun initially with minor protests which kept growing in numbers and in intensity until the police could no longer handle them, and the executive instructed the armed forces to take over the fight against subversion. Meanwhile the legislature was losing credibility. Senator Enrique Erro strongly protested military involvement, but his protest was ignored and the president decided to dissolve Parliament on June 27, 1973. The government continued to be a civilian one, but it lost its legitimacy when it refused to call elections on the dates promised.

The military took over the executive in phases. Our training and experience led us to value democracy and made the takeover a rather unusual one. There was no intention to remove the president; it was not a coup against institutions, it was an attempt to restore order. Two facts testify to these intentions. First, when the Council of State was first established it was chaired by a senior politician of the National Party, Dr. Martin R. Etchegoyen, and the other members were people of prestige. Second, President Juan M. Bordaberry maintained his political ideology and had no problem with us.

The problem started when Bordaberry tried to dissolve the political parties, which had just completed one hundred and fifty years of existence, on the basis of his new theory of organizing politics around "currents of opinion," rather than parties. This was the reason why the military leadership asked for his resignation. Our position was that while one could certainly disagree with what the parties were doing, preservation of the party system was indispensable. Once the survival of the parties was assured, the National Council, made up of members of the Council of State and the generals of the armed forces, appointed Aparicio Mendez president.

BOEKER: The military came in by stages. When did the step-by-step retreat from power begin?

MEDINA: At what point can it be said that the military government began to deteriorate? The answer lies in two factors. The first factor is the difference between "putting the house in order" and being able to govern while preserving that order. This was part of the military's dilemma. It is not that the military were incompetent, but rather that we were not the people best suited to do the job of governing. The second factor was the duration of the period of military rule. The exercise of power wears one out, and in our case the wear was on the institution. We did not have the usual change or relief which normally occurs with constitutional government.

We wanted the armed forces to be in charge, not any one person. When a general had to retire, the command was passed to another and thus there were several different periods of the military government.

I was selected by the generals to assume command on June 7, 1984. A series of meetings with the political parties were already under way and important agreements were reached such as that calling for internal party elections.

Just before these internal elections took place, the armed forces presented a plan for constitutional reform which was rejected by the people in a plebiscite. The military lost and accepted the result. They then proposed a schedule for a three-year transition period, culminating in the national elections set for November of 1984, with full participation of political parties and full guarantees. This set up the critical step for transition from de facto to constitutional government.

The most important steps during this period were: 1) the 1980 plebiscite; 2) the 1982 internal party elections; 3) the round of negotiations at the Park Hotel which failed probably due to an excessively formal atmosphere; 4) the less formal, but successful negotiations at the Naval Club, and 5) the presidential elections in November 1984. We were able to reach a compromise in the Naval Club negotiations because everyone had his say; we all made concessions and there were no hidden clauses.

Why did we not deal with the problem of torture or other abuses of human rights? Simply because if we had tried to sort out that issue no agreement could have been reached. Civilians were not in a position to offer the guarantees which we wanted, and it would have been unseemly for the armed forces at that time to accept anything less.

Bruising attacks against the military were coming at that time from all possible sources, the press, television, radio, and books. They tried to discredit the armed forces in the eyes of the public by naming people within the military implicated in the violations of human rights.

I do not deny that there were in fact violations of human rights. However, one needs to understand that this happened during a time of armed conflict. In a very short time we wiped out the armed element of the Tupamaro movement, we discovered a communist group holding large quantities of weapons, and we took over the university. All that made the people aware that the enemy was inside our house. This does not by any means justify any violation of human rights, but it does explain why some members of the armed forces were themselves in danger of assassination, and it validates the urgency of obtaining information from those detained. Many lives were saved on this basis.

Our method was to arrest a man, interrogate him to get any information he had, and then send him to a detention camp. We did not have a sadistic mentality; in these detention camps we took care of their health and they were allowed to exercise and to prepare their own food. It would have been easy, for example, to have four thousand deaths in a camp for five thousand prisoners. However, the number of deaths was under one hundred, and the number of disappeared under all circumstances was twenty during the entire period.

The military also suffered some "disappeared," and several deaths for which we don't know who the killers were. But the law of March 1985 forbids further investigations in these cases. There should be equivalent treatment (in a political amnesty); if one pardons one side, he should pardon the other as well. If the State wants to prosecute one side, then both sides have to be prosecuted. If one wants to draw a line under the past as is customary in this country, there has to be total amnesty. Under those conditions we could all look to the future and go back to work.

BOEKER: Is the debate in Uruguay over the amnesty law, and a referendum on it, going to create new tensions between the military and civilian authorities?

MEDINA: I doubt the number of signatures (on a petition) is going to be sufficient to hold a referendum. If a referendum were held, the response of the people would be negative. The amnesty law will be upheld and that will prevent a confrontation.[10] Some people would like the amnesty law to be revoked, but that would

---

[10]The required number of signatures was obtained and a referendum on the amnesty law for military officers was conducted in Uruguay on April 16, 1989, with a majority of the voters upholding the amnesty.

be beyond the scope of the referendum. Whatever the case, if a confrontation does occur, it is not going to be provoked by the armed forces. The responsibility will be on the shoulders of those people collecting signatures—the "Tupamaros," the "Frente Amplio," and some members of the National Party.

BOEKER: During the 1983–84 transition period the armed forces tried to find some way to perpetuate a role for itself, through a National Security Council in a civilian government. Was this objective achieved in part and is it still being pursued?

MEDINA: That has not been decided because the basic law governing the armed forces has not yet been revised in a way which would resolve all ambiguities. There is a draft under way which the president intends to present to the Parliament.

The armed forces do not and should not have any power of decision-making within the government. Our constitution specifies that the president, together with the minister of defense or the Council of Ministers, will command the armed forces. We do not ask for power, but we do demand respect which is quite different. The armed forces owe obedience to the executive and cannot share its powers.

I would not deny that there are elements within the armed forces which would like to hold power, but they are a small minority. The great majority of the military want a country in which order prevails, the armed forces remain under civilian authority, and their work consists of preserving our sovereignty.

BOEKER: The armed forces increased in size during the period of military rule. Have they decreased since the transition, proportionate with their more limited role?

MEDINA: We are now back to the 1973 force levels. There was an increase of five thousand men, but it was reversed by January of 1988, when our total force structure exceeded by only fifty-four the planned reductions: twenty percent for the army, sixteen percent for the navy, and fourteen percent for the air force. In June 1988, there were almost four hundred positions we could not fill. People are not joining the armed forces because the salaries are so low they cannot make a living.

BOEKER: Is it likely that the military will now remain out of government for the foreseeable future, or are there any circumstances under which Uruguay would have another military government?

MEDINA: I don't foresee military intervention in Uruguay's politics, unless there are serious disorders, or if we need to take action in self defense.

You in the United States have not personally felt the brunt of terrorism in your own country as we have here in Latin America. We go from one period of terrorism to another. I don't know when the next one is coming but it may be foreshadowed by current labor disorders and refusal to accept the authority of the government?

The members of the armed forces are not robots. They are conscientious men and when they think about an armed conflict they realize that it means making decisions that could result in loss of lives, not only their own but those of the men under their command. If terrorists are inactive here it only means the timing is not right for them, or that their international leaders do not think terrorist action would be to their benefit or lucrative enough at this particular moment. When they decide that the time is ripe, here or anywhere else, they will strike, and we need to be ready. It would be inexcusable for us not to be prepared. The raison d'être of an army is to be ready to defend the country from internal or external threats.

BOEKER: Do you believe that the policy and the attitude of the United States had any impact on the military during the transition process?

MEDINA: Yes, the impact on us of the policy of the United States under the Carter Administration was negative. It condemned our actions without knowing the causes, and it put the issue of human rights above everything else. This is why I was saying to you that your perspective is different because you don't live with terrorism at home.

The United States continuously displays ignorance and contempt when it comes to making policies that affect all Latin America.

I told former U.S. Secretary of Defense Frank Carlucci that the United States had to change its approach toward Latin America. He asked me how, and I said that it was beyond the two of us because it had to do with economic changes. The United States has put a number of obstacles in the way of my country's economic recovery. I told him that if our products had access to the large U.S. market, I would be there buying the arms we need. We also hope that men of the importance of Vernon Walters will visit more often. Vernon Walters did the U.S. a great favor with his visit here because the image of the U.S. had been deteriorating seriously, although I don't know if the U.S. noticed.

Neither I nor my country are pro-Western; we are part of the West. What we want is a place in the trenches to fight beside you, but you ignore us and don't allow us that place. Russia, by contrast, is launching an offensive to make its presence noticed.

BOEKER: What do you want specifically? Do you want closer relations between the armed forces of the United States and Uruguay?

MEDINA: At that level our relationship is excellent.

BOEKER: How do you see yourself in the role of retired general participating in a civilian government?

MEDINA: I was enjoying my retirement after forty-three years in the military, but if the president offered me this position it is because he decided that I had something to contribute and I did not feel I had the right to refuse. There was also my desire to collaborate with the armed forces and a very strong personal feeling that makes me want to reciprocate the president's loyalty toward the armed forces.

BOEKER: Your participation in the government was not something that came out of the transition negotiations?

MEDINA: Absolutely not.

BOEKER: Are you satisfied with the course of civilian government so far?

MEDINA: If I said "yes" I would not be telling you the truth. I am satisfied with the intentions and the objectives of the executive branch, but not with the results. That does not mean that I am opposed to them; it only means that one hopes for more. One wishes that both the attitude of the people and of the government would be different.

JULIO MARIA SANGUINETTI

Julio María Sanguinetti, a patient consensus-broker whom most Uruguayans seem to like and surprisingly many even claim to know, is perhaps the ideal president for Uruguay's still delicate democracy. This affable journalist-turned-politician, with a sonorous deep voice, has been a soothing tonic for a troubled people whose democracy looked to be a burnt-out case in the 1970s. Some of Uruguay's hopelessly lost politicians then abetted the Tupamaro urban guerrillas, thereby contributing to a slide of their country into a dirty war in which the military crushed the Tupamaros, and a takeover of the government by Uruguay's military, for the first time in this century. Sanguinetti is now trying to reestablish Uruguay's humane, democratic tradition after this bitter, divisive national trauma.

The presidential offices are themselves a symbol of the line Sanguinetti has tried to draw under military rule (1973–84). This neat modern office building was to be the military high command's new headquarters. But after Sanguinetti was elected president in 1984, he took over the building for the presidency and renamed it the "Liberty Building."

Julio, as many Montevideans call him, received me there, in his modern top-floor office, looking out on three sides over Montevideo, where close to half of this small republic's people live. On the one window-less wall hangs a painting of a colorful country outing by the modern Uruguayan painter Figari, about whom Sanguinetti has written a book. Sanguinetti's otherwise unremarkable face takes a dramatic cast under the shading of his thick, dark eyebrows, brushed straight-up and cut across the top, creating something akin to a romantic painter's image of Pan, who could be hovering at the edge of the campestrian scene on the wall. The eyebrows have given Montevideo's political cartoonists the motif they have used to create their popular image of a handsome, virile president.

Sanguinetti's own effort has been to humanize the presidency again in this historically quiet little country, where both the terror of guerrilla warfare and the tense regimentation of military dictatorship seemed strangely out of place. He shuns the presumptuousness and perquisites of presidential power by traveling modestly, going shopping on foot with his wife Marta, and jogging in public parks. Sanguinetti also tries to see everyone and gain everyone's confidence. He included some members of opposition parties in his cabinet and regularly took opposition congressmen on his foreign trips. When George Shultz came to lunch in August 1988, Sanguinetti invited the leadership of all opposition parties and their probable candidates for president in the 1989 elections. To him these gestures are part of an effort to restore a civil style of politics in a country where radical politicians and the military were killing each other in the Seventies.

In a striking innovation, Sanguinetti and his Argentine counterpart, Raúl Alfonsín, tried to bring the same touch of cordial informality to communication among Latin America's chiefs of state, who traditionally take themselves very seriously. Sanguinetti talked on the phone several times per week to Alfonsín, as well as to Brazil's José Sarney, and occasionally to other members of the Group of Eight democratically elected presidents. In their first meeting, in November 1987 in Acapulco, the Eight returned the favor by choosing Sanguinetti as their spokesman. His forceful and logical presentation of the Eight's conclusions served them well. Leaders who know Sanguinetti are consistently taken by both his eloquence and his down-to-earth grasp of the political challenges he faces. Several seasoned diplomats, on leaving Sanguinetti's office, have called him Latin America's most effective president of the 1980s.

Yet just getting to the presidency was a stunning achievement for this young leader, who emerged as a bright new face in a faded political class. In 1973 it was not only the military which saw its seizure of power as one precipitated in part by the political decline—some would say bankruptcy—of Uruguay's traditional civilian politicians. Later as Uruguay's inexperienced military lost its way in the tangle of governance, Sanguinetti represented a new generation, even breed, which gained the military's confidence and offered them a graceful exit. During a rocky transition laboriously negotiated over five years, Sanguinetti, leftist coalition leader Liber Seregni and General Hugo Medina were the three who cut the final deal, the "Naval Club Pact," which cleared the way to the 1984 elections won by Sanguinetti.

Completing the political healing process has been Sanguinetti's main achievement in office. His conservative economic policies, and some luck with international commodity prices, have also got Uruguay's long-stagnant economy growing again while paying its debts. But much remains to be done before Uruguay's extravagant system of public services and welfare is brought into balance with what Sanguinetti calls the more limited reality of the country's ability to pay for them. Many of Uruguay's institutions are also weak and sorely in need of reform: a public bureaucracy too large and still growing; chaotic labor-management relations characterized by continual strikes and work stoppages; a politicized system of higher education which is low on quality and relevance to the modern job market; and courts which are so slow they cannot protect citizens' rights effectively.

Now fifty-three, Sanguinetti could be back for a second term, five years after he finishes his first in 1990. (Uruguay's constitution prohibits two consecutive terms.) If he returns, his talents will still face much work to strengthen Uruguay's reborn democracy. The talent is there, as displayed in Sanguinetti's broadranging interview with me.

* * * * *

BOEKER: Some argue that the decline of Uruguayan democracy in the Sixties paralleled a deterioration in the quality of its politicians, including corruption, nepotism, etc. If so, would you say that your country's new generation of politicians has learned from that experience?

SANGUINETTI: Historically, Uruguay has not been a corrupt country. There could have been isolated cases of excesses but corruption has never been rampant.

The deterioration of Uruguayan democracy was due not to one single cause, but several. Without trying to establish an order of importance, I can indicate several.

First, economic stagnation. Since 1955 the Uruguayan economy had not grown. A country that enjoyed great prosperity during the war and postwar periods stagnated after 1955, when the import substitution model for growth exhausted its possibilities. This led to the next factor.

Our social security system reached a point of serious crisis. A country which already at the beginning of this century had a very modern "welfare state," confronted in the Fifties a sharp discrepancy between its cost and the economy's capacity to pay for it.

Third, the politicization of the labor union movement. Labor unions had not been very important in the past and the traditional political parties neglected them; and thus during the period of economic stagnation, a Marxist leadership was able to take over the unions.

Fourth, the political parties fragmented. Constant internal turmoil weakened their role further and reduced their credibility. Politicians could not come up with any clear proposals, and people did not understand the economic crisis and did not realize that the real problem was that we were following an obsolete economic model that needed to be changed.

Fifth, the country had elaborated a surrealist "democratic" structure to such a degree that it was dangerous. The structure of the executive branch itself was a good example. From 1951 to 1967, the presidency consisted of a committee of nine members representing both parties. It was like a mini-senate. This tendency weakened our governmental institutions. In 1967, we were finally able to implement a constitutional reform but it was too late.

Sixth, we had an intellectual class totally out of touch with what was happening in the country. It was as though the university were not in Uruguay but in another galaxy, talking about an imaginary Uruguay. As a result this intellectual class was the instigator of enormous confusion and agitation.

I could add some other facets, but I believe these provide the "why" of Uruguay's declining democracy at that time. Thus, we had a crisis, suffered a coup d'état, and now the country has pulled out of it. So what has changed?

First, the country has started to grow again economically, having convinced itself that the import substitution economic model had to be changed. The governing party, which was the initiator of the "welfare state," is now more liberal in the classical, economic sense, not in the North American sense. We have abandoned the traditional Keynesianism of our party and today we have an export-oriented, open economy.

Second, the university has not negatively affected the political health of the country.

Third, the situation of the social security system has improved, but is still a serious problem.

Fourth, the development of the political parties has been uneven, but this is not a subject which I can discuss since the president should not engage in partisan politics in his own country. I would say that there are many politicians who do not realize that the essence of politics is a competition for excellence, not a Roman circus where advantage is gained simply by destroying an adversary. However, there are also many others with a more modern vision.

Thus, there has been constructive change even though a lot still needs to be done.

BOEKER: Thanks to some persistent politicians such as yourself, a few realistic military leaders, and an energized electorate, Uruguay had a very impressive, if protracted transition from military rule to elected civilian government. In your opinion which of these actors played the most important role in the transition?

SANGUINETTI: Transitions from de facto to democratic governments are always difficult and must be the result of balancing two different forces: the impatience of political leaders on the way back, and apprehension of the military on the way out. In balancing these conflicting positions, one can achieve a peaceful and stable formula or, as has too often happened in many Latin American countries, accept a superficial transition which contains the seed of yet another conflict. The Spanish transition was a very important event which inspired us. From such historical experiences one reaches the conclusion that the intangible, psychological elements are the most important. We were extremely careful to keep this in mind.

Now that Uruguay's elected government is four years old, I can honestly say that it has succeeded and that it has the support of the vast majority. Of course there is never total unanimity. There are still some military officers nostalgic for power; there are also some civilian groups which have not adjusted to the rules of a democracy. Fortunately, Uruguay has a long tradition of democratic rule and political stability. There has been in this century only that one military government which ended in 1984.

For us the key was to achieve the transition through negotiation. At the time there were three important countries in the region changing from military to civilian rule, Argentina, Brazil, and Uruguay. They may have seemed identical from afar but each actually followed a different path.

The Argentine situation was similar to the fall of the Greek military junta. When a military regime suffers a military defeat the regime collapses. Democracy emerged in Argentina all of a sudden, and without prior negotiations, once de facto government broke down.

In Brazil, democracy broke out in a surprising way. The military set the rules for an intermediate period during which they expected their electoral mechanism to produce the "right" presidential candidate. The opposition headed by Tancredo Neves and José Sarney worked out a political solution which allowed a more democratic transition to play out within the rules set by the dictatorship. It was a good piece of political engineering which reflects the Portuguese temperament. The same process would be very difficult in a country without Brazil's long tradition of solving conflicts through negotiations.

Uruguay does not have a history of military "presidents." Even when the military was in power, we had civilian presidents. Only toward the end of the dictatorship did a military man become president. The Uruguayan transition occurred through direct negotiations between the political opposition and the military leadership, with the government per se relegated to the sidelines.

The negotiation of Uruguay's transition was long, with several failures along the way, but the situation moved forward. We started negotiations before 1980, but they were broken off. At that time the military were convinced they had the support of the population, and held a plebiscite on their version of constitutional reform. The opposition won with a majority voting "no," despite the fact that we had no access whatsoever to the media.

There were two unique developments during this process. First, that the military called a plebiscite and then accepted the results; second, that we could win without any publicity and without any ability to mobilize voters. Our situation was not comparable to that of Chile in 1988. In Chile you had functioning political parties with some access to television time, an opposition press, rallies, and other opposition activity. We had nothing. All we had during a three-month long campaign was one single television program where two government representatives and two spokesmen for the opposition held a roundtable discussion. But this had great impact throughout the country since it had been ten years since the people had witnessed any open discussion.

The plebiscite caused great commotion within the military, but they accepted the result and decided to negotiate. A timetable was set including primary elections within the parties in 1982, since the military would negotiate only with legitimate representatives of each party. In primary elections which took place on the same date throughout the whole country, the two major political parties elected their representatives. We then began a new round of negotiations to get to the 1984 presidential elections.

The first round of negotiations failed. Other, spectacular sessions also failed, creating a great deal of uncertainty since the election date was approaching and the terms for it were not defined. Finally in August of that election year a round of negotiations held at the Naval Club produced an agreement. It was a long process but it had one great advantage: it forced the politicians and the military to get together, to get to know each other, and to negotiate.

When we first sat down at the table we saw each other as enemies, but through dialogue we were able first to relate on a personal basis, and then to impart concepts which led us to a more authentic and satisfactory solution to which the military consented. The important point is that we did not end up with a resentful military leadership just waiting to get back into power. In the process, the majority of the military became committed to the success of the transition and felt as responsible as we for its leading to political stability. Looking at it another way, if the transition had produced a failure, the opposing minority in the military would have reproached its own leaders rather than the political parties. This phenomenon was the critical key to the Uruguayan transition.

BOEKER: Did the policy of the U.S., particularly on human rights, have any impact during this whole period of negotiation?

SANGUINETTI: Yes it did; without doubt, it had a positive impact. I can highlight one event. The timetable for the transition was set the day before Terence Todman, the U.S. assistant secretary of state for Latin American affairs under President Carter, arrived as an envoy to discuss human rights and a political solution for Uruguay. The military leadership met and set the timetable. Nothing was announced at that time. But much later the date

of that meeting became known and we were able to determine
without any question that the military's decision was made under
the pressure of Todman's visit.

To put this visit in its proper context we must remember that
while today Uruguay has a democracy and is very active internationally, at that time, after the 1973 coup, nobody came to Uruguay, and the military government had many differences over
human rights with the Carter administration. It is in this sense
that Todman's visit was quite a political event.

In the case of Uruguay, U.S. human rights policy had a very
favorable impact. I wouldn't say it was the decisive factor, but
it was a constructive influence and, without any doubt, an important one.

BOEKER: Do you believe that during the transition period the
Carter and Reagan administrations could have played a more constructive role?

SANGUINETTI: I guess one always feels that more could have
been done, but that goes for us too. But in general the influence
of the United States during our political transition was a positive
one.

The United States' role on questions of basic human rights is
very important because here it has the capacity to exercise a
moral influence, with significant political force. It is not so influ-
ential in other areas where its policies are either weak or unclear.
But in the area of human rights, the U.S.'s own political system
provides in its strong guarantees of those rights, a solid base for
its role. Why does the U.S. continually raise the flag of human
rights when negotiating with the Soviet Union? Because on this
issue the U.S. has credibility which strengthens its negotiating
leverage and I think it is a smart approach. The same thing holds
true in our part of the world. When the U.S. carries the flag for
human rights, it does so with political credibility and thus its influence is great.

Then we have our complex economic problems. Democratic
governments have to deal with a wave of rising expectations.
People associate democracy with economic prosperity, with a
"chicken in every pot," and while this is a natural way to react
it does not correspond to reality. The most difficult challenge facing democratic governments is managing these economic expectations. Uruguay is a typical example. During the first three and

a half years of our government we increased real wages by thirty percent, which is extraordinary. Nevertheless we suffered a lot of labor strife. It has a political component, but we cannot ignore a perception that people earn too little and that our economic policy is very restrictive. When one explains that it is not realistic to expect earnings to continue to increase at such a rate, one receives blank stares of disbelief. It is indeed a difficult situation for democratic governments to manage.

A critical aspect is that of the foreign debt. From the beginning Uruguay has held the position that the debt problem has to be dealt with through negotiations.

Uruguay is meeting its obligations and it will continue to do so, but it is a real burden. At times economic conditions may be particularly favorable, as in 1985 when the price of oil fell and interest rates were lower. However, at present we are facing the prospect of an increase in the price of oil and higher interest rates. Thus our situation is becoming increasingly difficult.

Even with sound economic policies, it is very difficult to keep up debt payments which represent twenty percent of Uruguay's total exports, and that is less than other Latin American countries have to pay. It is in this area that the United States, as well as the rest of the industrialized countries, have still ahead a very important role to play.

Just as important as the debt problem is the issue of protectionism. The Uruguayan position is that the problem of debt has to be seen as linked to the issue of free trade. This has been our position in all forums, especially in GATT[11] negotiations. The "Uruguayan Round" bears the name of my country because we made every effort to make GATT the organization which can achieve more liberal trade. Our position has been similar to that of the U.S. administration. However, protectionist tendencies in the U.S. Congress are worrisome; if these prevail, the effect for Latin American economies would be extremely negative. I can neither be too clear nor too emphatic on this point because the consequences would be extremely serious. A resurgence of protectionism in the U.S. would cause serious economic recession in Latin America, it would revive anti-American political currents, and it would severely hurt U.S.-Latin American relations.

Finally, the United States has a role in military cooperation. There is a theory that sees the U.S. as a decisive element in mili-

---

[11]The General Agreement on Tariffs and Trade.

tary coups, but this cannot be demonstrated objectively and historically. It could have been true on some occasions but this has not always been the case. Recent years have certainly not seen military coups in Latin America encouraged by the United States. Of course, the United States has exerted influence over the armed forces of certain countries, sometimes with a negative and sometimes with a positive effect. In the case of Uruguay we think it has been positive and today we would like to have more cooperation between both countries' armed forces. This is a controversial subject in Uruguay but I do believe that it would be favorable, in the spirit of respect for Uruguayan sovereignty.

BOEKER: You have a different, more informal political style from that of other heads of state; you like to take a walk in the city, go shopping with your wife, and travel without the usual perquisites of other heads of state. Is there a message in this style? Are you trying to present a contrast?

SANGUINETTI: It is more like restoring a country's tradition. Uruguay had always enjoyed a presidential style which was simple and authentically republican. When violence and guerrilla warfare erupted in the Seventies, presidents became increasingly isolated from the people and surrounded by security agents. Thus, our younger generation was not accustomed to being able to approach their president on the street, at a football game, or during a public ceremony. I have simply gone back to the way it used to be. It humanizes politics and the vision the people have of their leader. It also gives the president an opportunity to hear and see a lot that reports and statistics do not show.

BOEKER: The success of democracy in the larger Latin American countries has an impact on the rest of the continent. How do you view the prospects for consolidation of democracy in Argentina and Brazil?

SANGUINETTI: Uruguay has never had its destiny determined by what happens in neighboring countries. We had a democracy at a time when Brazil and Argentina were under military regimes.
   Of course we are not an island, and the fact that Argentina and Brazil are now democracies creates a very positive climate for us given the degree of social and economic influence these countries exert on Uruguay. Every day I read the Brazilian and Argen-

tine press, which I find as necessary for my work as the Uruguayan press.

I believe that democracy is consolidating in both countries which, of course, are very different from each other.

Brazil is a whole subcontinent which managed to maintain its unity. By virtue of its vast territory, Brazil has both great diversity and a tendency to isolationism. It is fighting to conquer its own borders, tantamount to what happened in the United States with its Far West. In this sense the history of Brazil resembles, more than that of any other country in Latin America, the history of the United States.

Brazil reflects the unity of the Portuguese Empire. While the Spanish Empire fragmented in twenty different pieces, the Portuguese Empire preserved its unity, which is still reflected in Brazil's military and diplomatic institutions. The Brazilian Army is the only army in Latin America that did not originate from wars of independence. It is a continuation of the Portuguese Army that came to America with John VI, King of Portugal, at the time of Napoleon's invasion of Iberia. This heritage makes Brazil different from any other country in the region.

Brazil is consolidating its democracy in its own fashion but on a solid foundation. Its industry and agriculture lead the country in an economic development which is unfortunately uneven and very unbalanced. On the one hand it manufactures airplanes which are sold in Europe, and on the other there is extreme poverty. Brazil is full of contradictions, but it is an extremely dynamic country.

Argentina has lots of problems, but President Alfonsín will transfer power to another elected president [Carlos Saúl Menem in July 1989] for the first time in sixty years, and this is quite an achievement. When something similar happened in Venezuela thirty years ago, people did not realize the significance of the event, yet it marked the end of Venezuela's endemic propensity to coups d'état. Something similar is happening in Argentina. It is a great country with a rich cultural tradition and a solid economic base which has gone through very serious spiritual problems.

While Brazil's and Argentina's democracies may seem to be in a state of agitation, I believe they are basically solid. Despite the problems, we feel very optimistic about the future of our region.

BOEKER: You have mentioned protectionism and foreign debt

as two subjects which in your opinion should be on the agenda of the new U.S. administration. Are there other challenges which you believe should be taken up by a new administration in the United States?

SANGUINETTI: I believe that serious consideration must be given to the image of the United States in Latin America. When my generation was growing up during the Second World War and postwar era, the United States was the great leader of the West, the country of greatest prestige, even admiration. However, this leadership role is now very much in question, perhaps to a lesser degree in Uruguay where what the U.S. represents is respected, even while U.S. foreign policy is criticized. Realistically speaking there could be very valid reasons to be critical, but I doubt that this in itself would account for the image of the United States being so diminished and questioned as it now is.

Spain is now the key model for us. My generation in Uruguay did not identify at all with Spain; forty years of Franco had totally alienated countries with a republican tradition. Spain had lost all influence and everything Spanish was viewed here with suspicion. Spain's return to democracy has restored it as a model, and the enormous prestige Felipe González enjoys in Uruguay helps democratic leaders here. Without any question, it would also help us to have a better image of the United States, a great democracy and still the leader of the West in scientific, technological, and economic advance.

BOEKER: Mr. President, in 1984, you said "the United States is an island unto itself, which understands little of the rest of the world, and therefore has made mistakes in its policies for the long term." Do you still believe that of the U.S.?

SANGUINETTI: It is generally believed that the United States does not really understand the psychology of Latin America. I believe this is true, but it is also hard for Latin Americans to understand the United States. We have to make a mutual effort. Latin Americans must accept that some of the things which are said about us are true; such as that our personal inclinations and our romantic tendency sometimes prevent us from pragmatically facing economic realities. However, North Americans should also understand the importance that Latin Americans place on certain spiritual or humanistic values and on the concept of honor.

OSCAR ARIAS

When I met with Costa Rican President Oscar Arias he referred continually to his talks with some of the most ruthless of Central America's practitioners of the politics of force: the Sandinista brothers Daniel and Humberto Ortega, contra leader Enrique Bermúdez and El Salvador's FMLN guerrilla leaders—with whom he was to meet the day following our interview. But Oscar Arias seems badly out of place among these hardened fighters of Central America's long civil wars. Arias is a small man, with a puckish face. He is an idealistic, almost pacifist intellectual who is proud of the fact that his country has no army. Yet this young president-turned-mediator feels confident that his assertion that Central America's conflict cannot be resolved on the battlefield will eventually be convincing to the likes of Ortega and Bermúdez, as well as Fidel Castro, whom Arias accuses of backing El Salvador's guerrillas.

For his tireless efforts so far, Oscar Arias has received the Nobel Peace Prize. His efforts have also put on the map his tiny country, which Arias believes has a claim to being the oldest democracy in Latin America. Costa Rica certainly is the Latin American country with the longest continuity in democratic government today. Elected civilian governments there have followed each other peacefully and regularly since 1949. Costa Rica is, as Arias recognizes, a different world from the poorer, racially mixed, and socially deeply divided Central American countries to the north—El Salvador, Nicaragua, Honduras, and Guatemala. Costa Rica is a country of largely European immigrants, a prosperous little country of middle-class burghers and small capitalists, as Arias says. He describes Costa Rica's advanced social legislation and programs as a "welfare state." In contrast, he characterizes Costa Rica's neighbors as "garrison states," ones in which the military has been used to protect the interests of a narrow ruling class. Far-reaching social reform and economic development are needed before stability can prevail in Central America, Arias says.

Arias is thus pessimistic about the prospects for early consolidation of democracy in other Central American countries. He believes in fact that only strong warnings from the U.S. to military leaders preempted one or two military coups in 1987 and 1988 against the struggling civilian regimes in El Salvador, Honduras, and Guatemala. Arias believes strongly that democracy and peace have to go hand-in-hand in Central America if stability is to be restored to this troubled region. He thus takes great pride in the fact that his peace proposals, in contrast to the previous Contadora mediation effort of five Latin American countries, addressed democratic reform, including in Nicaragua, as well as security. He still insists that guarantees of democracy and security must proceed together.

President Arias was not a logical choice for the ambitious efforts to mediate peace which he launched in a series of personal meetings with other Central American presidents on the Guatemalan city of Esquipulas. At forty-eight, he is Central America's youngest president, a somewhat bookish intellectual and lawyer with a degree from the University of Essex and studies at Boston University, as well as a degree in law and economics from the University of Costa Rica. He was already minister of planning and economic policy in Costa Rica at age thirty-one.

But Arias is an intense man, who takes himself very seriously and believed he, as a Central American, had a chance to help where outsiders, particularly Americans, could not. The accords he dramatically and unexpectedly got the four other Central American presidents to sign in August 1987 came as a shock to the Reagan administration, which was still trying to win congressional approval for new military assistance to the Nicaraguan contras. His efforts surprised Washington again in March 1988, when he helped produce a cease-fire agreement between the contra leadership and the Sandinista government in Nicaragua; and once again in February 1989 when Central American presidents agreed on a program which included disarming and resettling the contras, as well as holding elections in Nicaragua in 1990 under a reformed electoral law.

Arias, with reason, is intensely proud of these achievements as an effort by the Central Americans themselves to take charge of their own problems. He believes these accords have brought real, if limited progress, including the first extended halt of fighting in Nicaragua in a generation. He was perplexed that these efforts were not more warmly received by the Reagan administration and looks to greater appreciation of his initiatives by the Bush administration. Arias is also disappointed that other Latin American countries have seemingly lost interest in the Central American conflict. The original Contadora countries, whose mediation efforts in Central America came to nothing, have retreated from the field. Renamed as the "Group of Eight," these democratic countries have turned their efforts to increasing Latin America's voice on other issues. Arias resents that other countries have not denounced as vigorously as he, the Sandinistas' failure to live up to their commitments for democratization, including fair elections.

Yet Oscar Arias is not so discouraged as to diminish his efforts. In fact, he expected even before U.S. elections in November 1988, that the new U.S. administration would have to embrace the logic of the peace process he helped launch, the logic of Central Americans coming together to solve their own problems.

* * * * *

BOEKER: Mr. President, why has it been possible for Costa Rica to have a stable democracy, an achievement which still eludes other Central American countries?

ARIAS: There are many reasons, historic, sociological, and political. In the first place Costa Rica is historically different from the other Central American countries. It is a country of small entrepreneurs, with the exception of the banana plantations which are basically in the hands of transnational companies. Coffee production is widely distributed among small land holders. This gives us a much more egalitarian society than in the rest of Central America.

Then this is a country with a predominantly civilian, non-military mentality. Our first President was a teacher, and it has consistently been liberal civilian leaders over the past century who have taken the actions which give Costa Rica its different political structure and character. Local government in Costa Rica is very strong. We have led the way with important reforms such as abolition of the death penalty, and a legal system which was advanced even a hundred years ago. We have had compulsory free education for one hundred and twenty-two years. Finally, what has helped most in consolidating Costa Rica's modern democracy was the dissolution of the armed forces on December 1, 1948.

In October 1989, Costa Rica celebrates one hundred years of democracy. For that occasion I expect to inaugurate in the center of San José, "Democracy Square," to celebrate this event with some flair, because very few Third-World countries have such a record. Of course, over a period of one hundred years there were some interruptions in our democratic process—the last in 1948, when there was a feud which was rather like a civil war for us. Nevertheless, the predominant fact is that we have had one hundred years of democracy.

In the 1940s we began to build our welfare state, which contrasts to the garrison states in the rest of Central America. This welfare state has given us important social and political stability. We have a national health program which covers the entire population. Illiteracy is less than six percent; life expectancy is seventy-seven years, comparable to any industrialized country. Infant mortality is thirteen per one thousand, lower than in many regions of the United States. The most important priority of my administration is low-income housing, which is why I have said that Costa Rica will be the first slum-free country. Costa Ricans have set for themselves the objective of making our country not only one free of slums and drugs, but also the most developed in Latin America.

Looking back over the last forty years, our income per capita has increased six-fold, and population four-fold. We have had this growth without any Costa Rican being exiled, or imprisoned for his political ideas, or having to pay with his life for disagreeing with the government. In that sense we are unique in Latin America.

Costa Rica is an excellent example that a developed, fair society can be built within a democracy without having to pay the political price that so many of our neighbor countries have had to pay—without having a revolution, firing squads, filling the jails with political prisoners, or sending dissenters into exile.

BOEKER: How do you see the prospects for consolidating civilian, elected regimes in neighboring countries such as Guatemala, El Salvador, and Honduras?

ARIAS: I don't believe that these governments are going to be able to consolidate their new democracies unless they do what

Costa Rica has done; they must be able to meet within the framework of democratic governments the urgent and basic needs of their people: jobs, education, health, nutrition, and housing. The mission of any political system is to benefit human beings. Democracy alone is not enough if the system cannot meet the basic needs of society. Democracy is not an end in itself but a political system which allows people to change their government without violence. This is a nice definition of the democracy we have tried to achieve in Central America. In the past people have had to resort to violence to change their government.

Obviously, the war in Central America has meant that those basic needs cannot be met, and with the exception of Costa Rica, most Central American countries are poorer today than before the wars. If for Latin America in general, the foreign debt is the main obstacle to development, for Central America it is the war.

The essence not only of Costa Rican democracy, but of democracy everywhere is negotiation, deal making, knowing how to be flexible, being tolerant, rejecting absolute truths, and searching for consensus. This has been the spirit of the peace plan, and this is what we would like to bring to our neighbors.

There are countries which have always had powerful armies at the service of oligarchies defending the status quo, and the privileges of very wealthy minorities. Such alliances would overburden any democratic government. It is no secret that if it were not for Washington's strong support of the elected governments of the region, the military would have easily launched a coup or two. This has been the pattern in the past, always encouraged by the privileged few.

Costa Rica had the good fortune of persuading its most privileged groups that they had to share some of their power and wealth, so we could have the kind of social stability and political security which would allow us to hold elections every four years without fear of kidnappings and without having to walk around with bodyguards.

If we want to consolidate these incipient democracies, their economies must grow, but growth won't happen unless they implement internal changes essential to be competitive internationally. The Central American Common Market was the most dynamic factor for economic growth in the last thirty years, but no longer is, for political and economic reasons. But it is through a similar opening to the world market that we in Costa Rica are inducing needed internal changes and structural adjustments. The rate of domestic investment has increased; foreign investment and our exports have diversified; our industrial sector has become more efficient and more competitive in markets outside the Central American Common Market. The U.S. gave us a hand with the Caribbean Basin Initiative.

If other countries cannot overcome economic stagnation, it will be not only the military, but also the people who will wonder whether democracy is the system under which they want their children to grow up. That is the great challenge that our countries face and that is why we need a lot of help. For that reason the Central American peace plan has a chapter addressing the necessity of economic aid. The peace plan makes democracy a necessary condition for peace, but without economic aid the emerging democracies will not survive.

BOEKER: Speaking of the peace plan, its importance was as an effort of the Central American countries themselves to take their destiny in their own hands. Is it possible to continue along this road? Or has that effort been blocked?

ARIAS: If we analyze developments since August 7, 1987, we will realize that everything that has happened is due primarily to the peace plan and not to military action. Important events such as freeing political prisoners, bringing the Central American conflicting parties to negotiations, having the Salvadoran guerrillas talk to the Duarte government and the Guatemalan guerrillas talk to President Cerezo—all that is because of the peace plan and not because of military action. When the contra forces met with the Sandinista officers, first in Sapoa and then in Managua, it was because of the peace plan and not because of military action. When the newspaper *La Prensa* was reopened in Managua it was because of the peace plan and not because of military action. When Guillermo Ungo became a presidential candidate in El Salvador it was because of the peace plan, not because of military action. But whatever we have accomplished is not enough, because we have not gotten results as quickly as we had hoped, we have taken some steps backwards, and the whole world has watched with much indifference.

Everybody is asking me to raise my voice to pass judgment on what has happened since August 7, 1987, when we signed the Esquipulas II Treaty in Guatemala. I continually make such judgments before local and foreign press, as well as in communications with other political leaders. I am only sorry that I seem to be the only one called upon to raise a voice every time a step backwards is taken on the road to peace. I'll give you an example: the Salvadoran government stated that it would be very difficult to re-establish the dialogue with the guerrillas before elections. So I had to persuade both sides, the Salvadoran Government and the guerrillas, that they should talk before the elections. I had to do the same with the Guatemalan Commission for National Reconciliation and the Guatemalan guerrilla leaders. I talked for weeks with President Ortega about the importance of his dropping the prerequisite that the next meetings between the Contras and the Sandinistas take place inside Nicaragua, because I believed that such meetings would not be fruitful if they take place there.

I complained to Felipe González of Spain that he has not raised his voice against specific steps backwards and against those signatory countries which are not living up to the Esquipulas II Treaty. This also goes for many other democratic leaders. The democratic leaders who believed in and supported the peace plan should call Central American presidents to account for lack of compliance with the agreement. The stimulus and support we received from Europe and Latin America at the time of the agreement have disappeared.

I also mentioned to Felipe González that I was the only one who expressed great indignation when the Nicaraguan government imprisoned thirty-eight opposition leaders for a demonstration in Nandaime it had approved. I have protested again and again, and I have personally told Daniel Ortega that he must free these leaders because their imprisonment represents a step backwards in the peace plan. I also told Felipe González that Europe should play an important role and that Spain should be the advocate for the peace plan before the European Community.

I get very impatient because sometimes I think that no one should have a more firm commitment to the peace plan than the presidents who signed it. Whoever succeeds me, or Napoleón Duarte, Vinicio Cerezo, José Azcona, or Daniel Ortega will have less of a commitment to Esquipulas II than we do. We must honor that treaty because we thereby created a great hope for twenty-eight million human beings who want and deserve peace.

Your question was really whether the peace plan is dead; my answer is no. What we need to find again is the will to fulfill the plan which we had when we reached agreement on August 7,

1987. I don't see that will at present. For me there is only one road: to honor the Esquipulas II Treaty. The only other alternative is to continue the war, and I will never agree to that alternative which condemns Central Americans to being poorer every day.

BOEKER: Do you think it would be possible to put aside the commitments with respect to the democratization of Nicaragua and implement the rest of the plan?

ARIAS: I would not agree to that. I do not believe that there will be real peace in Nicaragua unless it moves toward pluralism and democracy. The Esquipulas II Treaty covers five countries. For me, democracy is the precondition for peace in Central America. I truly believe that lasting peace will not be possible unless our citizens can freely choose their leaders. One cannot exempt any signatory from being democratic, because the essence of the plan I presented to my colleagues is precisely the democratization of the whole region.

The main concern of the earlier Contadora Group's proposals was the security of the countries of the region; democracy was not seen as a requirement for peace. In contrast, the Costa Rican proposal requires that democracy be a prior condition for lasting peace.

BOEKER: Do you think it is time for the countries which signed the Esquipulas II agreement to implement a series of measures which have to do with security, such as eliminating foreign bases, asking foreign advisors to leave, and reducing the military forces of some of the countries? And is it possible to implement any "package" concerning internal and external security of the countries involved without participation of the United States and the Soviet Union?

ARIAS: For me, the sequence of measures to achieve peace is the following: first, democracy is a necessary condition for peace, which in turn will allow greater economic and social development, and thus eventually greater security for each country. would not want to reverse that sequence and negotiate security for each Central American nation, leaving democracy as the last step. A peace without democracy would be too fragile.

BOEKER: You have said that the Sandinistas have used the war against the contras as an excuse for not fulfilling the commitments they made to their own people, such as development of the economy and democratization. Do you expect a different political evolution in Nicaragua as the war with the contras ends?

ARIAS: The Sandinista government has used the contras as an excuse for not negotiating and to justify the failure of the communist experience in their country.

I have faith in what dialogue can accomplish. The peace plan brought the Sandinistas to the negotiating table, not the contras. The Sandinistas used to say that they could not allow any contra leader to enter Nicaragua because the country would have to be disinfected; today they want to meet in Nicaragua, although I prefer that meetings between the Sandinistas and the contras take place outside Nicaragua. The Sandinistas used to say that they would only talk to the "owner of the circus, not to the clowns," or that they could only speak through an intermediary, and I got them to accept Cardinal Obando y Bravo. That phase is over. Nobody would have thought ten months ago that Enrique Bermúdez and Adolfo Calero were going to sit down at a negotiating table with Humberto and Daniel Ortega.

Coming back to your question, I don't believe in using force; I have always been against it not only in Nicaragua but also in El Salvador and in Guatemala. The only way out is negotiation. The ideal solution in Nicaragua would be for the contras to leave Honduran territory and relocate in sites to be determined during the negotiations and gradually to re-incorporate themselves in the political life of their country. I think the same should be true for El Salvador and Guatemala. What we must do is overcome the impasse which now exists between the two extreme positions in these countries now mired in internal conflicts.

There are two key countries to achievement of peace in Central America: the Soviet Union and the United States. If Washington really believes in the peace plan and wants it to succeed it must stop military aid to the contras, and Moscow has to stop supporting guerrillas in Guatemala and El Salvador. That is what I asked of Fidel Castro and that is what I asked of the Reagan administration. I requested that personally of President Reagan, and in press conferences in the United States, and in a joint session of the U.S. Congress.

I spoke to Fidel Castro at the inauguration of President Rodrigo Borja in Ecuador. I expressed to Castro my concern that as long as the Salvadoran guerrillas continue to receive the help they now get from the Cuban government, he is undermining the Esquipulas II Treaty.

BOEKER: What was his reaction?

ARIAS: Fidel thought that I was exaggerating the influence he exerts over the commanders of the Salvadoran guerrillas. I told him that I didn't think so, that he has the power to convince them that a military victory is just not possible in El Salvador as it is not in Nicaragua, and that sooner or later there will be negotiations, and sooner is better than later. A truce as fragile and vulnerable as the one that now exists in Nicaragua has already saved five thousand lives: I am talking to the Salvadoran commanders about this same possibility.

BOEKER: What is your opinion of the mission of the Group of Eight and its evolution toward a political entity of democratic countries? Will it be useful and what does it mean for smaller countries like Ecuador, Bolivia, and Costa Rica?

ARIAS: I have no objection to some countries, like the Group of Eight, getting together regularly, with a flexible agenda, to analyze problems which are common not only to the group but also to other Latin American countries. Of course as a Central American I am interested mostly in keeping the issue of Central American peace on everybody's agenda. I have asked colleagues who are part of the Group of Eight not to forget that there is a Central American peace accord which is not being honored by some governments of our region, and to keep democracy and peace in Central America on the Group's agenda. I cannot justify any pressure other than political for implementation of the Esquipulas II accord.

BOEKER: Which actions and policies toward Latin America would you like to see from the new administration in Washington?

ARIAS: The new administration in Washington should address the issue of the renegotiation of the foreign debt, which presents the greatest obstacle to the development of our region. There has to be a much more assertive attitude on the part of the U.S. government, which has the power to persuade creditors to be much more flexible in future negotiations.

With respect to Central America, I would wish for a greater commitment to our peace plan. Whether or not the Esquipulas II plan is successful will depend a lot on both the United States and the Soviet Union. The superpowers should talk much more about Central America. I think that they are still not interested in taking more flexible positions on Central America; they are treating Central America differently from regional conflicts in other parts of the world such as the Persian Gulf, Afghanistan, and Angola.

BOEKER: As a friend of the United States, do you have some advice for the new president with respect to his personal role in U.S. relations with Latin America?

ARIAS: My advice would be that the President listen more to those who have been elected by our people to direct the destiny of our countries. Some policies should be formulated jointly, so that different points of view, and different opinions, held by Latin Americans are taken into consideration before a decision is taken.

Let's remember that the consolidation of democracy in Latin America depends on the efficiency of the democratic system in solving the problems of the poor and the needy. In that sense, rates of economic growth smaller than rates of population growth are condemning these democracies to greater instability day after day. It's been too many years of impoverishment for most countries and too many years of stagnation for others. There are very few countries whose economies are growing. That is the reason for my concern that the Latin American countries may not be able to strengthen and consolidate their democracies.

MEXICO

CARLOS SALINAS DE GORTARI

Carlos Salinas de Gortari has a chance to change his party and his country's politics in ways which might finally bring the words "Mexico" and "democracy" into a single clear focus. Yet in this effort, young Salinas faces formidable obstacles, in particular the old guard of his own PRI Party, which has grown corrupt and high-handed during sixty years in power. But Carlos Salinas has on his side a steely personal determination, the substantial powers of the Mexican presidency and a clear vision of why Mexico's political system needs to modernize to assure political stability in an age of democratic awakening.

Salinas has heard, and even anticipated, the strong protest vote of the Mexican people in the July 1988 elections, expressing their judgment that something is wrong in Mexico's governance. In coming years that protest vote is likely to defeat more PRI candidates in gubernatorial and mayoral elections, and threaten the party's congressional majority, a result the PRI old guard—the Mexicans call them the Dinosaurs—is likely to read upside down. The Dinosaurs will argue that electoral defeat calls for going back to the old system of stuffed ballot boxes rather than completing the transformation of the PRI into a modern party in a democratic system.

Carlos Salinas appears an improbable man for the role of modernizing Mexico's politics since he would not be president but for the old system. Under the self-perpetuating nature of that system, he was tapped personally by outgoing President de la Madrid to be the PRI's candidate at a moment when the party heavies and probably the membership would have chosen someone else, if they were asked in a primary. But de la Madrid chose his young protégé and budget minister precisely because he did not trust the older generation of party heavies, whom he blamed for many of Mexico's problems. By choosing Salinas, de la Madrid wanted to assure passage to a new generation of leadership and completion of his slow cure of orthodox medicine for Mexico's economic crisis.

Carlos Salinas still looks an improbable president. When I met him in his attractive transition office in Mexico's San Angel district, he was wearing a full, wide-lapeled, double-breasted tweed suit, with the jacket open. A slight, slender man with a smooth boyish face, Carlos Salinas somehow looked one size too small for this outfit. The image seemed to mirror the disparity between the tremendously powerful role of Mexican president and the mere mortal on whom the "Destape" system suddenly puts that broad mantel, before any political process has allowed him to grow into it by cultivating grass roots support and building his own personal political organization.

At forty, Salinas is already bald on top but still looks even younger than his age. He has a warm smile and can fire quick thrusts of ironic humor, both of which bring his lean face alive and make one feel he could like Carlos Salinas.

His transition office is attractive, but business-like and without the imperial trappings which usually surround a president of Mexico. His personal office where we met was small and traditionally furnished. The dark wood paneling and black leather chairs, edged with brass upholstery tacks, gave the office some of the atmosphere of the Harvard Club—if ever its furnishings were new. There was just one young receptionist between the front door and Carlos Salinas' office. This is clearly a very different president of Mexico.

Salinas is an intellectual of the type Mexicans like to call a technocrat—an expert who accumulates power on the basis of superior competence, not political skill. He holds a Harvard Ph.D. and loves the contentious but stimulating world of intellectual debate over analytical problems. He is a confident, secure person who surrounds himself with bright young talent not out of any sense of inadequacy, but simply because he can get more done through them.

Salinas professes a commitment to reform and to modernize his PRI Party by making its structure leaner and more democratic, its administration cleaner and its projection to the public more appealing through attractive candidates and respect for democratic practice. He faces a lot of other challenges as well, some of which must be confronted first, such as consolidating his control of his own party. Here he faces a protracted bruising fight in getting the complacent, corrupt organization he inherited into shape. An early step in that fight was his bold and forceful move to arrest the head of the petroleum worker's union, who flaunted financial and political muscle like the warlord of a state within a state.

Salinas reiterated to me his personal commitment to see that Mexico's next rounds of gubernatorial and mayoral elections are fair and transparent in the voting procedures and tabulation. If so, the PRI Party will inevitably lose some key governorships, as it did in northern Baja California in July 1989 and the leadership of some key industrial cities. The PRI Dinosaurs will certainly fight hard to prevent losing control of such rich municipal administrations.

Miguel de la Madrid, Salinas' predecessor, shared his belief that the PRI must become a truly competitive member of a democratic system, for the long-term health of the PRI and Mexico. In his first years de la Madrid was able to implement significant reforms, including increasing the number of deputies elected on the basis of proportional representation—the reform which allowed the opposition in July 1988 to gain forty-eight percent of the seats in the Chamber of Deputies. De la Madrid also managed to get an improved electoral code passed, as well as judicial reform and greater autonomy for state and municipal governments. By mid-term, however, de la Madrid's reforms stalled. With his impressive determination, his explicit commitment to reform in the campaign and the strong message of discontent from the voters, Salinas has a better chance to succeed, and six years to press on from the point where de la Madrid stopped.

Yet Salinas has other priorities which conflict with democratic reforms. Gaining personal control of the PRI apparatus and using it to back his economic reforms are in some ways easier if reform of the PRI is postponed. In this interview Carlos Salinas de Gortari does not project any sense that he intends to lose a game he is committed to contest. Yet he dodges the issues of defining the timing and nature of planned reforms of his party. His evasiveness raises the question of whether he plans to postpone political reforms until he has dealt with his economic problems. Such a strategy would imply using the party establishment to build support for economic stabilization plans and shaking it up only later. If so, the risks increase that his reform plans will be blunted or watered down, as de la Madrid's were.

* * * * *

BOEKER: Mr. President, your administration will have the problem of addressing three very important challenges with inherent tensions, even contradictions among themselves: economic recovery, political reform, and internal stability. Do you have a strategy as to how to pursue all three, and what are your priorities among them?

SALINAS DE GORTARI: I have indicated that the priorities are the defense of Mexico's independence and sovereignty, the promotion of democratic life, the defense of our liberties, and the achievement of greater justice through sustained development. These objectives complement themselves, and I am convinced that through the strengthening of our economy and our democracy we will preserve our independence. The strategy I plan to put in place will accommodate all these fundamental objectives, as it must, because they reflect the main demands of Mexicans today.

BOEKER: Given all the other pressures you face, do you think that your call for "more and better democracy" is still feasible?

SALINAS DE GORTARI: I am convinced that it is essential to extend and deepen the roots of Mexican democracy. This will also help our economic recovery because with increased participation of our citizens, the economic program can be carried out more effectively. I am, therefore, totally convinced that economic recovery and broadening of democracy can go hand in hand and thereby increase our efficiency in using the resources we have.

BOEKER: What are your specific plans to make the Institutional Revolutionary Party, the PRI, a more open political party?

SALINAS DE GORTARI: This is being discussed now within the party leadership and I have to wait until we have reached some conclusions. What I can say, however, is that the party will be strengthened through a process of modernization.

BOEKER: Do you think that the small margin of your electoral victory can be of help in pressing these reforms?

SALINAS DE GORTARI: No, I think that what the margin of victory reflects is the will of the people, and the degree of pluralism Mexico is experiencing today. The narrow margin is a result typical of a modern country and of a race with three main candidates. Yet I still won an electoral majority. The options were very clear. The progressive center, the right, and the extreme left competed, and we won, which creates a mandate for the program I presented to the Mexican people.

BOEKER: After sixty years of being fused, is it now possible to separate the organs and functions of the PRI from those of the state?

SALINAS DE GORTARI: Well, the PRI is a party in government, not a government party. This is a fundamental qualitative difference. I believe the job will be to modernize the party through the democratic process, and then to succeed in keeping the party in power with the support of a majority of the voters.

BOEKER: Do your plans extend to changing how your party's presidential candidate is chosen? Is a primary election feasible for the PRI in the longer term?

SALINAS DE GORTARI: We are just beginning my administration. I am now working on how to get it started, not on how it will end.

BOEKER: Can Mexico expect in coming elections, such as those for governors and local officials, the "clean and transparent elections" which you said during the 1988 campaign that Mexico should have?

SALINAS DE GORTARI: That is my commitment. I have said that out of conviction and in response to the demands of our citizens.

BOEKER: What do you plan to do to realize your goal of increasing the power of state and municipal government?

SALINAS DE GORTARI: I intend to decentralize significantly, to give more responsibility and resources to those levels of government where the people usually present their requirements and requests. To the extent we can strengthen state and municipal governments, we will increase government's capacity to deal directly with the needs and demands of the people.

BOEKER: President de la Madrid also had a concept of political reform, and carried out some significant reforms, such as increasing the number of deputies elected on the basis of proportional representation, adopting a new federal electoral code, carrying out judicial reform, and giving more autonomy to state and municipal government. Have the results measured up to the concept?

SALINAS DE GORTARI: This is only the beginning. We'll have to see how it continues to develop. We need to observe how it actually works over the next few years before we can evaluate the results.

BOEKER: Can you simultaneously run a "white revolution" of internal reform of the PRI from the top, the Presidency, and still keep the support of the old guard of your own party for your whole program, especially your economic plan?

SALINAS DE GORTARI: These are matters that are still being discussed within the party and I do not wish to comment until we have reached a consensus.

BOEKER: In general, do you have enough time and political space to continue your orthodox economic policies until the expected rewards are apparent to the people who have to support these policies?

SALINAS DE GORTARI: Yes, I am convinced it can be done, because there are already some positive results, in terms of the fall in the rate of inflation, the privatization of some of the semipublic entities and structural changes from our economic strategy, "the economic opening." I am convinced that the people are clamoring for greater modernization, in the form of more efficiency on the part of the state, and more governmental responsiveness to the demands of the voters; that is, "the economic opening" as we call it.

BOEKER: Do you think that a confrontation between Mexico

and its creditors is inevitable before you can get the breathing room you need to restart economic growth in your country?

SALINAS DE GORTARI: I think it will require decisiveness on our part and a hard negotiation. I am convinced of the virtues of negotiating, but also of the necessity for firmness in the renegotiation of our foreign debt.

BOEKER: Then, do you expect that negotiations will take place within the framework established so far?

SALINAS DE GORTARI: No, I expect that the kind of financing we have received in the past will continue but that additional, different steps will be taken as well. That is how I conceive of the negotiation.

BOEKER: Do you think you need a lower interest rate than the banks are charging?

SALINAS DE GORTARI: What we really need is for our countries to transfer less resources abroad so that we retain sufficient resources to finance sustained growth. This result can be achieved by various formulas. I would not want to narrow the possibilities down to one type of formula.

BOEKER: Given your experience, you may be the Mexican president who best knows and understands the United States. Do you have a concept of how you will approach Mexico's relations with the U.S.?

SALINAS DE GORTARI: On the basis of respect and by adhering to principles of Mexican foreign policy which have earned us a dignified presence in the international community. I will emphasize our similarities and respect our differences. It seems to me that there are four main issues which will be at the core of the relationship between our two great countries: the issue of trade, the issue of financial relations, the problem of drug traffic, and the issues relating to migratory workers. From the way the relationship has evolved up to now it seems to me these are going to be the most important issues.

BOEKER: In general American presidents haven't been very

successful at establishing rapport with Mexico's leaders. Do you have any advice for them from the perspective of your past experience with the United States?

SALINAS DE GORTARI: I have no advice to give. For my part I intend to strengthen dialogue and communication with my counterpart in the United States. I am convinced that through direct communication we can create the basis for a better relationship between the two countries. I expect a positive dialogue with the new U.S. administration on the core issues I have mentioned. I would like to stress that there should be respect for our differences and emphasis on our similarities.

BOEKER: Given that Mexico is not inclined to receive U.S. advice with respect to your political development.

SALINAS DE GORTARI: Because we don't give advice. We do not tell other countries how to conduct their domestic politics. We firmly believe in the right of self-determination for every country and in a foreign policy of non-intervention.

BOEKER: Is there any helpful role for the U.S. as you approach your task of political reform?

SALINAS DE GORTARI: More than help, what the United States needs is to be better informed as to what the Mexican reality is. I would emphasize the lack of information and knowledge about Mexico, and in addition the need for respect for our internal, sovereign decisions, which is the beginning of understanding. We in Mexico should also know more about developments in the United States. Better information and knowledge are indispensable for better relationships among countries, communities, and people.

BOEKER: With respect to drug traffic, the U.S. Congress, under pressure from its constituents, has awakened to the fact that the U.S. is too tolerant of drug use. This reflects, for the first time, a very strong reaction not only against drug traffickers but against drug users. Does this open some new avenues for political understanding on fighting drugs?

SALINAS DE GORTARI: It would be useful. I have indicated

that the responsibility for combating drug traffic within a country is on the shoulders of the people and the leadership of that country. However, recognizing that the drug traffic affects many countries we need a dialogue among governments to maximize our efforts and win this fight. I intend to redouble our efforts to fight drug traffic in Mexico, and to strengthen the dialogue among governments to better coordinate our fight against what can be truly called the cancer of modern society.

BOEKER: Would it be useful to have the leaders of the group of countries most involved in this fight issue a declaration with respect to what their governments intend to do about this problem, to present a stronger common front?

SALINAS DE GORTARI: It would be useful. I believe we need to work with greater coordination, but I repeat, what happens in Mexico is the exclusive responsibility of the Mexican people and the Mexican government.

VENEZUELA

CARLOS ANDRES PEREZ

President Carlos Andrés Pérez of Venezuela met me in his Caracas senatorial office, a penthouse atop several floors of harried staff scurrying to meet the demands of one of Latin America's most hyperactive and charismatic politicians. Carlos Andrés Pérez plays the part of statesman initially, responding to my first question in a measured, low voice and firmly gripping the arms of a leather easy chair with large hands in blue cuffs bearing the monogram "CAP," the nickname by which all Venezuelans know him. But CAP's voice soon rises in pitch and force, and his arms thrust forward and upward with increasing frequency as if to grasp an unseen parallel bar and revealing the true style of CAP the consummate stump-politician.

CAP was elected president of Venezuela for a second time in December 1988 and has been a prominent player on the stage of Venezuelan politics for the decade between his two terms. His lean, angular face, with just a thin garland of dark hair around his pate, has been Venezuela's most familiar visage for a generation. Yet Venezuela is too small a stage for all of CAP's energy and zeal. As president of Venezuela for the first time in the heady days of the oil boom, Carlos Andrés Pérez was known internationally as a firebrand asserting the Third World's right to a better shake from the rich countries. At home, Carlos Andrés Pérez completed the nationalization of the oil companies and abroad he set the tone for developing countries' pretensions, in the wake of OPEC's early success, to an international redistribution of wealth through commodity power. These pretensions evaporated when the collapse of commodity prices in the Eighties left all but a few large oil producers with scant new power and wealth.

A more sober and pragmatic President Carlos Andrés Pérez

today is still a fiery orator with incredible energy and superb skills as a political campaigner and organizer. He is the first president of Venezuela elected for a second term after the daunting ten-year gap mandated by the constitution. At sixty-six he can still in one day cut more ribbons, pump more hands, and give more speeches than anyone in Venezuelan politics. He was, in fact, not the choice of his party's establishment and the incumbent president for the presidential nomination in the December 1988 election. Carlos Andrés Pérez swept the nomination away from the favorites by a grass roots primary campaign which won him a wide majority of the Democratic Action Party.

CAP's status as an outsider under the previous administration of his party may have been critical for his election at a time of deep dissatisfaction with the government. After seven years of no growth, serious economic and social problems beset even wealthy Venezuela. Rapid inflation and lagging per capita incomes have increasingly put many acquired necessities of Venezuela's middle class beyond its reach. The oil boom left Venezuelans with an illusion of easy wealth and of a permanent right to subsidized food and transport the government can no longer afford. The shrinkage of this expansive horizon to a more limited reality today contributed to the sudden and violent explosion of popular frustration in Venezuela's bloody riots of February 1989.

For Venezuela's economically pressed voters, CAP still has the aura of "Mr. Good Times." During CAP's first term, 1974–79, Venezuela was raking in dollars faster than it could spend them. Under CAP the government made massive investments in petroleum refining, petrochemicals, and public services, while stashing away billions in monetary reserves. Venezuela's labor problem then was importing enough skilled labor to work in its burgeoning economy, rather than today's problem of dealing with the pains of growing unemployment. But some of "Mr. Good Times" accomplishments have endured. The nationalization of the oil industry has increased Venezuela's income, and its heavy investment in refining and petrochemicals has helped Venezuela hold its markets in an era of a crude oil glut.

CAP's managerial and political skills will now be tested in tougher times of resource scarcity. He professes that these are not the times for free-spending populism, and indeed his views on economic policy and trimming the government's expensive holdings in industry now sound more orthodox than populist.

CAP's concept of Latin America's role, as expressed in this interview, clearly stresses the quest for greater influence, particularly vis à vis the United States. He faults the U.S. for its clumsy efforts to unseat Panama's General Noriega and its perceived role in stimulating the buildup of Sandinista military forces. Yet CAP's interest today is more in how to deal effectively with the U.S. than to berate it. He wants the Latin Americans to return the Organization of American States to its original post war political function as an instrument for the then-fledging Latin Americans to increase their leverage in dealing with the U.S. by forging a common stand. CAP sees the new Group of Eight Latin American democratic leaders as a particularly promising mechanism for increasing Latin America's weight in international affairs. He believes that Latin American debtor countries can get a fair shake from their bank creditors only by joining forces in a coordinated demand for debt reduction.

The second presidency of Carlos Andrés Pérez portends an assertive foreign policy, reflecting in particular his conviction that Latin America's leaders have in recent years not pushed the U.S. hard enough on issues where the U.S. should respond in terms of its own interests. Reviving Latin America's growth and combating narcotics are top targets for the initiatives CAP foreshadowed in his interview with me. This vigorous veteran of Latin America's international politics is thus focusing his formidable energies on the right issues.

* * * * *

BOEKER: Venezuelan democracy has had an impressive continuity which few people anticipated thirty years ago. What are the weak points in your country's democracy today?

PEREZ: Without doubt the most important lesson our country and its political leadership have learned was a dual one: first, that the essence of democratic politics plays out within a framework of controversy, but second, that controversy must be ultimately limited by a consensus, tacit or written, among political parties to preserve the democratic system. Venezuelans and their political parties thus came to share values, no longer subject of debate, which solidified the base of our democracy. As a consequence of this consensus, the army began to play its defined role without interfering in the governance of the country. However, we are part of Latin America and I would not say therefore that we are totally immune from, or vaccinated against, dictatorship.

The most destabilizing element for Latin American governments today is the economic situation, including foreign debt. We are forced to repay loans on terms which paralyze our economic growth and development, and thus aggravate the social conflicts already present in our societies. Our problems did not start with the debt; we have had them for a long time. But with the burden of our debt obligations, the possibility of solving these problems has become practically nonexistent. There is no question that economic instability could result in recurrence of dictatorship in some countries.

BOEKER: Recognizing these economic pressures, should one consider the prevalence of elected governments in Latin America today a high point in an old cycle of alternating periods of military and civilian governments, or has a new phase begun in the region?

PEREZ: There is a theory which great powers have used to assuage their conscience with regard to their own complicity with dictatorships in Latin America. The theory holds that our countries are not suited for democracy and that dictatorship is our natural state.

Latin Americans have rejected this thesis with great indignation, as our own history rejects it. Throughout the life of our republics there has been a constant struggle to achieve democracy and liberty. But conditions to which the great powers contributed have nurtured dictatorships in some of our countries. The Somoza regime in Nicaragua, for example, was the product of a United States foreign policy decision, and was under U.S. protection, contributing to the Central American tragedy we see today.

That kind of situation is now a thing of the past. Our international relations today take place on very different terms. Today the major democratic countries encourage democratic processes in our countries.

Latin American societies for their part have changed significantly and positively. In the past, periods of civilian government were the result of pacts between progressive elements in the military and progressive elements in the civilian sector to displace a dictatorship. Now the process is different. The fall of the Brazilian, Argentine, and Uruguayan dictatorships, to take the important examples of recent transition to democracy, were not a result of pacts between some military and some civilians, but rather the result of a resounding triumph on the part of the whole civilian society, which withdrew all support from the military dictatorships. That is how it happened. If you visited Brazil at the time of the struggle for democracy you would have heard people in the streets, on the beaches, in cafes, shouting just one thing, "Direct elections!" In Argentina we saw the military government disintegrate under pressure from civilians. The same thing happened in Uruguay. This indicates that we are now living through a different process, the culmination of Latin Americans' long struggle to achieve democracy and liberty.

BOEKER: Some foreign analysts believe that the Latin American economic crisis will bring a wave of populist leaders, a surge in government spending and finally more instability.

PEREZ: This is a version of just the sociological pseudo-thesis about Latin America which I mentioned. In one form it has to do with racist complexes. It comes from considering us inferior countries which must therefore submit to being "protected." It holds that time stopped for us, that science, culture, and modern means of communication have not produced great changes within our societies. This is absolutely false. On the contrary, we see growing every day in Latin American societies the sense of civic responsibility and the force of public opinion. I absolutely and without reservation reject this thesis.

BOEKER: I agree with you. Many commentators say that the news in Argentina is populist Peronists returning to power, but the real news may be that Peronists today present a democratic alternative.

PEREZ: But consider the seriousness of the situation. I would say that the maladjustment and imbalances which the Argentine democratic process is facing today are a direct result of absurd and offensive measures which the International Monetary Fund prescribes. These measures caused a deep economic crisis in the country and thus the elections were a disaster for President Alfonsín's Party. Also, the nominating process of Argentina's political parties has not yielded the best results because of the divisions which prevail in Argentina's society.

BOEKER: What possibilities are there for democratic leaders to help encourage democracy in other Latin American countries where it has not yet been achieved?

PEREZ: This is one of our aspirations. The preamble to the Venezuelan constitution favors promotion of freely elected governments throughout the entire region. We do work at stimulating and supporting democracy. In fact we have now seen how vigorous action on the part of democracies in the region prevented military coups in Argentina, Peru, and Ecuador. This desire for democracy is growing very strongly all over our continent.

There has also been a change of attitude in the industrialized countries. Before, the attitude of the U.S. was suspect by virtue of its support for some dictatorships. Today the attitude of U.S. governments is one of frank opposition to military coups and strong defense of democracy in Latin America. Thus we find that the united backing of the Western world and the strengthening cultural and political development of Latin American societies create a very strong combination of forces sustaining the region's democracy.

BOEKER: What can be done in a specific case like Panama?

PEREZ: Panama is a sad and painful case. For many decades Panama was dominated by its original formation under the protection of the United States and the large American interests in that country. It is also obvious that the Panama Canal is of vital interest to the United States. These are some of the reasons why Panama has not developed its own democratic consciousness. General Omar Torrijos, more by instinct than design, began to develop both democracy and a deeper national consciousness in the course of his struggle to ensure Panamanian sovereignty over the Canal. He started from a military dictatorship, and unfortunately his untimely death, before he could complete this plan, left the dramatic situation we see today in Panama, one which leaves no room for optimism at least in the short term.

The attitude of the Reagan administration was not very smart either. It not only complicated the situation but further strengthened the power held by the head of the Panamanian armed forces. I believe it is the responsibility of all Latin American democracies to help find a solution that will allow the people of Panama to decide their own destiny.

BOEKER: In his last years Rómulo Betancourt put a lot of emphasis on the problem of corruption as the most serious threat to the hemisphere's democratic regimes. Do you believe this still to be the case?

PEREZ: The Democratic Action Party has always stressed fighting corruption in public life. At the time of the October (1958) Revolution one of the first actions taken by the revolutionary government was to create a civilian court with administrative responsibility to investigate the misuse or embezzlement of public funds which had occurred during previous administrations. This remains a serious issue. Corruption affects developing countries deeply and it will assume crisis proportions if we do not deal with it firmly.

Of course we in the developing countries have no monopoly on corruption; it is rampant all over the world. We are constantly hearing about corruption scandals in the United States and Japan.

Unfortunately the causes of the problem reside not only within our own countries, but also in some aspects of international commerce. Transnational companies are agents of corruption in our countries. I am not saying that we ourselves are not at fault. What I am saying is that the transnationals pay excessive commissions to their agents, way beyond what is reasonable compensation for their services, with the objective of providing resources to bribe and corrupt officials in countries where they are doing business. In 1974, several developing countries tried to get the United Nations to adopt a code of ethics for the transnationals to deal with this problem, but we failed. Corruption is deeply and painfully rooted in our societies, but it has been fueled by the aggressive policy of market penetration on the part of the transnationals.

Here in Venezuela we have taken various types of legal action against corruption, but the problem goes beyond that. There has to be a change of attitude by the population. All involved—industrialists, politicians, even cultural institutions—have to take a stand to fight corruption. We cannot euphemistically call it "administrative corruption"; it is generalized corruption. A civil servant, for example, could not engage in such actions without counterparts in the private sector.

BOEKER: Since you see debt and the larger economic crisis as the main threat to Latin America's democracy, how would you like to see the debt problem managed?

PEREZ: Fortunately, both the industrial and developing countries are coming rapidly to the conclusion that we are hurting each other by not working out a solution that would allow Latin America to meet its obligations without sacrificing growth. We are on the verge of new agreements. A solution will benefit creditor countries as well as borrowers. As the dynamism of Latin American economies revives, our capacity to pay and import will grow which will benefit creditor countries.

A sense of solidarity is awakening in Latin America. There is no question that the negotiating position of Latin American countries will be strengthened by a coordinated stance on debt. We seem to be on the right track. I thus see real possibility of a new deal on debt. No country can get there solely on its own. We need to define a global framework within which each country would renegotiate its own debt in light of its particular economic and financial circumstances.

BOEKER: Negotiate country by country, but within a global framework?

PEREZ: Yes!

BOEKER: Some see a loss of Latin American influence in the international scene. Do you believe this is the case?

PEREZ: Yes, I do, but this is due to temporary factors. The economic crisis, let's call it the debt crisis, brought about a strange and unusual phenomenon in Latin America. It brought out national egotism as every country turned inward to concentrate on its own problems. This sapped the force of earlier efforts at integration and concerted action in the region. Our countries became weaker and our image suffered. Our international influence declined as we all became entangled in the debt problem. We are just coming out of that.

The Acapulco meeting of eight heads of state and their decision to meet regularly is a unique event in Latin America. Latin American presidents used to meet only when a president of the United States called a meeting. Not even those leaders linked in regional pacts saw a need to meet regularly to consolidate those pacts, as the leaders of the European Economic Community do. Now the presidents realize we face a real common problem and if we do not deal with it together there is no way out of the malaise that affects our region. We are entering a new era in Latin America. The heads of state (of the Group of Eight) will continue meeting so we can enhance our capacity to influence important international decisions concerning Latin America.

BOEKER: In the interviews which I have had I have seen what could almost be called a regional "crisis of confidence" on the part of Latin American leaders. Many talk in tones of deep concern about Latin America being left behind technologically and economically because of the economic power of the U.S. and Japanese markets, the European Economic Community, and even the "four tigers" of the Pacific, as Latins call them.

PEREZ: This is true and it shows precisely that a new consciousness of our own reality is emerging and of our need to work together. We have seen this in Europe, when the countries felt "trapped," despite millenniums of civilization, by the industrial capacity of the United States and other nations. European countries, for instance, forged the Eureka Project to do space research which they could not have done individually. We have been taken by surprise that the European Economic Community has not only developed and gained strength, but moved toward political integration.

These are examples that we Latin Americans are witnessing, observing, and absorbing, while becoming more and more convinced that we have to intensify our efforts to unite as a region.

BOEKER: But Latin American integration still appears so far off.

PEREZ: Of course. Europe needed many centuries and had to fight two world wars which became part of the process of European integration. So we have no reason to feel disappointed or disillusioned. These are long processes, but the important thing is that we have already begun to develop a consciousness of the necessity of integration.

BOEKER: Some inter-American institutions, such as the OAS, have fallen into disuse, and even disrepair some would say. Can they be revived or is the emergence of new groups, such as the Group of Eight, a sign no one wants to revive the old ones?

PEREZ: No, the reality is the following. In the first place, the concept of the OAS was based on a mistake: pretending that the hemisphere is one region. This may be true geographically, but from the economic, cultural, and social point of view, there are two regions: one south of Rio Grande and another north of Rio Grande. If the OAS were to convert itself into the great forum where the two regions meet to identify common interests, work out differences, and organize their cooperation, it would improve relations between the two regions. This is what we should do, because the OAS cannot be the center of a region which does not exist. As long as this fact is not recognized, the problems between both regions will not be candidly discussed, as they are not now, and the OAS will not meet its objectives. It is certainly not doing so now. In a way, the OAS deals with appearances, not realities.

Then Latin Americans need a forum where we can discuss our problems, our affinities and our need to get along with the United States. Another aspect of the problem is the legacy of a historical misunderstanding between Latin America and the United States. All along this has prevented better, more productive relations and deeper understanding between Latin America and your great nation.

BOEKER: If the OAS had a new agenda maybe its first item would be drugs.

PEREZ: Let's talk for instance about the drug problem. We are engaged in a dangerous and useless controversy. Latin Americans are blaming the United States in the mistaken belief that only they, as consumers, are responsible. And then the United States reacts in the same manner. Latin Americans are seeking to avoid responsibility by saying that drug production is driven by consumption and financing in the United States. While this might be true, it is a problem we have in common, it is inter-American, it is international.

Drugs may be the most formidable threat that humanity has faced over the course of its existence. If we do not treat it as a major international crime, and if we do not forge a common effort to fight it, we will never resolve this problem. The U.S. could help a lot by prosecuting consumers, and by cooperating with Latin American authorities within a well thought out inter-American plan that would include intelligence, technical cooperation and economic assistance.

It might require a major Latin American conference to take some joint actions against drugs. We at least have to prevent the charade of drug traffickers hiding behind the protection of national sovereignty. An international police, whose effectiveness does not stop at borders, should be established. There has to be an all-fronts attack on the drug problem. The entire continent should participate in a world-wide conference to agree to such an attack on drugs. This is not an illusion because everybody— East and West—is suffering terrible and destructive effects from drug use.

BOEKER: You have criticized the ignorance of U.S. leaders with respect to Latin America. 1989 brings a U.S. president who knows more about Latin America than his predecessors. Is there not an opportunity for Latin American leaders here?

PEREZ: Here we must also share the blame. Neither the United States nor Latin Americans have really tried to establish a candid dialogue that would lead to better understanding between us. This is one of the things that must change. We should have more regular exchanges between congressmen, industrialists, cultural and other institutions, at all levels.

We also need to make the OAS a viable center where representatives of the two regions of the hemisphere can meet. Latin American presidents should also get together periodically with the president of the United States to discuss these matters at the highest level. Latin America must try to become known and understood in American public opinion. It is interesting that even though the United States is the country where more research is being done, and more information is available, about Latin America than anywhere else, the results seem to be limited to academic and scientific circles. We need to get the information and knowledge out in the streets for North Americans and Latin Americans.

BOEKER: What would you suggest to a new U.S. administration with respect to its policies toward Latin America?

PEREZ: I wish the candidates (in the U.S. 1988 elections) had been more precise as to what their intentions were with respect to U.S.-Latin American relations. We heard almost nothing from Vice President Bush. It would be good to be able to have a meeting with the new president soon. It would be very useful in trying to eliminate all the prejudices.

The whole culture of anti-Americanism (or as they say here, "anti-Yankee" culture) as it has existed since the early decades of this century has fortunately receded, opening the doors of our countries and our people to authentic cooperation. The moment has come to initiate this new kind of relationship between the United States and Latin America.

BOEKER: Mr. President, you are the first Venezuelan president to return to lead your country for a second term after waiting the constitutionally mandated ten years. What motivated you to try for a second term?

PEREZ: I am not the first to try, but the first to succeed. I am a politician by vocation but I did not enter politics to become president of Venezuela. If that had been my purpose I would have retired after completing my term. I am active in national political life because I am committed to my country.

Since I left the presidency I have continued to work in politics, and now the country puts this challenge before me. Before there was any talk of my being a candidate, the polls showed broad support for my being the next president. This made me think about running again. I am first and foremost a full-time politician, and I have a duty to meet whatever challenges are put before me. My candidacy was one of those challenges which I immediately accepted. Given the crisis facing the country, and the credibility that I enjoy among Venezuelans, my candidacy could be a national, nonpartisan one. I did not doubt even for a moment that I should run for the presidency.

BOEKER: Your first administration was made easier by the riches of the oil "boom." Now you face a very different challenge, trying to revive growth in an era of scarce resources. Can we expect a program very different from that of your previous presidency?

PEREZ: I was president at a moment when circumstances were favorable for getting things done; but not necessarily the right things. Actually more mistakes could have been made. I could have made worse use of the country's resources. We saw during the period following my term how with even greater resources bad decisions were made for which the country has paid dearly. I now return to the presidency under very different circumstances. One cannot cling to old formulas but must take advantage of lessons learned in the previous exercise of presidential responsibilities.

During my first term there were abundant economic resources, but the country lacked other things. Venezuela's human resources were very limited in 1974, as was the nation's understanding of its new reality. Today we don't have the economic and financial resources we had then, but we have the human capital which we lacked earlier. These are comparative advantages which facilitate other ambitious strategies consistent with our reality, with the same objective: the development of the country and the welfare of all Venezuelans.

BOEKER: The preceding administration of your Democratic Action Party tried to reduce the role of the state in the economy. Will you continue with that same economic orientation?

PEREZ: Some mythology confuses this issue. No government in Venezuela has ever been statist. None of the Venezuelan political parties has ever subscribed to such an ideological concept of the government's role in the economy. I nationalized basic industries because this had been a national aspiration all along, and formed part of the program of our party since it was established. Part of the inheritance we received from Simón Bolívar was the concept that the state owns the subsoil. But this has led to a very peculiar situation of state capitalism. With the oil boom the state became the real provider of the country's wealth and the largest lender, which created a distortion in Venezuela's economy. Because of deficient planning and lack of capacity to assess accurately the real feasibility of certain projects, enterprises ended up in bankruptcy courts, which handed over to the state corporations it never wanted and had never tried to get.

The over-valued bolívar also had made Venezuela very unattractive for investment in some industries such as tourism. The private sector was thus not interested in hotels, so the state developed and owns the hotel industry. The objective is to make them work and then return them to private ownership.

All this resulted in the state managing a whole series of corporations which in the opinion of all political parties are not the state's business. But the oil boom provided the resources to procrastinate on passing these corporations to the private sector. This has been bad for the country because the majority of these business have not fared well under government management. Many have been underutilized and now form part of an industrial complex that somehow has not been a part of the country's economic activity. This crisis has stirred up interest in solving this problem.

I am going to take advantage of the lessons learned from the poor experience of the previous administration. Mechanisms have not been created to make the transfer from public to private ownership quickly. We need to use private sector mechanisms to dispose of these holdings and will establish a large stock corporation for that purpose. This is one point on which there is no disagreement within the party, or in the country.

RAFAEL CALDERA

I met Ex-President Rafael Caldera in his mid-town Caracas office where he seated himself at a large conference table, which serves as a desk. The over-sized, highly polished table reflected the image of an elder statesman who still sees himself as one with more deals to make and more campaigns to wage, even if fewer people call these days. At seventy-three Caldera is one of the few surviving leaders from Venezuela's surprisingly durable transition to democracy over three decades ago. When Venezuelans overthrew the military dictator Pérez Jiménez in 1958, they were a people of weak democratic traditions and long history of dictatorship. But Venezuela's fledgling democrats, against all odds, launched a succession of peacefully elected civilian governments now in its seventh term. Caldera was part of the first government of this era, under President Rómulo Betancourt, but later took his Social Christian Party into opposition. When Caldera himself took over from President Raúl Leoni in 1969, this was the first time in one hundred and forty-three years that a Venezuelan president had peacefully transferred power to the opposition party.

Caldera's presidency saw the virtual end of a Marxist guerrilla threat in Venezuela. Caldera dealt with the guerrillas by a combination of open arms (offering amnesty to guerrilla leaders) and iron fist (wiping out those who continued to fight).

When I met Caldera he appeared all ready to go to church, in a solid dark blue suit, plain black shoes, white shirt and colorless tie. Caldera is a formal, sober man who presents a total contrast to the flamboyant Carlos Andrés Pérez, who succeeded Caldera as president in 1974. Caldera takes the values and philosophy of "Christian Democracy" seriously. On the wall beside his desk is a large wooden crucifix, hanging above a picture of Caldera's late father. Arrayed on the credenza behind his chair are large photos of his wife and children.

Today Caldera is not happy. He senses that even in his own party the younger generation of ambitious, pragmatic politicians does not share his militancy for Christian Democratic ideals. Caldera, who has written a passionate book eulogizing Simón Bolívar, ruefully quotes the strongman's curious axiom that it is not institutions and laws which guarantee good government but the character and moral values of the leader. Caldera the idealist and elder statesman is worried that what he sees as the materialistic and self-centered values of a new generation leave it susceptible to corruption.

Caldera is also distrustful of the market-oriented, growth strategies advocated by Latin politicians today, including the candidate of his own party in the December 1988 elections. Caldera continues to stress the moral imperative of redistribution of wealth, including internationally. His address to a joint session of the U.S. Congress in 1970 was entitled "International Social Justice for Developing Countries," and argues that Christian philosophy requires of nations a generosity consonant with their capabilities.

In 1988 Caldera once again offered himself to his party, ready to run for the presidency one last time, but he was out-voted and out-maneuvered in his party's primaries by a much younger candidate.

As we talked, Caldera gathered his thoughts and began his responses with his eyes half closed, looking pensive and withdrawn. But as his passion for his subject swelled, his eyes flared wide, revealing a man suddenly younger than his years and eager still to shape his party and the future of democratic institutions. The "Social Christian" name of the party he founded should not lead one to view him as necessarily a conservative, for many of his concepts are sweeping and provocative, such as suggesting that the Organization of American States adopt the standard of non-recognition of governments created by coups. Along with Colombia's Carlos Lleras Restrepo, Rafael Caldera is one of the most thoughtful of Latin America's elder statesmen on the problems of consolidating democracy, as his responses in this interview reveal.

* * * *

BOEKER: How do you explain Venezuela's record of unbroken continuity in its democracy over the past thirty years? Why has that been possible here and not in other Latin American countries?

CALDERA: I believe we have been lucky. Venezuela's political history has been very unstable.

From 1830, when the Republic was finally consolidated until 1945, we had fewer than eight years of civilian rule in one hundred and fifteen years. The rest of the time the head of the government was a general. Some of these were harsher, others more tolerant, some more liberal, others more severe, some more honest, others more corrupt. Venezuela's "General-Presidents" became such an institution that one cynical sociologist called them our "essential cops."

My generation and the generation before grew up with dictatorships. When I was born General Gómez had already been in power for seven years, and when he died I was almost twenty years of age. It was a harsh regime, isolated from the rest of the world, which grew out of the country's longing for peace and order after so many civil wars.

The process which began in 1945 was also very unstable. President López Contreras, who had been the minister of war under President Gómez, and President Medina who held the same position under President López Contreras, initiated an important transition toward democracy. It ensured freedom of speech, and encouraged political parties and labor unions. Some important institutions such as the General Accounting Office and the Central Bank were established. Progressive labor legislation was passed and the state became administratively more efficient.

Nevertheless, the understandable impatience of the civilian sector and of younger military officers led to a breaking of this so-called constitutional thread on October 18, 1945. There was a period of revolutionary government with socialist tendencies but it ended up with another military coup by the same officers who had participated in the earlier, liberalizing action of October 1945. After so much hope for a democratic system, civil liberties were curtailed anew on November 24, 1948, and even more after December 2, 1952. On that date the military government rigged the results of an election and made Colonel Marcos Pérez Jiménez, who had been minister of defense, president by decision of the armed forces. After that, the situation became much worse and we civilian politicians who had gone through that whole process finally learned our lesson. Despite our serious differences and the fact that we had fought each other very hard we understood that we had to make an effort to restore and preserve the democratic system on the basis of an understanding that would put the well-being of the country above our individual preferences.

On January 23, 1958, we launched our democracy with a broad national accord among the armed forces, the political parties, business representatives, and what was left of the labor union leadership. This pact was finalized on October 31, 1958, at my home "Punto Fijo," the name by which the accord is known. The pact committed the parties to govern jointly during the first constitutional government although each put forward its own candidate for president. The pact also committed the parties to a basic program including agrarian reform. That reform proved very effective in countering a guerrilla movement because the campesinos realized they could expect more from a democratic government than the guerrillas.

Venezuela's democracy was enhanced as well by both parties' acceptance of peaceful transfer of power; only then were the people assured that they could change the government and its policies by their vote. When President Raúl Leoni transferred power to me, the first opposition leader ever installed as a result of the popular vote, people realized the system worked.

Through all this experience Venezuela had to learn the hard way a lesson we would not forget. We were faithful to our promise to preserve constitutional government despite disagreements and controversies, to keep an ongoing dialogue between civilians and military leaders, and to respect the alternation of power. All this brought about the very encouraging result that our democratic system has now survived for over thirty years. All this occurred when democracies were going on the rocks in other Latin American countries which enjoyed a long constitutional tradition, such as Chile, and had a very rich cultural history, such as Argentina, Brazil and Uruguay.

BOEKER: Do you believe that these thirty years of democratic stability would have been possible without Venezuela's oil and high per capita income?

CALDERA: The question should really be how has democracy survived the effects of our oil? Oil income brings many benefits and opportunities, but instant and easy riches also bring greed, corruption, and turmoil. Former president Rómulo Betancourt, who had spent much of his youth as an exile in Costa Rica, once said there were no military takeovers in Costa Rica because there wasn't any money in the treasury to take over. Our oil has been a mixed blessing.

BOEKER: During your administration, you were able to overcome the guerrilla threat. Why has Venezuela succeeded where your neighbors in Colombia have not?

CALDERA: I had the good fortune to launch a pacification program which worked. But when I took over the presidency we had experienced ten years of guerrilla warfare, and the situation was ripe for a political solution. The guerrillas were suffering militarily and some of their leaders were in jail. The armed forces were also looking for a political solution. I got a solution by using the president's powers to grant pardons in individual cases. There were never formal negotiations. Some guerrilla leaders were pardoned and they convinced others that the democratic course was viable.

Our guerrilla problem lasted just ten years, from 1958 to 1968. Colombia's guerrilla problem started earlier and has lasted longer. In Colombia the violence began on April 9, 1948, with the assassination of the Liberal leader Jorge Eliécer Gaitán. At that time many leaders of the small liberal communities turned into guerrillas and remained guerrillas. It is in that sense the guerrillas have deeper roots in Colombia.

When the guerrilla movement emerged in Venezuela, democracy was new and evoked great enthusiasm and hope. The agrarian reform sent a message to the rural population which made it hard for the guerrillas to sink roots in the rural areas. The urban guerrillas, who became very violent, were slowly countered by community groups of the democratic parties which had taken their responsibilities very seriously. Colombia's democracy is older and because of that has been able to withstand this attack, but its people are growing weary.

BOEKER: What do you think is the greatest threat to democracy in Latin America?

CALDERA: All democracies in Latin America, whether brand new or restored, face two kinds of problems: the relationship between civilians and the military; and serious social and economic problems, aggravated by the debt crisis.

Many societies have not yet satisfactorily resolved the relationship between civilian authorities and the armed forces. This is easy to understand because traditionally the armed forces in Latin America have been seen in terms of either of two extreme positions. For the militarists, the armed forces represent their only hope for law and order. For the anti-militarists, the armed forces represent a constant source of turmoil and conspiracy against democracy, motivated by ambition, and egotism. Rarely does one find a balanced view.

I have heard some Latin American political leaders say that the solution is to do away with the armed forces, as Costa Rica has done. But that is not the answer. Costa Rica itself faces serious security problems from turmoil in neighboring countries. Costa Rican presidents have requested military aid from Venezuela and other friendly countries when Somoza threatened to attack Costa Rica. With time Costa Rica's own National Guard has become more and more militarized. This complex relationship between the armed forces and civilian authorities has to be solved once and for all.

Transition from military to civilian government in Latin America has occurred either by virtue of collapse of a military regime or by consensus. In Argentina the military government collapsed in the wake of the Falklands War, while in Uruguay and Brazil it left by consensus. Collapse leaves behind frictions and antagonisms with which Argentina is still struggling. Consensus, or negotiated transition, tends to leave pockets of resistance within the armed forces which do not sincerely back democracy, as we see now in some Central American countries.

The second threat to Latin American democracies is their serious economic and social problems and their inability to respond to the needs of their populations. This is critical. Authoritarian governments in Latin America took over on the pretext that they could do what elected governments failed to do. Yet a decade later the military has handed the hot potato back to elected leaders having solved nothing and made the old problems much worse.

Now the people once again demand solutions, and within the democratic forces there are still irresponsible demagogues who, without thinking of the consequences, take advantage of the circumstances to stimulate discontent. The strengthening of democracy is thus hindered by the poor economic performance of Latin American countries; democratically elected governments find it increasingly difficult to deliver on their campaign promises. This is where the phenomenon of populism emerges. Populism is not a doctrine, it is more of a drive for quick fixes, even if the relief is only temporary. In ten years or so, many populist measures yield only deeper poverty.

The debt problem has aggravated the economic crisis. Debt is a political problem of the first order, as people like Henry Kissinger and Jeane Kirkpatrick, hardly revolutionaries, have recognized. But reasonable avenues to a solution have not been opened. It is not that Latin America does not want to pay; we cannot pay, given the interest rates charged by the banks.

The solution, I believe, is the formation of an intermediary institution to handle the debt. Such an entity could buy the loans from banks at a discount and then concede reasonable interest rates and realistic payment schedules to the borrowers. It could be the World Bank, the International Monetary Fund or a new institution. Of course this presupposes subsidies from the industrialized countries to cover the institutions' own borrowing and any losses. It would be worth it. Many of us remember the Marshall Plan, and it is a good example that sometimes a sacrifice of this kind is small compared to the damage if the problem drags on indefinitely.

BOEKER: Rómulo Betancourt said that "administrative corruption is a more serious threat to democratic governments than conspiracies of the right or of the left." Do you think the situation has improved?

CALDERA: Unfortunately, no. On the contrary it has gotten worse, not only here but all over. One becomes alarmed when reading that corruption has penetrated even the Pentagon which is considered the bastion defending the Western Hemisphere. We also hear that corruption is growing in Japan which in many ways is an exemplary country. There is no question that corruption represents a threat to democracy. Betancourt's point is well taken.

Corruption has carried over from dictatorship to democracy. In fact there is a curious coincidence between what former president Betancourt said about corruption under democracy and what Pedro Estrada, chief of Pérez Jiménez's powerful National

Security Guard, said about corruption under a dictatorship. During the Pérez Jiménez dictatorship, I represented Estrada's wife in divorce proceedings. At one point, when we were discussing his wife's demands, Estrada said to me: "I am not a thief; I have told Pérez Jiménez that his worst enemies are those who steal within his administration, for they can do far more damage than his political enemies."

I am very seriously concerned that corruption in Venezuela is growing at all levels. There is a real crisis with respect to moral values. It is very easy to become rich when handling public funds. People in the private sector who handle huge amounts of money receive attractive salaries. In the private sector a manager in a relatively small company will have a higher salary than a minister or a president. Civil servants earn far less and feel themselves disadvantaged. It has been said many times that there has to be equivalence between private and public salaries, but this is unrealistic. A taste for luxury is stimulated every day by media advertising, enticing people to consume beyond their means. All this contributes to corruption.

BOEKER: Drug traffic has caused profound instability for young democracies elsewhere in Latin America. How has Venezuela been affected?

CALDERA: It is starting to hit Venezuela, perhaps to a greater degree than we are now able to perceive. Up to now Venezuela has been primarily a transit point between producing and consuming countries. The drug traffic problem is obviously an international one and requires an international response.

The most serious problem is a rather simple one: the United States is a very rich country and the billions of dollars which drug traffickers earn in U.S. markets give them enormous power. Such drug profits naturally bring proportionately even greater power in poor countries. In Bolivia and Colombia for example, some drug dealers have offered to pay their country's entire foreign debt in exchange for a free hand in their trade. Such power poses a very grave threat for Latin Americans, now and in the future.

Drugs are among the most serious threats to human survival, along with AIDS and the deterioration of the environment. There is no doubt that the "solution" which some suggest, legalizing consumption of drugs, is not a solution at all. We are not dealing with substances which are relatively harmful; we are dealing with substances which cause irreparable damage.

BOEKER: Many years ago you started a new political party with a Christian Democratic philosophy. How do you see the new generation of leaders within your party? Do you believe they share this philosophy?

CALDERA: Fundamentally yes, but governing creates incentives to become pragmatic and the rank and file reflect this "pragmatism," which worries me. The old party militants used to donate their services, for some psychic satisfaction. This no longer happens: everyone wants compensation. To remain strong, political parties have to encourage moral consciousness and ideological commitment. The parties are the pillars on which democracy rests and their erosion would present a serious threat to the democratic system.

BOEKER: Do you think the traditional Venezuelan political parties need some internal reforms to become more democratic?

CALDERA: I think so, though I am rather skeptical that one can solve problems by changing rules. I believe the problems are of a deeper nature and have to do with moral values. Bolívar said that: "It is not laws or the institutions that guarantee good government; it is the men of honesty, virtue, and patriotism, who make up the republics." Of course reforms are necessary and useful, but the most important reform is that of the inner self.

BOEKER: What do you think of the idea of electing mayors as Colombia has done? Has the time come to do that in Venezuela?

CALDERA: I think so. The demand for direct elections at this level has been growing and it should be satisfied. But responsibilities for specific services need to be sorted out so that autonomy of local offices does not result in increased bureaucracy and unnecessary expense.

BOEKER: What can the democratic countries in Latin America do to support democracy throughout the region?

CALDERA: Integration of Latin America must be oriented toward strengthening liberties and democratic institutions. I believe that regional organizations like the Organization of American States should be more active and conscientious with respect to their responsibilities. Without meaning this as a criticism of the present secretary general, I believe that the OAS should be headed by very strong political personalities who can carry a message and have a positive impact in the region. There was a time when secretary generals of the OAS were former presidents like Alberto Lleras (of Colombia) and Galo Plaza (of Ecuador) whose most important contribution was that of strengthening the institution.

If the community of Latin American nations would take a more clearly defined stand, we could achieve real results. The so-called Betancourt Doctrine advocated the principle of denying recognition to governments resulting from coup d'états. Venezuela proposed it but it did not succeed because we acted alone. This kind of measure could succeed if it were a regional commitment. It worries me to see that in the smaller countries there is still a number of governments resulting from coups. I thus welcomed the initiative of former Presidents Carter and Ford to form a council of democratically elected former heads of state, to try to use the moral authority which comes from having been chosen in a free election to counteract abuses against democratic institutions.

BOEKER: Would you say that besides being in need of new leadership the OAS is in need of a new agenda?

CALDERA: Yes. And even more we need a new attitude. Those of us who have been in the political leadership of this country have asked ourselves whether the OAS should be dismantled, and transformed into a union of Latin American countries. My answer has been that the OAS offers a great opportunity to change hemispheric politics because the United States, which is stronger than all the rest of us put together, is seated there sharing responsibilities and rights at least theoretically on an equal basis. This opportunity should not be lost.

When I visited the OAS in Washington, I said that "it is far worse for the Latin American countries to see themselves as colonies than for the United States to have an imperialist mentality toward Latin America." Regrettably some Latin American countries still act like colonies, instead of assuming the position of dignity and respect they deserve.

BOEKER: Under your government, Venezuela decided to join the Andean Pact. Are you satisfied with the results of this decision?

CALDERA: Satisfied no, but I am not so disappointed as to think the Andean Pact is not worth the effort. Despite its shortcomings there has been a considerable increase in trade. Yet the political will is lacking to implement the pact fully. When powerful economic sectors argue for protection at the expense of commitments to the pact, there is little pressure in favor of this pact. To a great extent the political parties are to blame. They ought to give a voice to the perspective that some sacrifice in the short term can result in enormous benefits for the country in the long term.

I personally am convinced that sub-regional integration is an indispensable stepping stone to regional integration. Latin American integration among such large states as Brazil and Mexico on one hand, and small ones like Bolivia and Honduras on the other, would now result in such disequilibrium that I doubt it can soon be achieved.

BOEKER: What would be your advice to the new U.S. administration on its policy toward Latin America?

CALDERA: I am an advocate of the idea of social justice. Just as the concept of social justice applies within a country so should there be some sense of obligation internationally between the "haves" and the "have-nots," between the strong and the weak. I presented this idea when I had the honor to address a joint session of the U.S. Congress in 1970. I do not believe in a paternalistic concept of development. Our development is our responsibility, but certainly the developed countries should remove barriers and provide opportunities for us (in their markets).

Problems sometimes are solved in terms of safeguarding the interests of the superpowers, and the smaller countries have to suffer the consequences. For instance, the most serious setback we have had in recent years has been the enormous increase in interest rates to incredible levels. After the Second World War low-income families could get housing loans at four percent. Today such credit is out of reach for low-income families, all because of the level of interest rates prevailing in the developed countries.

We have won political liberty, abolished slavery and officially ended colonialism, but in order for us to accomplish what needs to be done now we need capital and technology.

Finally a suggestion of a political nature. Some years ago, on the occasion of Andrés Bello's two hundredth anniversary, I visited Washington and was invited to the White House. President Reagan was in California but Vice President Bush received me. After a very cordial meeting he invited me to see the Cabinet Room. He introduced me to the Secretaries who were present, and indicating the president's chair asked me: what would I say to Latin America if I were sitting in that chair? I answered that I would tell Latin Americans that "never will a U.S. soldier set foot on their soil to violate their sovereignty."

PERU

FRANCISCO MORALES BERMUDEZ

When he wore the over-sized, high-peaked hat of Peru's military, this stern-faced officer looked like "Evita's" caricature of the Latin general absorbed in the corrupting games of power. But the essence of General Francisco Morales Bermúdez goes deeper, and his character is stronger. The essence of Morales Bermúdez's contribution was getting Peru's military out of power, not in. Today in retirement he writes on Peru's economic and security problems and works with a private institute supporting democracy. And in the most dramatic contrast from the stereotypical military ruler, General Morales Bermúdez remains a man of modest means and tastes, despite having been in charge of Peru's finances for twelve years and its de facto president for five more.

I met with Morales Bermúdez in the living room of the modest house in Lima's San Isidro suburb where he and his wife have lived for most of the last thirty-seven years, including the five years he was Peru's last military ruler (1975–80). At sixty-seven the general is still tall, fit and trim, looking younger than his years but for his silver hair, combed straight back, which dramatically contrasted with an all black outfit of narrow slacks and open-necked shirt. His large mouth, broad nose and heavy eyebrows give an initially austere impression, close to that of a youngish Leonid Brezhnev. But once the general warms to his subject his lively, light brown eyes grow round and offer a more friendly reception.

Morales Bermúdez was born into a military class with strong pretensions to rule. His grandfather, Colonel Ramirez Morales, was president of Peru from 1890 to 1894, and his father, also a military officer, was a rising star until he fell victim to a political assassination in 1939. But Francisco, the third generation, proved to be a talented economic policy manager and wide-ranging political thinker whose proudest achievements were restoring a func-

155

tioning liberal economy after the turbulent radical-populist regime of General Velasco and returning his country to elected, civilian rule. Morales Bermúdez reveals his disillusionment with the economic and political bungling of the civilian presidents who followed him. But he retains his pride in his role in restoring democracy and his conviction that it remains nevertheless the right system for Peru and Latin America.

The transition from military to civilian rule was not on Morales Bermúdez's or the Peruvian military's minds when they turned out the radical General Velasco Alvarado in August 1975, and put Morales Bermúdez in his place. Morales Bermúdez, who had been finance minister both under Velasco and the earlier elected, civilian government of Belaúnde Terry, was picked to clean up the economic wreckage of Velasco's administration. Velasco had nationalized nearly everything that worked in Peru and broken off relations with international financing agencies. Morales Bermúdez, an economic conservative, promptly straightened out the economic mess, selling off some nationalized firms and restoring financial relationships with the International Monetary Fund and Peru's other creditors. But by the spring of 1976, Morales Bermúdez turned to political reform, launching and managing with considerable finesse a gradual transition to elected, civilian rule.

Morales Bermúdez left the writing of a new constitution to a Constituent Assembly elected in 1978, and dominated by Haya de La Torre's APRA Party. The elected civilians were as anxious as the military to produce a constitution which would promise smoother military-civilian relations; thus, the Assembly included provisions critical to the military. For example, the military was given extensive administrative powers in any province declared in a "state of emergency" because of persistent violence, a provision under which the military by 1988 ran over thirty of Peru's one hundred and eighty provinces. In July 1980 Morales Bermúdez completed his transition plan by turning over power to an elected civilian President, Fernando Belaúnde Terry, the same man the military had deposed twelve years earlier.

Five years later Morales Bermúdez made a half-hearted effort to succeed Belaúnde by running for president himself, but he finished fifth in a crowded field—a painful rebuff under which he still smarted at the time of this interview.

Today Morales Bermúdez is sharply critical of the hyperinflation and declining incomes left in the wake of the failed economic policies of a civilian populist, Alan García. The general fears that Peruvians will punish García's APRA Party so badly at the polls in 1990 that the way to power could be opened for the Marxist-led United Left. Morales-Bermúdez clearly bares his fear that such an outcome could trigger another coup. Thus one of Latin America's more thoughtful generals draws in this interview a very tentative judgment on the future of Peru's beleaguered democracy.

* * * * *

BOEKER: What were the main reasons which led the military government in August 1975 to replace the radical populist General Velasco and start on a different course?

MORALES BERMUDEZ: It was not for personàl reasons or out of any "caudillo" mentality, as has been the case in other military coups throughout Peru's history. The armed forces decided to replace General Velasco as the head of state but that did not mean a change in the structure of the military government, which ruled under a decree of October 3, 1968, until July 28, 1980, when I left the presidency.

There were two main reasons for the presidential change. First, General Velasco's health. Toward the end of 1975 he used to go to the office only three times a week, by his doctors' orders, so all administrative actions were much delayed. Despite our efforts, Peru's government is unfortunately still very centralized, requiring the president to sign many documents, so this delay in administrative actions was serious. A vacuum of power resulted which is always dangerous in Peru or any Latin American country.

The second reason was clear and disruptive Marxist infiltration into a government which was never intended to be Marxist. The military government was revolutionary only in the sense that it aimed at changing structures. All the branches of the armed forces sensed this Marxist infiltration and decided to deal with it by initiating a second phase to rectify some of the decisions taken during the first. It was not a question of reversing the process of change, which was necessary for the nation, but of preventing a process of reform from taking a Marxist turn.

BOEKER: Were you already thinking in terms of moving to civilian government when you became head of the military government?

MORALES BERMUDEZ: Not when I first took over power. I spent the first months studying and analyzing the situation which I had to manage.

In political terms I realized that the armed forces had already been in power for seven years, but there were still economic problems and institutional issues to deal with. Once I had a clear vision as to how the institutional question should go, I started to consider the dangers if the military did not limit its stay in power. I use the word "limit" because it was clearly implied not only in the initial decree of 1968 but also in the governing plan that the armed forces would be in power until the structural reforms were consolidated and irreversible.

In May of 1976 I tipped my hand during a rally which filled the main square of Trujillo, the largest square in the country. It was a very spontaneous and enthusiastic rally which was not generated by the authorities. In speaking to the crowd I revealed two very important points about the process of transition to democracy. The first point was that we had to end once and for all the historical hatred between the army and the APRA Party. I emphasized that if Peru continued on that road, it would never achieve the consensus it needed to reach its objectives. The second point was a pre-announcement that the military government was considering a process of transition to democracy. Later that year there was a press conference at the Presidential Palace, in which it was said that "the government is reviewing its plans, in the belief that after seven years a complete revision of the situation is in order, and we are working on a new plan, including a transition to democracy."

BOEKER: What did you expect to get for the country and for the armed forces from the 1980 transition?

MORALES BERMUDEZ: Two things. First, during its initial phase the military government decided to stay in power until its reforms were implemented and irreversible. This key point precipitated long analysis, struggling with questions such as: how do we know we have reached the point where the reforms are irreversible; what are the criteria for deciding this; which political authority or group is going to decide? It was going to take forever.

A lesson we learned from this transition was the following: if an authoritarian de facto government does not announce a specific time for return to elected, civilian rule, it will just not happen. Of course another military movement could have taken over and repudiated the first, but that would have started a dangerous chain of events for the country. So if the armed forces were going to get out of power we had to force an answer to the question "when."

Then we had to give concrete form to the concept of "irreversibility." The solution turned out to be that it was not really the armed forces who could decide if the reforms were irreversible, but rather civilians, through a democratic process. This is how the idea emerged of a freely elected constituent assembly.

At this point we announced that the transition to democracy would occur in two phases. The first was to elect a constituent assembly so that the people, not the military government, would write the new constitution. Some thought that the military should write the constitution, as in Chile, and then submit it to a plebiscite. This was widely debated but I made it very clear that there should be no doubt that a transition would indeed take place, and that the best way to ensure its success was for the people to freely elect their own representatives, one hundred of them, to write the country's new constitution.

My belief was that a large pluralistic assembly was going to adopt most of the military's reforms. These could not be ignored because they were in place and had already made their mark on national life. The military's fundamental concepts dealing with labor, agrarian reform, and education were in fact adopted and form a part of our present constitution adopted in July 1979.

The only political party that did not participate was (Belaúnde Terry's) Popular Action Party, which felt that the process was too slow. But a hasty transition from such a long period of military government would have left a danger of a military reaction and its return to power. We did not want this to happen.

The constituent assembly was a "bridge" between authoritarian and democratic government. I am an engineer, so I am always speaking in terms of bridges. For a long time we had a military government and we needed a bridge to help us cross over to democracy. I firmly believed that the constituent assembly would preserve the necessary reforms and that above all Peru needed a democratic experience.

The second thing: it was essential to bring about a transition to civilian rule because the armed forces had been too long in power and were becoming politicized—compromised by power and exercising partisan politics. This was corrupting the armed forces and compromising their future stability and their role of preserving the security of the nation.

We had to be faithful to the concept of a democratic transition and at the same time cover the armed forces' retreat to their barracks with honor.

BOEKER: The constitution incorporated provisions for military control of provinces declared under a "State of Emergency," provisions which the military government had earlier adopted by decree. Was this a condition of the armed forces for completing the transition?

MORALES BERMUDEZ: Not really. What happened is unique in Peruvian, and perhaps Latin American history. The armed forces did not intervene in any way, neither by establishing conditions, nor by limiting the assembly in the task it had to accomplish. The writing of the constitution was left entirely up to a sovereign assembly. The military leadership was kept informed, and consulted on the articles dealing with the armed forces and the police.

BOEKER: Given the internal security problems Peru faces, the provisions for a state of emergency have resulted in the military having administrative powers in many regions of the country. Is this what you envisaged ten years ago?

MORALES BERMUDEZ: When we talked about a state of emergency during the military government, it had a totally different character from the one which prompted Mr. Alan García's government, and the preceding one of Mr. Belaúnde Terry, to declare emergency zones. At the time of military rule a state of emergency had to do exclusively with public disturbances, such as riots due to demands for increases in salary, or protests of increases in the price of consumer goods.

Now emergency situations have to do with terrorist subversion. They entail efforts by terrorist groups to control areas of the country and important cities. It is a very different situation.

How to deal with such an emergency situation in present day Peru is the key question being argued here, including in many panels and conferences in which I have participated. Many people believe that we should discontinue the position of a military political command for provinces where a state of emergency is declared. This would mean that in an area which is declared an emergency zone the essential action should be political, and thus civilian authority would be preserved, with the military carrying on only their specific function. I agree with that position.

There should be a national political plan; we still don't have one. We need to use the same system all over the country, with the military subordinated to civilian authority at all levels, because the problem is essentially political, not military. If there were a national plan against subversive violence, there would not be differences of opinion on its management. The handling of such a situation should be first and foremost a political action. When Shining Path and other groups, such as the Tupac Amaru Revolutionary Movement and lately the Leftist Revolutionary Movement, use violence, then the armed forces have to be ready to respond. This does not mean that force can be the only response; it has to be part of a broader fight against violence.

The national political plan should coordinate a series of responses. The plan must address economic problems, which plant the seeds of terrorist subversion, and psychological factors, which should be combatted by modern means of communication. The administration of justice is also of enormous importance; without it we will never solve the kinds of problems we have. Education is fundamental because ideological infiltration and terrorist influences penetrate the schools—elementary schools, high schools, and of course universities. Right now our educational system is not cultivating men and women who will build this country's future; we are allowing the system to plant the seeds of terrorism in the minds of our youth.

BOEKER: Would the regional authorities be elected or appointed by the government?

MORALES BERMUDEZ: The possibility of electing governors is still very immature and we cannot lose any more time. Because of subversion we have already lost eight years since the transition.

According to the existing structure in Peru, the government appoints the prefects of the departments and the governors of the provinces. These political authorities should take responsibility for executing the law. Political responsibility must not be lost, because the military needs to operate within political decisions by civilian authorities.

There have been officers at all levels who have been indicted for using violence to combat violence, which makes our armed forces reluctant to carry out their military duties. The armed forces act by use of force, even though we know that this is not how the problem is going to be solved. Let me give you an example. If subversive elements attack an installation, the army has to kill. They cannot take prisoners because if they do, the next day they will go free. That is how our judiciary operates at present, very inefficiently.

BOEKER: What is the attitude of the armed forces in the face of the painful economic situation which Peru faces?

MORALES BERMUDEZ: Much concern and uneasiness. The lack of foreign exchange due to the misguided economic policy of the García government affects the entire country, including the armed forces. When you lack the basic needs to maintain the army at an operational level, morale gets very low. On this, I have every reason to speak for the armed forces.

Salaries are extremely low. When I left the presidency in July of 1980, my salary, in dollars, was approximately one thousand U.S. dollars per month. At today's rate of exchange the same amount would be the equivalent to just two hundred dollars, and that for a general. Imagine the situation of a captain with a wife and two children. Military families are suffering very seriously from the impact of this economic crisis. Morale is low and naturally this is reason for great concern.

I have lived in this house since 1951 when I was a captain. My wife inherited it from her father. Whatever decorative objects you see have been accumulated over many years. This is what you would consider a middle class home. We own the house but I still have to pay the servants. I live with my wife and one of my children and I can barely make ends meet. We have had to do without things we were used to having. I cannot read as much as I used to because my pension is not enough to pay for books and subscriptions. From this personal situation we can see how delicate is the economic situation of the rest of the country.

BOEKER: What is your evaluation of the civilian governments Peru has had since the transition?

MORALES BERMUDEZ: I had hoped for the success of these

two civilian governments, but unfortunately they have not succeeded. The García administration came to power without a program, which is ironic because APRA is a political party which
has been struggling for fifty years to win the presidency; yet it
arrives with no plan. Everything has been improvisation, and the
country is suffering the consequences.

I was once asked which country was more difficult to govern,
Peru or the United States; my answer was that it is much more
difficult to govern Peru. I was of course comparing it to the
United States of today, with a productive structure that makes
it a world power. The goals the U.S. has set can be pursued under
known criteria without great difficulties. But to manage a country
as complex and confused as Peru one has to devise a plan first.
There are such different regions in Peru that they can in fact be
thought of as nations within a nation. There has been a chronic
pendulum moving back and forth between de facto and civilian
government. In no way can Peru be managed by improvising. I
am convinced that the García administration arrived without a
program and unfortunately the same can be said for the previous
government, that of the Popular Action Party, which in my opinion also failed.

When I left office in July of 1980, the rate of inflation was
twenty-four percent, and the consolidated public sector deficit
was only .5 percent of Gross National Product. Our exports had
reached four billion dollars, of which one billion were manufac-
tured goods. Peru had net international reserves of 1.8 billion dollars. Peru's foreign debt amounted to 6.9 billion dollars, including
all expenditures of the armed forces.

During the Belaúnde administration, the foreign debt reached
fourteen billion dollars, and today our debt is fifteen to sixteen
billion. Now there is much talk about the foreign debt burden,
but it is a self-imposed burden.

I cannot say that we have had much luck. This is unfortunate
because people are losing faith in democracy. They have to understand that democracy is a civilized form of governing a country in order to find the courses which are best for the well-being
of the whole nation. Now, many say that they were better off
under the military. This is the prevailing attitude in the popular
market places. This does not mean at all that the military is planning a coup. If I had wanted that I would just have stayed in
power, as in the Chilean case. We could have tried what Pinochet
has tried to do: call a plebiscite to lengthen the period we would

retain power, retire some military figures, replace them with more civilians, etc. That is not the road we decided to take. We took the direct path to democracy, though not in haste, as that would have been dangerous.

Democracy is akin to a ship on the high seas which has to be steered without ever reaching port. By that I mean, we have to work hard, and it is a continuous effort. Democracy is not a system which can arise in Peru by improvisation. We must work to perfect such a democratic system.

BOEKER: Do you see any way out of this difficult situation? Another elected government? Another military government?

MORALES BERMUDEZ: Until 1990 it will not be possible to improve our situation. Two main factors are contributing to the instability of Peru's democracy, the mismanagement of the economy and terrorist subversion. All the energies of the democratic system should be directed to resolving these two major problems. The strength of our democracy will depend on how well these two challenges are addressed.

I do not believe that the answer is to return to military rule. In the long term a military government just won't solve these problems. We have to learn how to put out fires within the democratic system, and to reach a democratic consensus for the long term.

In Peru every group, every party, is looking out for itself. This kind of thinking could destroy democracy. It is one thing to disagree with what the current government is doing, but criticism should be constructive, for the good of the country. The kind of destructive criticism that we are seeing here can only weaken democracy. Democracy is a constant process of dissent and consensus. Dissent can be useful if it is constructive, working toward a new consensus.

The political parties are the pillars of the democratic system, not the armed forces. The armed forces can contribute to the system by maintaining their constitutional role. This means, of course, that the important thing for 1990 is that the democratic political parties reach some agreement to defend democracy. I believe the situation is so critical in Peru that the democratic political parties—the three in the Democratic Front, the governing APRA Party and maybe others—have to get together and reach some kind of consensus with respect to key issues now facing the country, especially the economy and the control of terrorism. They should unite through a "national accord."

The threat is that the Marxists might attain power here through the election, as happened in Chile when Allende came to power. Sooner or later that kind of situation is going to provoke a reaction on the part of the armed forces. There could be a coup with tendencies similar to those which took over in Chile. Who can prevent a coup? It is not up to the armed forces; it is fundamentally up to the democratic political parties.

BOEKER: Do you consider your public service as finished, both as a general and as a former president, or do you believe that you might have the opportunity to serve your country again?

MORALES BERMUDEZ: At one point I was involved in partisan politics, but I had second thoughts and decided to leave politics. However, as someone who was chief of state at the historic juncture in Peruvian history of transition from military to democratic rule, I cannot be satisfied with retirement. I keep up to date on everything that is happening in our country, with the economy, politics, and the problem of terrorist subversion.

I couldn't say that I have no political ambitions. Naturally the only position I could ever go back to would be the presidency. Needless to say this would have to be won through the electoral process which means I would need a political party willing to endorse me; it would be too difficult to form another party. This is not going to happen in 1990, because the candidates are already decided.

I still have the vitality needed to be in the race five years from now, for the elections in 1995. Belaúnde is now very active politically, and he is ten years older than I. There is no reason why I should not think of running for president. What I do not want to do is to complicate further Peruvian politics. If my presence would make the situation more complicated, I would not enter the race. However, if my candidacy would contribute to the defense of the democratic system, then I would certainly enter politics again.

BOEKER: What would be your advice to friends of Peru and its democracy, such as the United States? What can be done to help Peru consolidate its democracy?

MORALES BERMUDEZ: We have two main challenges: to improve our economy and to restore peace. As far as terrorism is concerned, I think it is an internal problem and I doubt that anybody could help. It is up to us to resolve this problem. The U.S. could help us with the drug problem, and I would urge that the United States cooperate with our country in this area.

Drug consumption in the States has to decrease, because as long as this strong demand persists, it will incite production in Peru. We could also use economic and technological help to make some headway with crop substitution. This is not something that can be solved quickly. Plans have to made for the medium and long term.

If Peru comes up with a program reflecting a serious effort toward solving the economic crisis, the United States and the international organizations could help financially. Until then it would be like trying to fill a barrel with no bottom. I think the government has come to realize that if no serious effort is made to deal with the economic crisis, there will be no international financial support. If the government presents a serious economic program I would hope there would be a more favorable attitude on the part of the U.S. State Department and Treasury.

My own experience with the International Monetary Fund, which some consider a ruthless organization, has been favorable. I dealt with them when I was finance minister for five years and then as president. When one presents to the IMF a macroeconomic plan with all the elements, and perfectly clear objectives which lend themselves to technological analysis, it is very difficult for them to raise obstacles or to demand more. I never faced demands from the IMF which interfered in domestic issues. When we established the agrarian reform program, the Fund had nothing to say. When we had a serious economic program we got the resources we needed from the IMF and the World Bank.

FERNANDO BELAÚNDE TERRY[12]

Twice elected president of Peru, Fernando Belaúnde Terry is still charging today, at seventy-five, full of enthusiasm, even optimism, for his country's prospects, which most Peruvians view in despair. When elected to his first term twenty-five years ago the handsome, dynamic Fernando Belaúnde was the dashing darling of the Alliance for Progress, at least in American eyes. An architect before entering politics, Belaúnde loves grand plans and visions such as those which inspired the framers of the Alliance for Progress. He still looks back wistfully at those years as the model of what U.S.-Latin American cooperation can be.

King-sized engineering projects like the Marginal Forest Highway, linking the interior regions of the Andean countries, riveted Belaúnde's imagination and attention as president. But his two terms (1963–68 and 1980–85) were also ones of prodigious efforts to build family-sized projects—housing, schools, roads, and smaller community-development works.

Today Fernando Belaúnde is still proud of these efforts, despite the political frustration in which his two terms ended. (He was deposed by a military coup in 1968, and his party's candidate gained just six percent of the popular vote at the close of his last term in 1985.) When I met with Belaúnde in his attractive, highrise apartment in Lima, he took me to the window to point out his favorite housing complexes, constructed during his terms. Soon plans for several more were taken down from the bookcases which line his apartment, and before I left, Belaúnde had called a car so that he could personally take me on a housing tour of Lima. It is not just a bit of vanity in Fernando Belaúnde; there is a genuine positivism in his attitude toward Peru's development which is a refreshing current under the stale

---

[12]The absence of Peru's oldest party, APRA, in this book reflects only the fact that its leader in 1988, President Alan García, could not keep his appointment with me.

cloud of political ennui and despair which hangs over Lima.

An honest man of principles, who refused to make any deals with military dictatorship, Belaúnde is personally one of the most appealing figures of Peru's turbulent and often seemingly self-destructive political life. Political fortunes have also helped make Belaúnde an urbane and cultured man of the world. His father, a minor politician, was deported in 1924, so young Fernando got his secondary education in Paris and a degree in architecture from the University of Texas. Belaúnde himself was deported twice by Peru's military in 1968 and 1970, and spent most of the years of Peru's military government in the United States and Canada, lecturing and teaching. He returned to Peru in 1976 and in 1980 had the unusual satisfaction of winning election to return as the first civilian president of Peru since the military deposed him twelve years earlier.

Belaúnde's two administrations compiled a mixed record in trying to confront Peru's confounding complex of seemingly intractable problems: overpopulation, abject poverty and malnutrition in the countryside, vast disparities in income distribution and degree of integration into a national society, chronic inflation and capital flight, and accelerating loss of government control in rural areas where terrorist insurgency and narcotics trade grow unchecked. His political achievements have been positive. At the beginning of each of his terms, both after periods of military rule, Belaúnde restored freedom of speech and press as well as other civic and human rights. He also both times re-instituted municipal elections in an effort to give greater legitimacy to government in rural areas. But his attention to economic policy did not match his commitment to urban planning and construction. Rising inflation and currency depreciation plagued both his terms. In his second term Belaúnde also suffered some poor luck. In 1983 the El Niño phenomenon caused a sharp recession and the Shining Path terrorist guerrillas ironically launched their insurgency just on the return of Belaúnde and civilian government in 1980.

Yet the two governments which succeeded Belaúnde, the radical populist government of General Velasco after 1968, and the recklessly populist government of Alan García after 1985, have contributed to some reevaluation of Belaúnde and a revival in his political fortunes. Both those populist governments seemed to produce less success, at much greater cost, than Belaúnde's more genteel governance. Always a speaker of exceptional eloquence, Belaúnde surprised himself and many Peruvians by attracting a crowd for a rally he suddenly convened in July 1988 to commemorate the twenty-fifth anniversary of his reinstitution of nationwide municipal and village elections. Still in exceptional health for his age, except for trembling hands which have bothered him for many years, Belaúnde prompted widespread speculation in Lima as to whether the old juices were flowing again and would prompt Belaúnde to launch a candidacy for president again in the 1990 elections.

In his interview with me Fernando Belaúnde made clear that was not his intention. He pleaded that his own age and political realism indicated another course: aligning his party with two others in the center-right coalition which launched the candidacy of Mario Vargas Llosa, Peru's premier literary-giant-turned-politician in mid-life. The energy and eloquence of Fernando Belaúnde are still formidable assets to such a coalition. The grand designer is still going strong, as in this interview, when he spins out the Belaúnde plan to solve the debt problem or Latin America's capital flight—naive in part perhaps, but full of the positivism and optimism Peru needs.

* * * * *

BOEKER: You have had the unique experience of returning to the presidency after having been ousted by the military.

BELAUNDE TERRY: Precisely, yesterday was the twentieth anniversary of that coup which some thought would be the end of my career, though I never believed it. In 1980 the people reaffirmed their trust by electing me to the presidency once again.

In my opinion, the coup had very negative consequences for Peru. It created discord and divided the country. It also created conditions which later spawned the terrorist movement. Ironically, the coup also gave me a historical opportunity when it suppressed free expression and confiscated the newspapers and radio and television stations. I was given the opportunity to restore all those liberties and properties, which I did the very same day I was inaugurated president for the second time.

BOEKER: You did not feel that your hands were tied during your second term?

BELAUNDE TERRY: No, because during my second administration I had broad electoral support and a parliamentary majority. During my first term I did not have a majority in Congress because of the alliance between the remaining followers of the Odria dictatorship and the APRA Party. This unnatural alliance caused me great difficulty with Congress.

BOEKER: I know that you believe that General Velasco's government inflicted great damage on the social and economic structure of the country. Do you believe that the consequences of Velasco's rule are still being felt in Peru's problems today?

BELAUNDE TERRY: It is obvious we are still suffering the consequences of Velasco's major creation, a giant state bureaucracy. Our problem in privatizing these industries is that they are overstaffed bureaucratic monsters which thus necessarily lose money. If they were privatized there would have to be extensive layoffs. That is the obstacle we now face. There are public enterprises of all types. A public electric company is justified, but the nationalized merchant marine is operating at enormous losses, as is the steel industry and the fisheries.

   The case of the fishing industry was the most dramatic example of the failure of Velasco's statist government. The nationalization was an abuse against the country because the fisheries were in the hands of Peruvians. The fishing industry was thriving when Velasco made the terrible mistake of nationalizing that industry which now is an enormous bureaucratic money-losing machine. I tried to cut the staff by offering early retirement bonuses to many employees but the present government is building them up again.

BOEKER: During the last months of the military rule, General Morales Bermúdez decreed some far-reaching provisions for a "State of Emergency" which the Constituent Assembly later included in the constitution. Were you consulted regarding these rather unusual provisions?

BELAUNDE TERRY: Well, my Popular Action Party did not participate in the Assembly. We voluntarily stayed out and we were consulted on some issues, but not the state of emergency. The state of emergency is a logical provision because any government has to face public disorders.

BOEKER: But under this provision administrative powers have

been granted to military authorities in various regions of the country?

BELAUNDE TERRY: That is relative. When there was a state of emergency in Ayacucho, there was coordination between the civilian and military authorities. Civil authority was not suppressed. In Ayacucho, as always, there was a civilian prefect who then needed to coordinate his actions with the military authorities. In that case the military did not infringe on civilian authority.

BOEKER: Why are the prefects not elected?

BELAUNDE TERRY: The Peruvian system of government until now has been very centralized. I did restore the practice of municipal elections on assuming the presidency in 1963, and again in 1980. Municipal elections were well established in Peru before 1919, when they were discontinued. Our municipal elections now cover all districts in Peru, about two thousand of them, and approximately two hundred provinces.

The prefect's authority is limited and concerns mainly public order, which is now largely under the federal police. There is now under consideration a plan for new regional authorities, including an elected president of the region and a partially elected regional assembly.

BOEKER: The degree of pessimism expressed by many Peruvians today is amazing, to the point that many say there is no way out. What do you think?

BELAUNDE TERRY: I think there is a way out; we have the fundamental assets. First, we have a vast territory with low overall population density, despite some very congested areas.

There has been a disproportionate concentration of population around Lima which bears no relationship to the capital's economic growth. When I was born, Lima had a population of one hundred and seventy-five thousand; now it has six million; the first time I became president (1963) the capital had a population of two million, and the country had twelve million; the second time I became president (1980) Lima's population was five million and the country's, eighteen million.

This rate of population increase nationally is a challenge. An annual rate of population growth of 2.6 percent means an additional five hundred thousand new citizens per year. We must feed, educate, and protect this growing population.

What is needed is a government that creates jobs for people. "Work and let others work" was the motto of my government. The situation now seems to be that the government not only does not work, but it does not create jobs. There are no new public works of any consequence. Since I left the presidency our population has increased by almost two million and energy production has not kept the same pace. The same can be said with respect to agricultural production, which was our main concern.

My government extended our agricultural frontier, as for instance with the so-called Miracle of San Martin. When I assumed the presidency the first time, San Martin was our most economically backward region. Now it is the most advanced, in terms of viability. When the Marginal Highway reached that region, it became a source of wealth, rich in livestock, rice, and corn. To see growth in Peru you have to go to the center of that region, Tarapoto, which has been transformed by colonization. There is an atmosphere of the frontier there, like your Far West, and of course there is no unemployment.

BOEKER: Some foreign observers say that Peru lacks the preconditions for a stable democracy; they frequently cite the wide disparities here in the income distribution.

BELAUNDE TERRY: The inequality of income distribution in Peru is basically the same as in Mexico or our neighbors Ecuador and Bolivia. Of course we should not be resigned to this evil, but it has been with us for a long time. There are no magic formulas to reverse this trend. There are those who are disappointed by democracy, but look at my personal case as an example of the mobility in the system. I do not represent wealth, industry, agriculture, or exports. I do not own any newspapers or media, and I do not direct any unions. Yet I have been legitimately elected twice and served as Peru's president for ten years. If I were five years younger I could get the votes to win again.

The reason why I have declined to be a candidate is my age. I'll be seventy-six years old soon. We need a younger alternative, younger people who will go into the government to work, not to make the spectacles we see now which only result in tremendous expenditures. That is why I am in the Democratic Front, a coalition formed by Luis Bedoya Reyes (Popular Christian Party),

Mario Vargas Llosa, (Movement for Liberty and Democracy), and myself. Because of his youth and other circumstances Mario Vargas Llosa is the right one to carry the standard for our movement in the campaign leading to the 1990 elections. The Democratic Front's program is a synthesis of its three parties. The fundamental propositions of my Popular Action Party are included.

My party draws on a strong legacy of old Andean traditions. We think that a mixed economy would be the answer to many of our problems: the marriage of an archaic system of communal work with a modern monetary economy. That's where we strongly disagree with the communists and the social democrats. They do not have any Andean roots and their ideas are foreign. Our mixed Inca-Hispanic culture has yielded very positive results for us. In my last election (1980) I defeated the APRA Party candidate, Armando Villanueva, and Dr. Luis Bedoya, leader of the Popular Christian Party, who has now joined us, and thirteen candidates of different branches of the extreme left. That is evidence that people respond to what we preach. The Democratic Front includes all the forces of order, without necessarily being conservative. We have been attacked by labeling us conservative, but that is not exactly true.

The United Left had its first municipal victory only in 1983 in Lima during my second administration. By then the left had learned its lesson and most of those thirteen different candidates who had opposed me got together in the United Front behind the mayoral candidacy of Alfonso Barrantes. But in the presidential elections of 1985, Barrantes ran way behind Alan García, with only twenty-five [percent] of the vote. Now divisions have again emerged within the United Left; it could split in two.

BOEKER: If the United Left came to power in 1990, despite its deep divisions, do you think there would be a possibility of yet another coup?

BELAUNDE TERRY: The danger of a coup is always there. It is a common occurrence in Latin America. I do believe the risk would be greater if there were a government of the extreme left. We know what such governments are like because we have other examples to contemplate. We have the case of Cuba, Chile under Allende, and Nicaragua. In Peru we have tried to avoid any experiment of this nature in foreign ideology.

BOEKER: How do you explain the point of complete frustration Alan García's government reached?

BELAUNDE TERRY: When it came into power, the García government should have continued those programs that were obviously working. For instance in the economic area we had a policy of mini-devaluations, nothing traumatic. Given the conditions of our economy we had no choice. We had not discovered new wealth, and demagoguery had prevented the oil industry from flourishing as I had hoped.

During my second government we brought in the Shell Corporation, which has now made an important find. But the current government is afraid to make decisions in general.

The worse crime against Peru has been all the demagoguery centering around the petroleum industry. We have been left behind, with insufficient oil exploration or production. Why? Because whoever takes a step in that direction is accused of giving up the national patrimony. That was the gimmick used against me in 1968 in the famous case of the IPC (International Petroleum Company).

When I was able to get IPC to give us back free not only the land, but also the installations, including three thousand wells, the real IPC problem was solved. The military, however, used the fact that the IPC refinery was not included as an excuse for their coup. This was absurd because we already had a modern refinery, La Pampilla, here in Lima, while the IPC refinery, Talara, was junk. The issue had nothing to do with national sovereignty. When the military "took" Talara, what they took over was the payroll and pension obligations and a fully depreciated, worn-out plant. Now when a payment is made to the IPC we have to ask, for what? The refinery was not worth much. Besides there had been previous payments made under the table.

In the United States I discovered how dishonest was the manner in which the IPC concession was canceled. It was a shady deal for both countries, involving dissimulation and bribery. I had in my own hands a Xerox copy of the earlier pay-off check, yet there were people who believed that I had acted to defend a foreign company, instead of the interests of my country.

BOEKER: Do you believe that the United States and the international financial institutions treated Alan García fairly?

BELAUNDE TERRY: No, I don't think so. They have not been very understanding. I have suffered from that same lack of understanding, but I always kept the dialogue going with the IMF. I warned the IMF that we needed to renegotiate our foreign debt, but they were unresponsive.

As for the U.S., when I visited the United Nations in 1984, President Reagan asked me to the White House. I insisted then that our most serious problem was foreign debt, and that it was going to affect his government. It was not that serious for me personally because I had only one year to go in my term, but President Reagan still had four more (after his reelection in November 1984). The problem of the foreign debt is enormous and affects most of the commercial banks. Yet there never was a serious desire in Washington to help.

I have no doubt that the U.S. State Department always favored the APRA Party in Peru. I did not get any help even though all my actions were geared toward close collaboration with the United States. But it was (the late APRA Party leader) Haya de la Torre, despite his anti-imperialist platform, who always got a warm reception in the United States. Alan García thus came thinking he could improve a situation which has only grown worse.

BOEKER: Is a return to military rule possible, as some believe?

BELAUNDE TERRY: It would be most regrettable because a de facto government would confront the same economic crisis. What could a military government do now? The crisis would be even worse. That is no solution.

According to the 1979 Peruvian constitution, any financial transaction of a de facto government does not obligate the nation. Thus any bank lending to a de facto government is not going to preserve its assets that way.

BOEKER: Could not Peru's internal security problems—the guerrillas and drug traffic—provoke a military reaction against elected civilian government?

BELAUNDE TERRY: I believe that terrorism would continue regardless of who is in power. The only advantage a military government has in restoring public order is its capacity to hide what is happening; when people get killed no one knows how many. With a democratic government everything is open.

I don't think that the situation with regard to the public order would be improved. On the contrary if there were an illegal government our own constitution provides for a "right to rebellion." That government would be just as illegitimate as the Shining Path guerrillas. I personally want the present system to continue with all its faults, until a new government is elected in 1990.

Besides, I don't believe in genies. Here (in Peru) we have a profound structural problem. The solution is to be found not in one political alternative or another but in a plan and a lot of hard work over many years.

BOEKER: Is there a threat of "dirty war" in which various groups use illegal means to try to impose their own solutions?

BELAUNDE TERRY: Well, that is always a risk.

Drug traffic has weakened the society by creating much turmoil. The international drug trade is causing corruption here and in consumer countries, where there is great corruption and tolerance for drugs on the part of the police and the society.

The other day someone who is very well known in international circles told me, absolutely horrified, that when he attended a reception in Palm Springs, the host first passed the drinks and then cocaine.

BOEKER: Public opinion is changing with respect to that. What would you advise the new U.S. government with respect to the debt problem?

BELAUNDE TERRY: I believe the worst mistake of the United States is to insist that the problem be dealt with bilaterally, under the thesis of "divide and conquer." There should be a global refinancing through multinational bonds, internationally guaranteed. We would acquire a new obligation for a twenty-five or thirty-year period. Through a formula based on the economic indicators a debtor country would pay part in such bonds and part in cash each year. One year Peru might pay eighty percent in bonds and twenty percent in cash; another year it might be thirty percent and seventy percent, and later, fifty percent and fifty percent. Cash payments would grow as a country recuperates.

Another aspect of great interest to us in which the industrial countries, especially the United States, could be of great help is the recovery of flight capital. When the money that has been taken out of the country illegally comes back we will recover economically. I understand that there are ten billion dollars invested outside Peru. If only five billion came back, our economy would recover. Venezuela has thirty billion dollars outside the country; the Dominican Republic, a small country, has three billion. This is why Miami has become a Latin American city.

The Inter-American Development Bank (IDB) could issue bonds to recover this capital. There would be a Peru Issue, an Ecuador Issue, etc. In the case of Peru the government would offer the appropriate incentives so that instead of buying dollars and hiding them in their mattress for fear of inflation, Peruvians would buy these bonds to help their country. The commitment on the part of the IDB would be to invest in each country all the proceeds derived from the sale of bonds issued for that particular country.

MARIO VARGAS LLOSA

Novelist Mario Vargas Llosa finds himself thrust into the role of the emerging leader and presidential candidate of a center-right coalition which is trying to present a new face to the tired and decaying world of Peru's democratic politics. It is a new and unexpected role for Peru's distinguished writer and intellectual. Mario Vargas Llosa, against great odds, is now devoting all his energy and talent to keeping the Marxist-led United Left from gaining power.

Writing and politics are equally intense and personal for Mario. Some of his conflicted feelings about a failed first marriage flowed into a depiction of his ex-wife in his novel "Aunt Julia and the Draftsman." She fired back with her version of him in her own novel "Dear Mario." With the same intensity Mario has launched a withering barrage of criticism at Peru's floundering populist president, Alan García. García has been less effective than "Julia" in defending himself, in part because attacks against Peru's respected literary giant do not seem politic.

I met with Peru's new political phenomenon at his seaside home in Barranco, a posh Lima suburb. Mario Vargas Llosa is in many ways the image-maker's ideal candidate. He is a tall, ruggedly handsome man at fifty-two with bright, dark eyes and thick salt-and-pepper hair which looks best not too well combed—which it usually is not.

He speaks in a loud clear voice, full of passion for his new political cause, which he sees as rescuing Peru from its profound economic crisis and terrorist-guerrilla insurgency without sacrificing its democracy to either Marxism or a new military dictatorship. His message is that a "parasitic" state, grown fat under both military and civilian populists, saps the economy of its vitality. The economic freedoms of a true market economy, he preaches, are both the best basis for Peru's economic revival and its political liberty. As a stump politician Peru's premier novelist has been strikingly effective with his free-market, anti-big-government message.

Mario Vargas Llosa sharply criticized Alan García's provocative and costly declaration in his inaugural speech of a virtual suspension of payments to Peru's creditors. "One doesn't declare wars one can't win," says Vargas Llosa, who saw the action as unnecessarily breaking Peru's relations with all the international agencies which could help Peru. But the incident that provoked Mario Vargas Llosa into a political crusade was Alan García's sudden nationalization of Peru's banks and insurance companies in 1987. A grandstanding measure which would have been a sure winner in the heyday of Latin populism was a political bomb for García with the more jaded public today.

Mario Vargas Llosa considered the nationalization one last straw on the back of an economy already carrying a bloated public sector. He took his protest message to the people and found himself addressing rallies with massive turnouts and galvanizing bank employees and managers to pursue sit-ins and passive resistance which have effectively staved off implementation of the nationalizations.

Mario's prescription for Peru is the opposite of García's: free up private initiative, rather than regulating it further; shrink the government's role in the economy, don't expand it; integrate Peru with the international market, don't cut it off; slash government expenditures to starve a raging inflation, don't feed it. His prescription may be more popular than García's, which has brought Peru to the brink of economic breakdown.

But Mario doesn't need to run against García. García cannot succeed himself and his APRA Party fears it will finish third at best in the 1990 elections. To gain power, Mario's center-right front will have to beat the Marxist-led United Left—which is not really united, but could conceivably stay together for the purpose of winning an election. It is a polarized, bitter contest. But Mario says he feels a moral responsibility to help preserve the democratic values and practices he believes in.

In one sense, Mario is the heir of Belaúnde's centrist philosophy, but the desperate state of Peru's economy and security are not susceptible to the cautious governance of Belaúnde's years. If one listens carefully, Mario is offering tougher, more radical cures. He talks of arresting Peru's hyperinflation by the cold-turkey treatment Victor Paz Estenssoro applied in Bolivia (bringing inflation down from twenty-five thousand percent to twelve percent in three years by a harsh contraction of government spending, including the layoff of tens of thousands of government workers). Mario advocates mobilizing the villagers, not just the army, to fight the Shining Path guerrillas, a potentially bloody if possibly effective course. Beneath the inspirational message, the essence is: no free lunch, work harder, expect less, and risk something yourself. It is a hard message to deliver to Peru's poor, even in an era of new realism in Latin politics.

*   *   *   *   *

BOEKER: Why does a renowned writer, like yourself, turn to politics?

VARGAS LLOSA: For the most part circumstances pushed me into it. For many years I have preached the need for development in the context of democracy, for my country and for Latin America. I have forcefully expressed my conviction that only democracy can guarantee the integral development of our society, not only in terms of economic growth but also in terms of the growth of a national culture, with a sense of social responsibility, of the dignity of the individual, and of liberty. For the last eight years, this opportunity has been open to Peru—but for various reasons the country has instead fallen into great danger.

There is a possibility that the alliance of Marxist parties in Peru could win the 1990 elections which would mean, sooner or later, the destruction of our democracy. This is one of the reasons why I believe that those of us who believe in democracy, and want to make it a dynamic tool for change, are obliged to enter politics.

The specific event which motivated me to enter the political arena was an attempt in 1987 by the García government to nationalize the financial system. Seen from abroad it is hard to appreciate the devastating consequences such a measure can have in an underdeveloped country. In contrast to what may be the case in an industrial state, state ownership in a developing country necessarily politicizes the operation concerned. Thus, when the state nationalizes the whole financial system, the government begins to exercise extraordinary control over the economic life of the country. That is a deadly threat for democracy. If all credit is in the hands of the government, how can any industry, such as communications, function with any degree of autonomy? What chance for real independence do television, radio, and newspapers have if in order to survive they need credit which is in the hands of the government? I strongly protested this proposal because its essence was obviously totalitarian in nature.

To my surprise a huge sector of the Peruvian people reacted forcefully against the legislation and formed a strong protest movement which stopped the implementation of the nationalization law. The government had already approved the law but has been unable to put it into effect because of the popular protest. That gave me great hope about the possibility of revitalizing Peruvian democracy by adding to the political freedom we have had since 1980 an economic and social dimension. I believe strongly this is Peru's real hope.

BOEKER: When you say that a victory for the United Left, which includes Marxist elements, would be a defeat for democracy, are you thinking that such a victory might provoke a military coup or are you thinking of the leftist government per se?

VARGAS LLOSA: Both. When I speak about a serious threat to the democratic system I am referring to both sides of the coin; either its destruction by a military dictator, or its degeneration toward Marxist models of social organization. If the Marxist alliance wins, the military's fears of a Marxist government could bring their intervention. Any such break in the constitutional order would be unacceptable to me. In the event that the United Left wins the election, I will oppose any kind of coup and I will defend the people's decision. I do believe, however, that if the United Left takes power, the Marxist model of development will inevitably erode, undermine, and ultimately destroy, Peruvian democracy.

The United Left's brand of Marxism, with a few exceptions, is pre-Gorbachev; it is Stalinist, dogmatic, Third-World Marxism in every sense of the word. It is a Marxism still feeding on all the old Marxist myths—socialization of the means of production, absolute hegemony of the state in the economy, inquisitorial practices with respect to opposition, etc. It would start a process which sooner or later would transform our potentially liberal democracy into a "popular democracy" and socialist system which has nothing to do with genuine democracy.

BOEKER: Your decision to participate in the Democratic Front draws you into a long, nasty struggle until 1990. Are you ready to see this through, despite the obvious cost to your other activities, including the intellectual ones?

VARGAS LLOSA: Politics means a sacrifice for me. It is not something I do because I have any vocation or taste for it. I don't crave power. Power has always incited great suspicion in me. Furthermore, I have always understood my vocation as a writer as one which serves as a counterweight to power. The idea of sallying forth from that redoubt of resistance to power, which literature has represented to me, and of becoming a part of the structure of power, is a great sacrifice to me. I not only have to give up my vocation for some time, but I also have to re-stack my personal values so that I can play a different role.

It would not be honest for me to remain merely within the intellectual realm because I believe that what is needed now is political action. While there is a risk that Marxism might win a victory in Peru, many people have opened their eyes and see the roots of the malaise. This gives us an opportunity to correct the political course of our democratic system. This opportunity arises from the terrible crisis we face and from the errors of President Alan García, particularly his insistence on such demagogic measures as the nationalization of the banks.

It would be a formidable achievement for my country and for Latin America if out of Peru's present crisis emerged a movement of democratic renewal which would take liberty beyond its political context and make it a tool for social and economic transformation. This would help free Peruvians from a series of myths and stereotypes which still confine our social and economic development and are the cause of the economic and social disaster which now plagues us. One must try to take advantage of the current opportunity to change the roots of the Peruvian problem.

BOEKER: Several political leaders with whom I have spoken in other Latin American countries consider that Peruvian democracy may be the most endangered in the hemisphere, and certainly in South America. Would you agree with that?

VARGAS LLOSA: Unfortunately, I believe that is true. Peruvian democracy is at a critical stage because of two factors: a very deep economic crisis and increasing political violence, which has received new stimulus from the economic crisis itself.

Alan García's administration also had raised such great expectations and hopes that disillusionment has been a very rude awakening. It has produced demoralization and distrust now being directed not only against the government but against the system. Many people hold the system responsible for what is happening, and there are some sectors where the idea of a coup is surfacing once more. I think these are in a minority, but recent opinion polls indicate segments which believe that Peru must be governed by a strong hand. Other, poorer sectors of society, are being hit brutally by the economic crisis, and their desperation drives them toward the apocalyptic vision of extremely violent groups such as the Shining Path, and the Tupac Amaru Revolutionary Movement.

For its part, the government is an immense inefficiency, totally incompetent to deal with the present crisis. This administration gives the appearance of being adrift, trying desperately not to drown, and having no plan whatsoever to get the country out of the whirlpool. Undoubtedly all this has considerably debilitated the basis of our democracy.

There is no doubt that the threat to democracy is probably worse here in Peru than in any other Latin American country. That is one of the reasons why I believe that those of us who want democracy to survive must take action. We must demonstrate that there is a democratic alternative to the present government, that it is Alan García who is to blame and not the system.

BOEKER: In light of the very deep social and economic divisions in Peru today, will it be possible to contain most of the tensions within a framework of democratic competition, without increasing violence, and social disintegration leading to a "dirty war" between various actors, including the army and the guerrillas?

VARGAS LLOSA: Yes, I believe that it is possible as long as we come up with an alternative which will give some hope to the people, one that will suggest there is light at the end of the tunnel. It is going to be up to us to make of the Democratic Front this kind of an alternative. The nature of our movement has to be new and reformist, and at the same time serious and technical.

One must not be naive, of course, because the situation is very difficult. Economic deterioration has gone beyond the most pessimistic predictions, including my own. I was never a supporter of Alan García, because he appeared too immature, irresponsible, and demagogic. I never had any illusions about him and criticized his economic policies which struck me as very dangerous. However, even I who had so many reservations about a García government, never imagined that the collapse could be so complete as we have now seen.

All this creates a condition of social disorder and suffering for people who have already had more than their share of misery. This is bound to cause social turmoil and increased violence. We don't know whether the system can survive until the end of his term in August 1990. Our obligation is to try to make it survive, but one cannot have illusions when the situation is so grave.

BOEKER: There was so much optimism and enthusiasm when Alan García came to the presidency, and now the country is rapidly reaching a point of total frustration. What happened?

VARGAS LLOSA: In the case of Peru there was initially a grand euphoria because his policy of subsidizing consumption artificially invigorated the economy and for about a year and a half created the illusion of a bonanza. We were on a binge which was really the equivalent of the primitive ritual in which the tribe consumes all the provisions for a whole year in one great orgy. That is exactly what the policies of Alan García did.

Alan García adopted economic and social policies which could only lead to this disaster. There was nothing new in his policies. They are orthodox, big-government, socialist-style populism which have been tried by many Latin American countries, always with disastrous results: for Allende in Chile, for Siles Zuazo in Bolivia, and for Daniel Ortega in Nicaragua. The result of those policies has always been the same: rampant inflation which turns into hyperinflation, exhaustion of monetary reserves, and the near-destruction of national economic life, creating ill will, mistrust, and social upheaval.

His irresponsible demagoguery also cut us off from the international financial community. He declared war on all the international credit institutions so that he could assume the image of a revolutionary, Third-World, anti-imperialist leader. Peru has thus become ineligible for credits from international lending organizations and will have to survive this crisis without any international aid to alleviate the tremendous adjustment we have to make.

The only thing we still don't know is how aware was Alan García of the cataclysmic consequences of his policies. Did he really think, despite all evidence to the contrary, that his policies were going to be beneficial for the country? Or didn't he care as long as a resulting radicalization of society made him a Peruvian Fidel

Castro? That did not happen. He frightened people and they rejected his policies.

A reaction within his own party stopped the radicalization, but the crisis was already upon us. What might have happened is that Peruvian democracy could have been destroyed from the top by massive nationalization and total socialization —which García at one point probably wanted to attempt. But he did not anticipate the resistance which arose even within his own party, which is no longer revolutionary. Most of the party members wanted to enjoy the fruits of power and live in peace. García misjudged the nature of his own APRA party.

BOEKER: You have mentioned your desire to involve not only the army but the people in the fight against the guerrillas. Specifically what do you mean by that?

VARGAS LLOSA: The concept is that if the civilian society does not recognize that guerrilla-terrorism is everybody's problem and not just one for the police or the army, it will be very difficult to resolve. The threat is against all who want a civilized, democratic life, with tolerance and pluralism in a system of laws. War has been opened on us and we must defend ourselves through active and effective mobilization organized in such a fashion that the people can participate at all levels.

In northern Peru we have the phenomenon of the watch patrols (ronderos) which is very interesting. In the region of Cajamarca the campesinos have organized themselves in patrols and have succeeded in decreasing to a great extent the problem of violence in the countryside. The people took effective action to defend themselves when the state was not able to do so. I have just returned from Cajamarca and have seen it for myself. These self-defense groups work. The communists and the APRA Party have tried unsuccessfully to take over this civilian self-defense movement.

At one point we had a spontaneous campesino movement to fight the Shining Path. Unfortunately it ended with a tragedy in which eight journalists were murdered. In a moment of great confusion the campesinos of the mountains near Ayacucho killed the entire group without realizing who they were. The killings caused great commotion in the country and were exploited by the extreme left to create great hostility toward the campesinos and to paint the movement as a satanic one. A genuine counter-terrorist movement at the popular level was thus stopped short.

If we can generate enthusiasm for an alternative offering change within a democratic system I believe that we can revive a spirit of popular mobilization against the guerrillas. Undoubtedly the army and the police have to be in the fight, always under the control of civilian authorities, but with the very active participation of the people in the fight against extremism as well.

I often think of the only conversation I had with Rómulo Betancourt (Venezuela's first president after the fall of the dictator Pérez Jiménez in 1958), after he left government, when he said something I have never forgotten: "Look, in the Seventies Belaúnde Terry and I both had the problem of guerrillas. Belaúnde called the military and told them to solve the problem, and they did; they liquidated them. However, later on they also liquidated democracy and took over the government, in Velasco's revolution. In Venezuela, when the guerrillas took to the hills, I did not call out the army. I, the government, fought that battle. I went on television and made myself the leader of the fight. The army was a tool, but I led the battle." Now Venezuelan democracy is thirty years old, and it is solid because it was based on the triumph of civilian power. I have never forgotten that conversation and it is very relevant to Peru today.

Our governments do not want to get their hands dirty in such a messy fight. They prefer that the fight retain the character of a police or military action. You cannot defeat guerrillas that way, especially in regions where the power of the state does not reach. Whoever is strongest imposes his authority there, and in many such regions that is the guerrillas. The campesino has a strong instinct for survival and accommodates to whomever is effectively in control. The power of the guerrillas has to be contested by civilian authority, not just military force.

BOEKER: Representatives of several foreign companies have asked me when one might expect that stability will be restored to Peru, as they have interest in investing here. When do you think that might be?

VARGAS LLOSA: It would not be fair to blame (Peru's instability) on just the policies of one president, because Peruvian democracy is defective. It needs to be reformed so as to change the direction of Peruvian society. If the Democratic Front wins a clear mandate from the people to make these changes in 1990, from that moment on things could change radically, including the ethic which dominates the life of this democracy.

Peru is a country with great natural and human resources. Peruvians have demonstrated many times that they can be very creative and that they have enormous productive energies. There are countries which are poorer, and with fewer resources, than Peru, and yet they have been able in just a few years to reverse their decline and become truly progressive and modern. There is hope!

BOEKER: But I am impressed by the disillusionment prevailing in the country.

VARGAS LLOSA: Can you imagine what it is to have a twelve hundred percent inflation rate? Peru has never experienced anything like this before. People are hurting. After two years of thinking that the luck of our country had changed, that we were entering a period of growth and prosperity, the disillusion has been devastating.

BOEKER: Do you think that the international financial institutions and the governments of creditor countries have been too harsh on the García government?

VARGAS LLOSA: Well, I would not say that has been the case. The policies of the García government have been irresponsible and totally senseless. Imagine declaring war on the international financial system! One should not declare a war one cannot win, and that is what we did! It would be different if you were asking whether I believe that the policies of the international financial institutions toward the Third-World debtors make sense. Then my answer would be they don't make much sense.

It is obvious that our countries cannot meet the debt obligations initially incurred. Demanding rigid compliance with those debt obligations will precipitate a social crisis totally incompatible with democratic life. There could be a collapse of democracy unless an understanding is reached. I am not advocating writing off debts or a policy of charity which would not solve anything. What we need is to realize that countries with imperfect democracies and tremendous social problems cannot be expected to have the capacity to carry the kind of burden they now have. Just to meet its interest payments, Peru would have to sacrifice sixty percent of income received from its exports. How can a poor country like Peru survive under those conditions?

There has to be an intelligent, sensible negotiation that will allow us to make payments without sacrificing our growth or our democracy. This should be the main criterion. There is no better guarantee for creditors in the long run than to have the debtor countries able to conduct their business within a stable system of government and law. Democracy provides that guarantee; military dictatorship does not. Military dictatorship does not ensure security or stability. There should then be a more flexible and intelligent policy, a long-term policy that would reinforce democracy.

I agree with the Western democracies which wish to penalize dictatorships. It's a good idea. In general, policies should clearly discriminate against dictatorships and in favor of democracies. Bolivia, for example, is making a tremendous effort to restore discipline to its economy and is working very hard to establish a genuinely free-market economy. That country needs to have the support of the Western democracies and the international financial institutions in its efforts to create a solid economic base for Bolivian democracy. [Paraguayan General Alfredo] Stroessner, on the other hand, should have been penalized as a dictator. If democracy is to be promoted in the Third World, it is wrong to deal on the same basis, using purely technical criteria, with dictators like Stroessner and democratic leaders like [Bolivia's] Paz Estenssoro.

BOEKER: Is it possible within the inter-American system to give preference or special status to democratic governments?

VARGAS LLOSA: I believe so. My criterion is that what is needed is what the French call "two weights and two yardsticks" (deux poids et deux mésures). Democratic governments should get effective support from the developed Western democracies. If the United States, France, or England wish to make sure that democracy, the great contribution of the West to mankind, "takes" in the Third World, they have to show an active solidarity with those trying to implant these ideas and institutions in these countries. I am not talking about charity or paternalistic policies; what I am saying is that it is important to avoid looking at our countries in merely technocratic terms, as one does with dictatorships.

Democracy in our countries is deficient. There is much corruption and that should not be condoned. For that very reason it is important that foreign aid and cooperation not pass necessarily through the state, which is the most deficient part of our democracies. It is not the people. Our people are honest and have good instincts. Peruvians proved it when they resisted the nationalization of the banks. Ancient practices and a certain ethic have made the government a source of corruption; therefore, the less aid that passes through the hands of the state, the better. Aid should go directly to civilian society, to the independent sector. That would be the best contribution to democracy. This would be a good policy for international institutions as well—to leap over the state organs, because the state is a source of great ineptitude and corruption.

BOEKER: You have already mentioned debt renegotiation as one way to help consolidation of democracy, but are there any other actions you would like to see from a new U.S. administration toward Peru, and Latin America?

VARGAS LLOSA: A policy of active solidarity with democracy. It is very bad that the United States takes an interest in Latin America only when it perceives a threat to its own national security, as in the case of Central America. It is bad that the image the U.S. in Latin America is that of country which seems to react only when its interests are at stake, and not out of conviction, in the spirit of good neighborliness among democracies. It is important that the U.S. take initiatives that give it the image of a country continually promoting democracy in Latin America, rather than just defending its security. Democracy must be promoted not just against the Marxist threat but also against military dictatorships or anything else that will destroy the constitutional order. Symbols and gestures play a significant role for us who are fighting for the survival of democracy, in order to show that the United States is with us because we share important principles.

BOEKER: Do you have any ideas on confronting the drug problem?

VARGAS LLOSA: This is a subject which causes me great anxiety. It is a terrible threat to a democratic system; it damages and corrupts healthy and pluralist political organs. I also realize that once drug traffic takes root in countries like Peru, Colombia, or

Bolivia, there are certain ways of life which cannot be eliminated merely by repressive action. Even if thousands of soldiers were mobilized (which won't happen) to burn coca plantings on a daily basis, the problem won't be solved. At the producer's level it is a social and economic problem.

The economic incentive will prevail. Coca growing brings an income superior to that of any other crop. Growers get a lot more money for coca than they get for potatoes or tomatoes. Enforcement, without taking into account a social and economic perspective, won't work. If the industrialized countries cannot eliminate consumption, then they have to help create an alternative that would not entail a brutal sacrifice for the campesino.

The power of drug traffic is terrible; it creates a source of power which conspires against democratic authority. Drug traffickers acquire such great economic power that they can defeat institutions responsible for enforcement by corrupting the military, police, judges, and politicians. All that is already happening in Peru. But the core of the problem is economic and social.

COLOMBIA

VIRGILIO BARCO

Colombian President Virgilio Barco received me in his sun-splashed office in the stately Casa de Nariño. The straight-backed, hard chairs in second-empire style discourage one from staying too long, but keep one awake while there. Barco, an engineer by training, shares Jimmy Carter's penchant for managing detail, and his love for statistics. Barco had dictated the night before most of what he wanted to say to me and started a filibuster before I sat down. A reflective, somewhat introverted person by nature, Barco is not comfortable with the give-and-take of interviews or in dealing with the press. He prefers to work it all out logically with lots of flanking data and lay it on his audience all at once, as the complete report on the guerrillas, or narcotics traffic, or human rights problems. But on second reading, Barco found some of the data in his own initial unburdening to me to be inadequate. He popped up several times to order more before I could settle down to a conversation with one of Colombia's most distinguished public men.

Virgilio Barco, like the best of Colombia's political class, has spent a lifetime in public service. As president he felt personally responsible for tending all aspects of the commonweal, from the staff work to final tactics of implementing a decision. At one point he stopped in mid-sentence to voice his preoccupation with the then on-going talks with the M-19 guerrillas over the kidnaping of Alvaro Gómez, his opponent in the elections which gained him the presidency in 1986. A succession of violent assaults on Colombia's politicians and judicial officials weighed heavily on Barco and kept buffeting his efforts to concentrate his government's efforts on his own agenda.

Yet drug traffic, sinking its roots continually deeper into Colombia's flesh, is Barco's principal fear for the future and the reason for his anguished calls for the U.S. to curb its massive appetite for drugs. Barco despairs of Colombia's being able to curb the drug mafia's corrupting power as long as the U.S. market provides such strong suction and enormous profit for drug trade.

For anyone who knew Barco as ambassador to the United States in 1977–80, the first impression had to be one of how much he had aged. A shock of now-white hair pointed skyward and his skin was pale from long hours and no escape from the continual calls reporting the latest assault by the guerrillas on Colombia's economic sinews—power lines, oil pipelines—or by the narcotics mafia on Colombia's democratic institutions, particularly its courts. I have never seen a man more in need of a vacation, or less likely to get one soon.

Governing Colombia is a job which would strain anyone to the limit, but it seems to be almost a killing job in Barco's time and in Barco's style. He is a straight-ahead, some say stubborn, politician with little interest in his press or the bobs and weaves which might curry favor on both flanks of his course. More a manager than a politician, he believes good government should bring its own political reward. The course he set for his government was a true one, calling for a tough campaign against narcotics traffickers and guerrillas with no unilateral concessions. At the same time he tried to accelerate delivery of social services and utilities to remote villages in areas where guerrillas operate. But his unwillingness to spend beyond the government's means limited the funds flowing to the program. Barco's efforts to stay his course were also continually diverted to the latest crisis provoked by the disparate groups using violence to sow anarchy or weaken the structures that could punish their crimes. Barco had to take on each crisis personally, not only because that is Barco's way, but also because Colombians expect such personal feats from their presidents.

Barco's major contribution to Colombia's long-term political stability could be his rupture with the tradition under which Colombia's two major parties had shared patronage appointments to government jobs. This move toward a truer division of governing and opposition party could prove a significant prod to more aggressive vote-seeking and grass-roots political mobilization by Colombia's traditional parties.

Barco was elected with the greatest majority of any postwar Colombian president, but his mid-term ratings in the polls showed scarcely half as many Colombians approved of his efforts. Yet Barco was anything but a bowed man. He was optimistic, almost Panglossian, in his faith that Colombia is stronger than its internal enemies and capable of overcoming them still if a steady course is kept.

*   *   *   *   *

BOEKER: Colombian democracy has the greatest degree of continuity, if not stability, in South America. What accounts for this?

BARCO: There is no reason why democracy should not be stable. By permitting everyone to pursue his legitimate interests, democracy provides the peaceful means to deal with inevitable social conflicts. All sectors of society, political and economic leaders, the armed forces, the political parties, and the people, have demonstrated their irrevocable commitment to democracy. Thanks to the attachment of the people to the legitimacy of established institutions, minorities attempting to bring chaos through violence have consistently failed.

Our armed forces have never had a tendency to engage in military coups. Our civil wars were in fact fought by civilians who put on a uniform. Our army was effectively established only at the beginning of this century. It is a bipartisan and professional army, despite attempts at one point to make them an instrument of the Conservative Party. Colombia is a country rich in resources which has developed in all sectors. The percentage of the population living in rural and urban areas has reversed itself. Seventy percent of Colombians have moved to cities, and that migration has transformed our cities. Bogotá had a population of ninety-eight thousand at the end of the past century, one hundred and eighty thousand on its four hundredth anniversary, and now five million just fifty years later. But Colombia is not a one-metropole country. We have four major cities, Bogotá, Cali, Medellín, and Barranquilla, and many more which are quite large. The economy has become modernized, with much more participation on the part of women and the rate of population growth has declined to less than two percent. All these factors have helped strengthen our democratic system at the same time that they present us with new challenges that must be met.

BOEKER: Despite the continual presence of brilliant minds in Colombian politics, some observers feel that political leaders have not kept in touch with the people, leading to concern that the legitimacy of Colombian political parties is deteriorating. Would you say that this is a legitimate concern?

BARCO: Yes, indeed. The National Front, an agreement to share power, led to the erosion of the mechanisms that usually assure proper representation. Now we are going back to direct democracy. We are seeking citizen participation at every level: in rehabilitation committees, in social development commissions, and in municipal councils.

On March 13, 1988, our first popular election of mayors was carried out with the greatest voter participation in our history. We have also amended our constitution to allow for the possibility of municipal consultations. The constitutional reform project which we are putting before the next Congress will include a provision for plebiscites and referendums on specific issues. With these initiatives, we hope to strengthen our political system by increasing participation and assuring that decisions reflect greater justice for a majority of the population. These initiatives do not substitute for political parties, or the Congress, but these institutions can be strengthened through increased competition, participation and acceptance of the political system.

I believe that Colombia must also put an end to the restrictions imposed on our democracy toward the end of the Fifties as a last resort to end the violence between parties at that time. A National Front was established to restore democracy after the 1957 crisis and Rojas Pinilla's short dictatorship. The Front was to last for twelve years, three four-year periods, to ensure parity within the ministries and rotation within the Cabinet. Then there were complications, and it was extended for a further twenty-year period. The result was to freeze the democratic process as we knew it for thirty-two years. Quite a few people remained in power merely because there was no viable opposition. Now that we have overcome that phase, I firmly believe that we must return to competitive, absolute democracy.

BOEKER: With such impressive democratic continuity in Colombia, how do you explain the continuous violence?

BARCO: The nature of the violence is not continuous: it has changed fundamentally. The violence which started in 1957, as you will remember, was the result of political confrontation. There was much discontent among the general population, due particularly to land-holding issues. At that time we were able to deal with the problem. As minister of public works during the administration of Alberto Lleras and with help of the minister of the interior and the attorney general, we formed a Commission for Peace. During one of the meetings held, three thousand guerrillas, for the most part campesinos, turned in their arms in return for titles to land. Today they are prosperous farmers.

The type of guerrilla we are facing now has different characteristics. It is not political. FARC (Fuerzas Armadas Revolucionarias de Colombia) has some thirty "fronts" or cadres. They buy and sell cocaine using their profits to purchase weapons. Then we have the ELN (Ejército de Liberación Nacional), operating at the Venezuelan border and dedicated to attacking U.S. interests. The company under contract for the construction of a pipe line is culpable for having paid them protection to be able to complete the job. The EPL (Ejército Popular de Liberación), is the harshest one of them all; its leaders are two Spaniards who are former priests. Then we have the M-19 (Movimiento 19 de Abril); it is very small, but operates very actively in Bogotá. They are responsible for the takeover of the Supreme Court, and the Dominican embassy (when the American ambassador and other diplomats attending a reception were held hostage); they also stole the sword of Simón Bolívar. At the present time the M-19 probably has about five hundred members. The ELN started in the Sixties with fifty people. When Belisario (Betancur) began his peace process there were six hundred of them and now there are even more.

BOEKER: So in your opinion the guerrillas used the cease-fire to strengthen their position?

BARCO: Exactly, the FARC (the largest guerrilla group and one which accepted the cease-fire) was able to grow from approximately one thousand to five thousand people with the money they got from cooperation with drug traffickers. That is the effect of the connection with drug traffic.

BOEKER: But up to now the ties to the drug traffickers have been weak.

BARCO: It varies.

BOEKER: And the guerrilla groups themselves are not united.

BARCO: During Belisario's (Betancur's) administration some of these groups formed what they called a "National Coordinating Alliance" (The Green House), with the intention of exercising central control, but it did not work out. There is much discord among these groups. Sometimes they form alliances, sometimes they engage in bloody battles. The term "narco-guerrilla" which implies a permanent alliance is misleading. But at the same time there are as many opportunistic alliances among these two groups as there are bloody confrontations. As to the FARC, its size grows in direct proportion to the profits it makes from growing coca and from processing the paste. Of the thirty-four fronts it has, fourteen are located in coca growing regions. Money from the drug trade has allowed the FARC to grow but has also led them into disputes with the drug traffickers and bloody cycles of revenge between guerrillas and drug traffickers. From the end of 1986 to the middle of 1987 the confrontation between FARC's seventh front and drug traffickers of the Plata family led to a wave of violence which cost the lives of the wife of a police chief and two mayors of San José. That there are disputes in some regions and confrontations between FARC and the coca traffickers does not mean that the functional, opportunistic alliance has ceased to operate.

Another problem is that some of the drug traffickers, especially the ones in Medellín, have invested heavily in land. Last December the Ochoa family celebrated with a party the closing of the deal which extended the land they own in northern Colombia to two million hectares (four hundred and ninety-four thousand acres). As property owners, however, they have suffered extortion at the hands of the guerrillas. They have reacted by forming vigilante groups for their own protection and to try to clean out guerrillas from their estates, leading to serious confrontations. The drug traffickers believe that some campesinos are part of the guerrilla groups and thus many have been killed.

The ideological confrontation between the drug traffickers and the guerrillas is interesting. Drug traffickers, who are among the richest people in the world, consider themselves representatives of capitalism, and in many regions they have organized to fight against the left. Thus, the drug traffickers assassinated a senator who was serious, courageous—and a communist.

BOEKER: So with all this fierce rivalry between guerrillas and the drug traffickers, you do not foresee the possibility of a real alliance as such against the government?

BARCO: Not at all. At this time the drug traffickers are fighting against the guerrillas. By the way, I understand that one of our most widely recognized drug traffickers went to the United States for a meeting in Atlantic City on the night of the fight for the heavyweight championship (in 1988). There were so many drug dealers present that they held a meeting to discuss cutting up the market for New York, Miami, and other cities. My point is that someone like that, known throughout the world as one of the largest drug traffickers, can manage to visit the United States as a "tourist."

BOEKER: Among Latin American nations, Colombia presents a marked contrast in terms of its enviable economic growth while besieged with internal security problems. Do you think that economic growth can continue under these circumstances, or is violence going to reach a point where economic growth will suffer?

BARCO: True, there are domestic actors which persist in using violence and spreading terror, thus creating obstacles for economic growth and development of our natural resources. However, there is no reason why we should not expect to defeat them. Other Western democracies have faced similar threats such as terrorism, guerrilla warfare or organized crime, and they were able to overcome these difficulties without giving up either their civil liberties or their economic development. Colombia too can strengthen its institutional stability and modernize its economy. It is not something that can be done overnight. But we are fighting a battle which we will eventually win, although paying high immediate costs.

We are also fighting social inequality and trying to eradicate the absolute poverty in which a quarter of our population lives. We are extending our agencies to regions previously ignored by the state and are working out a reconciliation with this neglected and important group of our society. We are adjusting our institutions to meet the needs of our people while striving to perfect and broaden the base of our democracy. At the same time, we are fighting terrorists and drug traffickers with some degree of success, which would be greater if we had more cooperation from the international community.

In the short term these measures, even when successful, will cause some instability and some violence. This does not mean, however, that development and modernization have stagnated. We will succeed.

BOEKER: At what point would you say that the violence, emanating from different sectors, threatens Colombian democracy?

BARCO: Out of a population of twenty-nine million over ninety-nine percent respect our institutions. Our armed forces, with a twenty percent increase during my administration, have now reached two hundred thousand men. The guerrillas are fewer than nine thousand. Do you think, given the numbers, that they represent a threat to Colombian democracy? In Colombia we are fighting terrorism with methods which have been successful in other countries such as England, Canada, Spain, and Germany. There is no reason why they should not work here.

There is clear evidence that our society is against terrorism. There was overwhelming voter participation in the March 13 (1988) mayoral elections, and there was total unity in repudiation of the kidnaping of Alvaro Gómez (a former presidential candidate). To the degree that our legitimate institutions become stronger, thanks to the changes being implemented, both the extreme left and extreme right are going to find it increasingly difficult to engage in violent activities.

BOEKER: With all these internal security problems do you see a danger that Colombia will become a country impossible to govern?

BARCO: No, I'll admit the country is difficult to govern, because of all the changes it is going through, but if there are two hundred thousand troops, some of them especially trained, and only nine thousand guerrillas, the country has a tremendous advantage in the balance of forces. The polls also indicate that approximately ninety percent of the general population is against drug traffic.

BOEKER: Does the general population support a tough policy against the guerrillas?

BARCO: According to the opinion polls, yes.

BOEKER: And the masses don't back the guerrillas?

BARCO: No, but I think that in some places they feel compelled to do it. When the guerrillas arrive in a village there is pressure. Guerrilla groups organize marches, tell the people where to go and in exchange they give them a small flag and a meal.

During its peace negotiations the past administration cut the army's budget, while the cost of living increased twenty to twenty-five percent per year. At the end of the four-year term the soldiers practically had no boots. We have restored two things to our army: morale and equipment. It is a democratic army. The officers are mostly career personnel, but the soldiers for the most part are young draftees.

BOEKER: Would you say that civilian authority over the military is secure?

BARCO: Absolutely. During our one hundred and eighty years of independence, we have had only two coups d'état: one lasted six days; the other, led by General Gustavo Rojas Pinilla in 1953, was actually at the request of the political parties, as a solution to their own violent confrontation.

BOEKER: Is there something that the new United States administration and other friendly countries could do to help Colombia consolidate its democracy and contribute to its stability?

BARCO: The worst threat that confronts Colombian democracy is the drug trade. This is a problem generated in the major centers of consumption, not in Colombia. The organized drug trade embraces a large international network with branches in many countries. It needs to be attacked with determination at every step of the way; at the stage of growing the raw materials and transporting them to the processing centers, and of marketing the product in the consumption centers. We also need to attack it at the level of the final consumer and at points where the profits are moved.

The worst threats to Colombian democracy are the tolerance which cocaine consumption enjoys in the United States and other countries, as well as the tolerance for growth and transportation of raw materials to processing centers, and for laundering the profits generated from all these illegal activities. Greater cooperation from the international community is required to end what is an international scourge.

BOEKER: If you were going to suggest an agenda for those in charge of policy toward Latin America during the new administration, what would you consider the first two or three priorities?

BARCO: I believe that with respect to the drug problem support is needed to combat consumers. Some headway has already been made in the United States; I have been reading the press a lot and I know there is a continuing debate which did not exist before. It has become a presidential campaign issue.

Secondly, I believe you need to give more support to those countries that are fighting the problem. No country in the world has paid a higher price in the war against drugs than Colombia. We have suffered the assassination of a chief justice, a minister, an attorney general, fourteen members of the Supreme Court, some members of the Council of State, and a large number of judges and police officers. We have paid the price.

Colombia has been getting from the United States approximately eight million dollars worth of aid in herbicides, helicopters, etc. But more help with intelligence is needed. Radar equipment must be installed at the borders with Peru and Brazil to detect the small aircraft which come from those countries with the cocaine base to be purified here. We have captured many small planes and dismantled many processing plants. The effort we have made is tremendous. Most of the activity takes place in the areas of manufacturing and purification of coca. To combat coca we could use more help for our military, especially for training specialized units.

BOEKER: Do you think there is something dramatic that governments could do to bring more attention to the urgency of attacking the problem at the level of the consumer?

BARCO: Yes, and I do believe the United States has opened that door; there is at least debate about what to do. But some argue for legalization and others for stricter penalties. Some are tempted by legalization because you have the experience of prohibition which produced Al Capone, and marijuana is grown in several U.S. states. Yet cocaine is much more dangerous (than alcohol and marijuana). That is why you must help fight it, and arrive at a better understanding of how to deal with it.

Colombia is determined to exhaust all the resources available in order to get more international cooperation for our fight against drug traffic. We have reached several agreements within the framework of the Group of Eight, and bilaterally with Peru, Brazil and Argentina. What we need is the commitment that the consumer countries are going to combat drug consumption with the same energy and efficiency with which they have achieved unqualified success in other areas.

In the United States a malicious campaign against Colombia has been started at the instigation of some members of our Communist Party, who went to the United States ostensibly to talk about drug traffic, but what they were really doing was attacking the Colombian government. They have persuaded some at Amnesty International.

BOEKER: Are you satisfied in general with the role the armed forces have played in this fight?

BARCO: In the struggle against guerrillas they have regained the advantage and their equipment has improved. Yes, their role has been most satisfactory. In the fight against drug traffic, the role of the military is very important.

MISAEL PASTRANA BORRERO

I met with former President Misael Pastrana Borrero in his attractive Spanish-style home, stair-stepped on the steep slope east of the city of Bogotá. He received me on a Saturday morning in a living room decorated in a masculine style. Two zebra skins covered the floor in front of a large stone fireplace in which a loud crackling fire accompanied our conversation.

With straight wet hair flattened across the top of his forehead, long, graying hair at each temple brushed back over the ears and a strong aquiline nose between dark, narrow eyes, Pastrana appeared the quintessence of the classical Roman statesman he so admires. His dress placed him more in the Via Veneto today: dark blue blazer over pinstriped shirt with a red Gucci tie. Apart from a metronomic movement of one foot as he speaks, Pastrana appears a man at ease, completely in control of himself and his party. His smiles come frequently and hold a long time—apparently in part as a result of a childhood facial injury.

At the end of the 1980s Misael Pastrana remained Colombia's most powerful politician. While Pastrana's party is in opposition, President Barco finds a quiet dialogue with him essential to the search for solutions to Colombia's crises, including at the time we met, the kidnapping of the Conservative party's candidate in the last presidential elections, Alvaro Gómez Hurtado.

Elected president at forty-five in a contest he almost lost to populist ex-dictator Rojas Pinilla, Pastrana is a politician who grew up fast. That close call shook the confidence of Colombia's political elite in itself and in Pastrana, who had been groomed for the presidency by the old lions of Colombian politics, Liberal Alberto Lleras Camargo and Conservative Mariano Ospina. A victory by the followers of Rojas—Colombia's last caudillo and only military dictator in this century—would have reversed the conservative economic and political policies Colombia has maintained for twenty-five years. Yet just two years after this narrow brush with radical populism, Pastrana led Colombia's traditional parties to a solid victory which ended, once and for all, any threat of a comeback by the followers of Rojas.

A scion of one of Colombia's great political families, Pastrana was brought up on politics by his father, a congressman and governor. Pastrana in turn has passed on the legacy to his son Andrés who became in 1988 the first elected mayor of Bogotá. Andrés was kidnapped by narcotics traffickers before his nomination, prompting Misael Pastrana's remark to me that entering Colombian politics these days is more of a sacrifice for others than a quest for personal power.

Pastrana presides over a united Social Conservative Party with a bevy of talented young figures like his son. He gives no hint as to whether he will use this position to try to regain the presidency himself or to have a decisive voice in picking who of the next generation will have a shot as young Misael himself did in 1970. (Many of Colombia's presidents have tried for a return to the presidency after four or eight years, but none has made it since the formation of the National Front in 1959.)

The answers come quickly and smoothly for Misael Pastrana, but the substance is deep. One leaves, as from most of Colombia's ex-presidents, with a copy of his latest book—but also with a profound admiration for the caliber of political leader the Colombian educational system and political parties produce. Despite the powerful disintegrative forces of prevalent criminal and political violence, Colombia's traditional parties have always found a way out, as Pastrana says, and they just might again—against the odds.

* * * * *

BOEKER: You almost lost an election to a strongman, Rojas Pinilla, who in his time was an attractive figure to many Colombians despite his anti-democratic convictions. Could Colombia once again turn to a strongman, one who would offer to end violence even at the cost of civil liberties?

PASTRANA: In the 1970 elections the National Front was divided. There thus were four candidates in the elections, not two. My position was also weakened by the fact that I was not in the obvious line of succession. I was forty-five years old while the old warriors of my party, sixty to sixty-five years old, claimed their own right to succession, regardless. If I had not broken that generation's hold, the party would have suffered traumatic defeat. As it was, we gained a new and more open outlook.

After the first two years of my term, ANAPO (Rojas Pinilla's party) lost the mid-term election resoundingly and simply vanished from the national political scene. When Rojas Pinilla and his followers launched their quest for return to power, Colombians still heard the echo of his autocratic government and with that memory, ANAPO disappeared. Their demise was an important event that transcended Colombian politics. In Latin America this type of populist movement had developed deep roots which have still not withered, although some have been modified, as in the case of Peronism in Argentina.

As a Colombian said many years ago, dictatorship is a plant that does not "take" in Colombian soil, as history shows. We have had only two brief dictatorships in this century and the transfer of power has occurred every four years. I do not believe we will again have that type of government; there would be too much resistance. It would almost be like being under foreign occupation.

Furthermore, Colombia has proved that in time of great difficulty, when the country appears about to dissolve and there seems no way out, the country pulls together to save itself at the last moment, as is happening now. It happened at the time of Rojas Pinilla with the formation of the National Front, and at the beginning of the century in the face of another strongman with the movement called Republicanism. The winds of democracy are the prevailing ones, and the right ones for Colombia. I do not foresee any circumstances under which the constitutional institutions would break down.

A small example: In June 1988, recognizing the difficult situation we are facing in Colombia, my party met and declared a "pause" in opposition politics. The reason was that we felt the situation was so delicate that our normal opposition stance might affect the stability of our institutions and the government. It was a gesture to create expectations of political stability.

BOEKER: Foreign observers fear that with all the problems Colombia is facing—violence and drug traffic in particular—there is danger that the country may become impossible to govern. You seem to be saying that pessimistic judgment goes too far.

PASTRANA: We are living through a very difficult period. That is why I fault the Barco administration's interruption of the dialogue with the opposition, thus aggravating a situation already critical because of social problems and the economic crises. With respect to our economic crisis the foreign debt has a lot to do with it. As to the guerrilla forces, they are not that powerful except for the element of surprise. Theirs is the power of the terrorist, to strike when least expected, with brutal traumatizing acts like kidnapping. But I don't believe that the country is headed toward either military rule or anarchy.

BOEKER: In your opinion, how healthy are the two traditional political parties? Do you think they are losing legitimacy or are they adequately meeting the challenges?

PASTRANA: I speak only for my party, but I will also give you my opinion on the Liberal Party. My party is living through a good period. It may be the first time in history that we are totally united. It was this unity which led us to victory in the mayoral elections, after a big setback (in the presidential race).

My party is convinced that in the final analysis the root of the conflict which exists in poor countries is the social problem. Thus we have a new name, the Social Conservative Party, as we pragmatically apply old principles and values. Political pragmatism is required because the problem of our contemporary world is not caused by a conflict of ideas, but of conflicting responses to the demands of our people. Our party is going to run in the next election, not with a partisan message but a national one. We are convinced that it is convergence of the parties on actual problems that will yield a solution to the nation's crisis.

The Liberal Party is at a different stage. I don't know whether it is one party or several parties: it is more heterogeneous and more diffuse. The nation gave them a clear mandate and they have not responded. Nevertheless, I hope that the unity of our party might inspire unity in the Liberals, which would be a good thing for the country. The country needs two strong parties.

BOEKER: What do you think of the present experiment of broader competition between government and opposition parties? Do you believe this competition will reinforce or weaken democracy?

PASTRANA: I accepted the plan proposed by the party in power, given the clear electoral victory of President Barco, even though we have a constitutional provision stating that the party which loses the election has a right to participate in the administration. However we did so under the condition that there be agreement on three fundamental points: the approach to peace (vis à vis guerrilla groups), the problem of drug traffic, and foreign policy. The government would not accept these conditions.

On two or three occasions President Barco asked for my help on concrete issues such as drug traffic, and I agreed to cooperate. Then we signed the so-called Casa Nariño accord to change our judicial structure through constitutional amendment. This proposal was widely acclaimed but the administration, in my opinion, lacked the necessary will to implement it. The plan for greater competition is valid because in the final analysis democracy is about one party which governs and another which holds out a future alternative, but without either party cutting lines of communication or pretending the other has lost its role in the country's political life.

From the very beginning I said that the plan would need to be changed by the popular will as expressed in the election of mayors and that is what has happened as we won four hundred and fifty of the mayoralties including the two most important cities, Bogotá and Medellín. Therefore today we can have different parties sharing power. In the case of the mayoralties won by my party we decided to grant participation in the municipal government to the Liberals and members of the Patriotic Union, where they obtained votes. Thus, we have now a member of the Communist Party appointed by the Social Conservative mayor of Bogotá to head one of the city's districts. The problem is not in the essence of democracy, that is government by one party and responsible opposition by another, but rather in a breakdown in communication.

BOEKER: Do you think your son went into politics because of the same family legacy and vocation which motivated you, or was it something different?

PASTRANA: In his case there are two important factors. One was his grandfather, who ran for president as the candidate for the Liberal Party, the opposition party, and cut a wide political swath during his public life. He was also mayor of Bogotá.

Andrés always admired his grandfather's ideas and way of thinking.

Another factor, without any question, was that he has from childhood watched me pursue politics. When I ran for the presidency, and he was only thirteen years old and attending Georgetown Prep (in Washington, D.C.), he asked to come home so that he could campaign with me. Later, to my surprise and to the surprise of the whole country, he organized a march which mobilized national attention on social causes. This gave him a very good public image and encouraged his political inclinations.

Andrés made an audacious move in running for mayor of a traditionally Liberal city, Bogotá, leading to the first win for the Social Conservative Party here.

All my children have been devoted to public service and have entered public life instead of going into other more remunerative fields.

BOEKER: Will talented young men and women continue to run for office despite the problems and the real personal risks?

PASTRANA: To be a politician in Colombia nowadays entails tremendous risk. It is an act that should be admired rather than criticized. Many times we are unjustly blamed for circumstances beyond our control when we are in positions of responsibility, without taking into account the politician's implicit act of courage. In reality what one is trying to do is to give to one's country and not desert it in time of danger.

But despite the circumstances, the risks, the challenges, those of us who are into politics persevere, hoping to overcome a moment of tremendous difficulties. One must keep faith in democracy. I like to quote to Colombians what Roosevelt said, "We have nothing to fear but fear itself." A person who is afraid of fear should not go into politics. Traditionally, Colombia's leadership in the social, economic and civic fields has been committed to public service. During my administration I had a saying: "I do not 'offer' cabinet positions or appointments, because I know whoever is appointed will accept," and that was really the case. Many left lucrative businesses to come into public service.

I believe that the mayor of Bogotá as well as the mayors of other cities brought a new message for the young. Election day is a happy day, when people go into the streets to celebrate. Bogotá's mayoral election was a spectacle of new voters and new contrasts. I saw family cars displaying the flag of the Liberal Party, but the young people of the same families with Andrés Pastrana's signs. There was definitely a new enthusiasm.

When I was president my theme was "power to the young." I was forty-five years old and I named cabinet members as young as twenty-six years old, one of whom, Luis Carlos Galán, was a possible presidential candidate for the Liberal Party. (He was assassinated August 18, 1989.) The average age of my cabinet was thirty-five, and I believe that in a coalition government I trained both liberals and conservatives of the new generation.

I see now that Andrés Pastrana has appointed very young people to positions of responsibility in Bogotá, which has generated a great deal of enthusiasm. The young need to know that they won't be held back because of their age, that they can get ahead by virtue of their merits, their honesty and their beliefs.

BOEKER: In Bogotá some say that the amnesty and cease-fire with the guerrilla groups have proved an unequal deal for the government because the guerrillas have taken advantage of the truce to increase their cadres and consolidate their positions. What do you think about that?

PASTRANA: One has to start from the point that the amnesty was an action which enjoyed the largest degree of political consensus in our history. It was a law passed with unanimity by the two traditional parties in the Congress.

I also believe that the incorporation (into open electoral politics) of the group called the Patriotic Union has been positive for the country. It has made our democracy more pluralistic and given a voice to elements which turned to armed conflict with the system, feeling themselves suffocated and without a way to express their opinions. For the first time they have their own representation in governance, and so far the apocalypse which was predicted if they were included in the system has not occurred.

Colombia has a wide spectrum of guerrilla movements: Trotskyites, Stalinists, Castroites, to which we have to add drug traffic as a new factor.

The FARC, which was the strongest guerrilla group, has some factions which are active and others which are passive, which is an improvement. The present administration maintains telephone communications with the leaders of this group, despite its having opposed the peace plan of the previous administration.

The ELN which had disappeared ten years ago is now destroying the pipelines. The transnationals revived this group. In Colombia, the transnationals were responsible for the same situation they created in Angola, Mozambique, and other African countries. They financed extremist groups by buying protection so they could complete their installations; later these groups continued to operate on their own.

The M-19 never entered into political negotiations. From the beginning they had a negative attitude. Sometimes they employ an idealistic message, sometimes they use undue pressure or terrorism.

In Colombia today our problem is more terrorism than guerrillas. Even the "guerrillas" in the countryside operate more as terrorists than anything else. They blow up pipelines and destroy power lines.

Why do I make this distinction between guerrillas and terrorists? I quote Gorbachev's phrase in *Perestroika*, "There cannot be revolutionary action without revolutionary theory." Nowadays the guerrilla groups in Colombia do not have a revolutionary theory. They are not seeking to participate in government; their intention is to destabilize and terrorize society.

I have just returned from an international meeting in Moscow with twenty-five former heads of state where I heard from the lips of André Gromyko that the intention of the superpowers is not only to work toward disarmament, but also to end regional wars. I believe that once regional conflicts are settled, these internal conflicts can more quickly find a resolution.

BOEKER: A question on democracy elsewhere in the hemisphere. In 1978 you and two other Latin American leaders participated in the Commission of the Organization of American States which assisted as observers in the Dominican elections. Did you discover significant fraud by the government or the military?

PASTRANA: I have participated on two commissions as an observer, once in the Dominican Republic and once in the Philippines. These have been two important experiences. In the Dominican Republic there was a moment of uncertainty and I believe our presence was definitive in settling the issue. At that time Balaguer was the incumbent, but he was defeated. There was confusion because the vote count had been delayed and because the opposition candidate had gone into hiding. We were cordial but firm and I think that was a definitive factor in clearing up the initial confusion which had totally vanished the next day.

If such commissions could be institutionalized, without any implication of intervening in the internal affairs of a country, it would create a great deal of calm for both the incumbents and the opposition at election time. It would stress the fairness of the process, and it would prevent difficult situations such as the one Mexico faced in 1988. This type of collaboration would greatly strengthen the democratic system.

BOEKER: What would be your advice to the new administration in the United States, in terms of specific policies and actions regarding Latin America?

PASTRANA: Some of our problems have, with time, been superseded: for example, the concept of foreign aid, on which friendly relations between Latin American countries and the U.S. used to be based. But we have two serious, intertwined challenges, one political and one economic.

As for the political challenge, Latin America needs to strengthen its regional mechanisms and procedures so it can solve its own problems. Latin America has a very old tradition of seeking its own solutions.

I know, for instance, that the Contadora Group has been criticized by some in the U.S. Contadora prevented Central America from becoming an explosive volcano as happened in Lebanon. Even though the Central American problem has not been solved, there are glimmers of light.

Mediation in Central America by the Latin American heads of state has helped to a very large degree to ease the tensions. This demonstrates that we need to strengthen both regional institutions and the use of ad hoc mechanisms operating in the region. In my opinion this is very important. Ironically, the Central American problem has consolidated Latin American unity.

As for the economic challenge, we cannot close our eyes to the foreign debt. Latin America cannot pay it. We are making sacrifices above and beyond our capacity. Besides having to meet our financial obligation we also have to meet what I call our social obligation, which has increased while we neglected it during the past six years.

During the past six years Latin America has suffered a profound deterioration, reflected in the statistics. The world has grown accustomed to reading statistics with a mathematical perspective, not a human and social one. That the (per capita) income in Latin America, a poor continent, has declined for eight years is a cruel and hard social statistic. It is now at 1970 levels.

This has happened in Colombia, as well. We have been called a good debtor country, but the cost of paying the debt has been immense, and the lack of funds for investment in many fields and whole regions of our country has fueled the armed conflict which we now endure.

Take the case of the city of Bogotá, with a population of six million; sixty percent of the income of the municipality goes to pay the foreign debt. Of course governments have to try to charge public services to the consumers, but it reaches a point where the consumer cannot pay the increased charges.

Resolution of the debt problem is a dire necessity. If the United States does not help find a solution, debtor countries will reach a point when they cannot "tighten their belt" any more and will impose unilateral solutions. Latin America has never wanted to do this, and all we ask is that realistic conditions of payment be established. The debt problem goes beyond just being able to pay it; the real problem is to revive growth in our countries.

BOEKER: With respect to strengthening regional collaboration, are formulas without the participation of the United States better?

PASTRANA: To pretend, within a geographic area, that one should become isolated from a country with so much wealth and technological resources would be absurd. In reality, Perestroika is the recognition on the part of the Soviet Union that it needs contact and collaboration with the West. The developing world needs it just as much as the socialist world.

Within this geopolitical reality, however, the commitment of the United States to this continent is not so strong as that of Europe to Africa because this continent was not in a political or geographic sense a colony of the United States. We see Europe's preoccupation with Africa's debt, and the aid they are prepared to give. For the United States the need for such links does not exist with respect to Latin America. The most serious experiment, with its successes and failures, was the Alliance for Progress. It was the most integrated plan formulated for Latin America. In the case of the foreign debt problem, which is concentrated in this continent, there has not been any real plan. The Baker Plan was directed at the entire Third World, and more at protecting the banks than the debtor countries.

We also need a plan for the transfer of technology. We cannot be at the mercy of limited transfers of technology by corporations which may or may not be willing to invest in our countries. A continent which remains far behind does not have a plan to incorporate new technologies in the fields of agriculture, industry or telecommunications. It is utopian, therefore, to think of foregoing cooperation with the United States.

BOEKER: Much is being said about economic integration in Latin America. But isn't this a very remote possibility since the prerequisites do not exist? Doesn't one need closer alignment of political and economic systems first?

PASTRANA: I must stress one thing. With the consolidation of the European Common Market, possible renovation of the Soviet economy and the new openness within the socialist groups, Japan an economic superpower, and the United States and Canada more closely tied, if Latin America does not do something to become part of this interdependent world, it will be off the map. As it is, we lack the capacity to defend our raw materials, establish adequate competition and reach foreign markets. If Latin America does not integrate, it will remain a foreign body within a world of integrated economies.

BELISARIO BETANCUR

Former Colombian President Belisario Betancur received me in a small apartment building perched precariously on a hillside which rises almost as steeply as the building's walls. The building was once his home but has been converted to offices for himself and his family. The large back windows opened onto the striking view of a floor-to-ceiling slope covered with flowers only a few feet away, giving the impression of a brilliant floral tapestry hanging on the wall. On the other side of the building, bay windows offer a striking view of the deceptively peaceful looking city of Bogotá spread across the valley floor.

Belisario, as everyone in Bogotá refers to him with affection, is different. But it does not immediately show. A handsome, fit man, with dark hair left gray at the temples and a ruddy face, Belisario looks younger than his sixty-five years. In a well-cut blue blazer and solid dark blue tie, Belisario's casualness appears as one which has to be just right. Beyond his well-groomed appearance, his manifest interest in painting, music, and literature place him apparently among Colombia's cultured political elite. But Belisario is different, and deeply proud of the humble origins which set him apart. Belisario was born into a working class family, one of twenty-two children (of whom only five reached adulthood). After working his way through a Jesuit university in Medellín to a law degree, Belisario pursued a classic Colombian route to the top, an early career in journalism, increasingly mixed with politics.

As head of a minority faction of a minority party, Belisario made it to the presidency (1982–86) with the help of a split in the opposition Liberal Party and charges of corruption against the previous Liberal administration. But he also was the first candidate to target successfully the growing group of undecided voters in Colombia, a country where party affiliation has been inherited and inflexible. A fiery orator, his exceptional ability to address

219

Colombians in a populist and moralistic tone also struck chords with resonance among the poor. One of his favorite paintings is a vast, naive painting in brilliant colors of Belisario himself delivering a campaign speech in the square of an imaginary, perfect Colombian colonial town in the mountains. It hangs in the meeting room of his offices.

Belisario immediately insisted to me (as to anyone else) that he had imposed silence on himself in any public discussion of Colombian politics. In particular he refused to defend his vaunted peace process with guerrillas, in the face of President Barco's criticism that it provided a cover for the major guerrilla group to double its cells. "Wait for my book," says Belisario. But he is in no hurry to deliver the book to a publisher, because Belisario hopes there is still another political chapter to be written.

Why, I asked, does this avowed Christian Democrat find himself in the oldest conservative party in the hemisphere? Because, answered Belisario, his family did not allow sons to change party. But, he quips, he did have leave to change the nature of the party into which he was born. And so he did. Belisario is responsible for the "social" in the newly re-christened Social Conservative Party of Colombia and for its emphasis on delivering social services to the rural areas as part of a long term strategy for defusing the causes of violence. Yet his own administration was criticized for putting too few resources into the program.

The other prong of Belisario's strategy, dialogue with the guerrillas and bringing their political cadres into the party structure, was dealt a devastating blow in his last year in office. In November 1985, the M-19 guerrillas launched a bloody assault on Colombia's Palace of Justice, which after a counterassault by the Colombian army, left dead twelve of Colombia's Supreme Court justices and one hundred people in all. Belisario then shifted to a tougher stance on fighting the guerrillas and the narcotics traffickers, despite death threats against him and his family.

Yet he remains proud of the one remaining achievement of his peace process, the advent of the leftist Patriotic Union Party in Colombia's electoral system as an open arm of Colombia's largest guerrilla group, the FARC. The important initiative to elect directly all of Colombia's mayors was another milestone of Belisario's effort to broaden avenues for participation of alienated elements in Colombia's political system—not a bad record for one round in a tough corner.

*   *   *   *   *

BOEKER: I have the impression, Mr. President, that although you are an outstanding member of Colombia's "political class" you see yourself as different from the country's traditional leadership.

BETANCUR: Yes, I was born and raised in the country, and of humble origins. I was the first in my family to get a formal education. As a child I studied in the seminary, not because I wanted to be a priest but because it was the only place where I could pay for tuition with work. I thus grew up with Greek and Latin, the classical philosophy of Aristotle and Plato, and the social philosophy of the church, later earning degrees in law and economics from a Catholic university. While still quite young I began writing for magazines and newspapers, and teaching in universities.

I traveled all over the world, including the Soviet Union, trying to learn from different cultures. The conclusion reached from this very personal experience can be summarized as follows: it is within the democratic system that the human being can realize to the fullest the values which reaffirm and enhance human dignity, among which, of course, is liberty.

After studying different systems and examining democracies in the United States, in Europe and, of course, in socialist countries, I have come to the conclusion that what comes closest to the truth is the symbiosis of social democracy which exists for example in the United States, present day Spain, or West Germany. The virtues and values of this kind of democracy present Latin America its greatest opportunity, if we are able to put them in practice and not just mouth them.

It would not have been easy for me to chose between Colombia's two political parties, but the choice was already made for me. In those times one just didn't switch from the party affiliation of one's family. Some of my concerns were not being addressed by the Conservative Party, but I tried to work them out within the party and at present I am totally satisfied, from an ideological standpoint. Of course, it is difficult for all Colombian political parties to convert their vision into reality—that is another story.

Mine was a minority party, with a largely rural base, slowly becoming more urban. If we were to win the presidency we had to have the support of other groups. I put forth some proposals, not necessarily all that conservative, and invited some liberals

*　*　*　*　*

and some communists to join me. I had the support of most of the liberals and my party perceived that probably only someone who could attract votes from other sectors could win a presidential election. Now I work closely with my party leader, former president Misael Pastrana Borrero. Our name is now the Social Conservative Party indicating that our mission is not to safeguard privileges but liberty, and to achieve social change within the democratic order.

BOEKER: Is there a risk that the traditional political parties will lose their legitimacy?

BETANCUR: Yes, they stand a risk of losing their legitimacy to the extent that they do not address the anxieties of the population. However, paradoxically, before elections take place here there is a perception that the communists and the leftists are going to win by a landslide, but in the end the votes are cast for the Conservatives or the Liberals. The legacy of the traditional political parties from one generation to another is very strong, especially in the rural areas. In the cities there is now more fluidity; for instance my children have no affiliation to a particular party.

BOEKER: Do you think this new fluidity is positive, given the fact that the parties have to compete harder to win the votes of the undecided?

BETANCUR: Yes, it's a positive development. Our recent move to popular election of mayors, and the increased community participation during my administration, are a breath of fresh air in our political life and will produce even more fluidity.

BOEKER: A change in administration in the United States is an important moment for the United States and for Latin America in the sense that it is really only every four or eight years that we have the opportunity to reconsider our agenda with respect to Latin America. I would like to know what you would recommend to a new administration in Washington.

BETANCUR: In order to understand the characteristics of the subversive movements in Latin America you have to look into the reasons why these movements originated. When I think about it, I find that there are always subjective and objective factors, or agents. The subjective agents are leaders such as Rubén Zamora (Frente Faribundo Marti) or Mario Guiñada of El Salvador, the contra forces against the Sandinistas, the Sandinistas against Somoza, the Shining Path in Peru, as well as the Tupamaros in Uruguay and the Montoneros in Argentina, or many years ago Luis Carlos Prestes in Brazil. These are extremely different groups with totally different leaderships, each with unique motivations.

When in the United States and Europe people speak of "Colombian guerrillas" they are being terribly simplistic. There is no such thing as "the Colombian guerrilla"; there are several distinct and very different groups.

As for objective factors or agents, these are more homogenous and one might say valid throughout Latin America. These include malnutrition, illiteracy, poor health, lack of education, unavailability of credit, the foreign debt, etc.

What should be the attitude of the U.S. in the face of these Latin American processes? I would begin by saying that first of all one has to understand that each country is unique and has its own personality. The weaker the country the more forcefully it tries to compensate by assertions of its cultural authenticity. From the United States' point of view it should be understood that Latin America is not an appendage of the United States, and that it certainly does not warrant the "backyard" treatment that it has traditionally received from U.S. foreign policy makers.

President Reagan's policies toward Latin America presumed that we are countries unable to govern ourselves. Thus the usual attitude has been one that looks down on us and on what is going on in "your backyard." This attitude naturally produces negative reactions in Latin America. It also produces misguided U.S. aid policies. Aid is seen as "gracefully" giving to lesser countries which, it is believed, cannot survive without U.S. aid. But what really happens to these smaller countries is that they are goaded to assert their individualism and independence. That is my first point.

U.S. aid is contingent on "good behavior." Who decides what "good behavior" is? The State Department with its "Mother Superior" mentality. In other words the State Department does not know how to give.

Countries such as Germany, Holland, or France, give help with the perception that on this side of the Atlantic there are real

human beings living in equally sovereign states which rightly belong within the community of nations. We are treated by them
as states with the potential to pay back our loans and to work
out of our problems through building wealth and use of our intelligence. This help is received in the same spirit as it is given, with
dignity. But aid from the United States is given and received with
disdain and even anger. This fundamentalist attitude of the
United States is reflected in statements such as: "we need to help
Latin America because it is necessary for U.S. national security"; "we need to reinforce democracy in Latin America so as
to preserve our national security..." Every time aid is given on
those terms the reaction is immediate and parallel. The second
point I would make then, would be that U.S. foreign policy deal
with Latin American countries as juridically equal members of
the international order.

BOEKER: But don't you think this has changed? For instance
if we speak about Central America, the Esquipulas II agreement
is essentially an effort by the nations of that region to assume responsibility for their own destinies and the United States has not
discouraged that.

BETANCUR: But the support of the U.S. for that process is offered on the basis of what is convenient for its own national security. This is why I said that it is resented even by elements which
are friendly to the United States. In other words, in Latin America, the U.S. is its own worst enemy. Your policy toward Latin
America determines the reactions of Latin America toward the
United States. Some of the most important reactions in Central
America, which I know very well from participation in
Contadora, have come as a response to Washington's attitude.

The Presidential Palace in Bogotá displays a quotation from
Simón Bolívar: "The good friend of the ruler is the one who tells
him the truth." In my case I have wanted to be a good friend of
the United States, but these kinds of truths are not understood
by the persons responsible for policy making. They are usually
better understood by whichever party is in opposition. In general
this has been my experience with the U.S. leadership in its dealing with Latin America.

It seems that both superpowers took Central America to be a
good place to pursue their conflicts. This is why during our
Contadora meetings the leitmotif was: "Why don't we give Cen-

tral American countries the opportunity to decide their own destinies?" Thus, get the Soviet Union out, get the United States out.

In the case of Nicaragua, for instance, there were times when agreements could have been reached, but they were blocked by the U.S. On those occasions when the United States decided to stand back, the interference came from the Soviet Union. Of course one could say that the United States is part of our hemisphere, while the Soviet Union is not. But that does not support the kind of "backyard" policy followed by the Department of State in Latin America.

BOEKER: Are there any specific actions that you would recommend?

BETANCUR: Yes, to contribute to addressing the objective factors or conditions in Latin America without political preconditions, other than establishing and preserving democracy. For instance, one of the most dramatic subjects right now is the foreign debt. The United States should contribute to constructive solutions such as reducing rates of interest or creating the necessary mechanisms for the individual countries to meet their debt obligations without having to sacrifice their own growth. If development is arrested, as has occurred in some countries, the democratic process is weakened. Is there any doubt for example that Argentina's democratization will be threatened if its economic crisis persists? We have already seen the party of Raúl Alfonsín, one of the greatest and brightest leaders of Latin American democracy, defeated by the Peronists. Why? Because the debt problem is charged to his account. That is the reality. It is difficult for the poor, and probably not very well informed, to understand the consequences of the debt burden otherwise (than the responsibility of those now in power).

How to contribute to re-starting growth? Through multilateral credit institutions. Up to now the U.S. has declined to replenish the resources of the Inter-American Development Bank and the World Bank. Another excellent institution that could be strengthened is the Central American Bank for Cooperation and Development.

BOEKER: Is there still a concept of a community of democratic countries?

BETANCUR: Yes, we have the Group of Eight. The Contadora Group was initially Mexico, Venezuela, Panama and Colombia. During the inauguration of President Alan García in Lima, we realized that Contadora was worn out and I proposed that some new countries join in. At that moment presidents Raúl Alfonsín (Argentina), Julio M. Sanguinetti (Uruguay), José Sarney (Brazil), and Alan García (Peru), offered to join in the Group.

The Group of Eight continues to have a great degree of convergence. The Core Group—Mexico, Argentina, Brazil, Venezuela, Colombia, Peru, Uruguay and Panama—is solid but needs to expand. A great leader, Rodrigo Borja, has already suggested that; however, we do have the difficulty that the Group of Eight is very homogeneous. If we expand it much more it would become a small OAS, which would represent even more of a threat to the United States, which already looks at the Group of Eight with some suspicion and distrust.

CARLOS LLERAS RESTREPO

Carlos Lleras Restrepo, Colombia's most articulate elder statesman, received me in his red-brick Tudor home in the middle of
Bogotá. The gracious old house with soaring ceilings is typical
of Bogotá's old family houses, now rapidly disappearing as security concerns and land prices pile even the wealthy families one
on top of another in apartment buildings.

I awaited him in a library filled with leather-bound volumes,
which could have been in a British manor house—except all these
leather bindings had real books behind them. When Lleras entered he appeared to me even shorter than I remembered. He
wore a black three-piece suit and tie, in mourning still for the last
of his two daughters who died prematurely a month before our
talk. Her portrait was on the desk, honored by a fresh pink rose
at her side. With his heavy dark-rimmed glasses completing the
framing of his white skin, Lleras presented a somber appearance
until a coy, almost mischievous, smile brought to life the counte-
nance of one of Colombia's great presidents (1968–72). The political and economic reforms of his administration set the foundation
for a generation of steady economic growth and filled in the structure of political amity among Colombia's traditional political parties set in the National Front Accord of 1957.

The stability thus achieved has now been overtaken by other
sources of conflict, guerrillas and narcotics, which leave Lleras
deeply concerned. At eighty, his bi-monthly columns in Bogotá's
liberal papers are still political "events" in Colombia. Those columns reflect his anguish over succeeding governments' inability
to find resolutions for the baffling and disparate new sources of
violence. Lleras himself fears that no political deals are feasible
with Colombia's contemporary guerrillas, because they are not
political creatures with a political program, except in the sense
of anarchists.

Despite his assistant's admonition that I speak loudly, Lleras did not miss a single word and responded in soft, but clear, tones. Age has still left him a clear mind and sharp judgment, which leads him to a harsh assessment of the current state of his own Liberal party. He sees weak leaders and a dearth of new talent. Lleras is also skeptical of the current corps of Latin American leaders, whom he sees as too pragmatic and deficient in the sweeping concepts he admired in Argentine economist Raúl Prebisch and Chile's Christian Democratic leader of the Sixties, Eduardo Frei.

As Colombia's Cassandra, Lleras in his later years is calling for national mobilization and international support to face a confounding array of sources of violence for which he sees no single or ready solution. As a nexus, he views Colombia's challenges today as more difficult and dangerous than the deadly violence and destructive party warfare of the Fifties. Lleras offers a hard-line approach which emphasizes toughness on two fronts, to use deadly force against both the guerrillas and the traffickers and to shore up a judicial system under siege to restore a reasonable probability of punishment for both types of violence.

*   *   *   *   *

BOEKER: Mr. President, I remember one of your columns in *El Tiempo* in 1987 in which you told Colombians to "open their eyes to reality and recognize the internal and external dangers the country faces. Never before has the country been under such a threat as it is now." Are you as worried today as you were then?

LLERAS: Yes, very much so. Unfortunately the country had to go through a period which might be called the "first violence," but one with totally different characteristics from the violence we now face.

At that time there was a confrontation between the two traditional parties because neither was willing to concede power to the other. There were also personal vendettas and lesser factors, but basically we knew what it was all about. There was a struggle for power which continued until the Conservative administration declared a state of siege and closed the Congress. The Liberal resistance then took more violent form and guerrilla groups formed in those regions where Liberals felt they were being hounded. After the assassination of Jorge Eliécer Gaitán on April 9, 1948, I agreed to be leader of the Liberal Party under most difficult circumstances, to the point that I had to leave the country after this house was attacked and almost burned down.

The seizure of power by General Gustavo Rojas Pinilla (in 1953) calmed down the fierce competition for power on the part of the liberals and conservatives. Rojas' suppression of freedom of the press and other such mistakes impelled both parties toward reconciliation. Thus, this temporary military dictatorship spawned an accord between the parties. Both parties kept their part of the bargain, the country respected it, and we had a National Front Accord which lasted sixteeen years. In contrast to what the country is suffering now we knew what had happened and why we had been fighting.

What is so serious now is that no one knows the motives for the violence, and without knowing what is causing the violence it is very hard to find a way to stop it.

BOEKER: Is this violence the greatest threat you see for Colombian democracy?

LLERAS: Yes, the problem has reached critical proportions, and it is incomprehensible. There seems to be no motive for the killings and we don't know who are the perpetrators.

BOEKER: It seems paradoxical to me that this problem of violence persists in a country like Colombia with such a stable democratic tradition. We have seen it emerge at different times, taking different forms, and for different reasons.

LLERAS: In my opinion, the present situation is the worst. When there was a confrontation between the two parties there was always the possibility for reconciliation, and it usually happened at the first opportunity. Now it is another matter, nobody seems to understand anybody else. It is a mixture of banditry, greed, kidnappings, ransom, and drug traffic which has corrupted the country. To me it looks like a much more serious situation than anything we have faced in the past. Different administrations have made efforts to achieve a peaceful solution. We passed an amnesty law for the guerrilla groups. It seemed logical that this generous gesture of not holding them responsible for their criminal actions would be sufficient. Not at all. The amnesty law worked only in a few cases.

BOEKER: Guerrilla violence and drug traffic, with its tremendous corruptive power, must be exerting pressure over the armed forces in your country. Do you think this pressure might weaken civilian rule over the military?

LLERAS: No, I have never seen that situation occur since Rojas Pinilla. To the contrary, I know from personal experience that the military do not want to rule. At one point when I was facing serious difficulties during my administration, and when the problems I had with the opposition party seemed beyond solution, I met with several generals to let them know that I may need to appoint a few of them to replace the conservative members of the Cabinet. They asked that I leave them to deliberate in private for a few minutes. When I returned, they informed me that if I ordered them to take the posts they had no alternative but to obey under the law; they also urged me not to do it, as they did not have the necessary experience and because the reputation of the armed forces would be tarnished. I must now admit that they were right.

BOEKER: This attitude on the part of the Colombian armed forces, over many years, has been very beneficial.

LLERAS: Yes, it is truly a professional army with no involvement in politics. Indeed Colombia is fortunate that way.

BOEKER: Is there any danger in your opinion, that the traditional political parties will lose legitimacy in the eyes of the people?

LLERAS: I don't think so. Our political parties enjoy a long tradition; they have guarded their political power for centuries, and they are rooted in the spirit of the people. At times there have been failed attempts from the right and from the left to do away with our traditional parties. In all likelihood our political parties as they now exist will survive.

BOEKER: Is Colombia becoming a country too difficult to govern, given the persistent violence and security problems?

LLERAS: Of course, there is no doubt that our governments have had to face increasingly difficult situations. There is a lot that we do not understand. One doesn't know, for instance, why a bus full of people from the countryside is attacked. The only possible motive that I can think of is the intent to create fear and uncertainty in the population. Frankly, I can't think of any other explanation.

BOEKER: Under these circumstances don't you think that it would be a good idea to establish a National Front with a broader base, including some of the elements that have not participated before?

LLERAS: Well, it might be useful, but the problem does not lie in lack of understanding or cooperation between our parties. The parties can now work together. We have violence for exogenous reasons. Violence will not vanish by virtue of signed agreements.

BOEKER: As president, you implemented a series of political and economic measures which have served Colombia well for over a generation and which have resulted in exceptional economic growth for your country, while most of Latin America suffers an economic recession. Do you think Colombia can continue its economic growth, or at some point will the problems we've talked about stop economic progress?

LLERAS: There is always that danger. There is danger for instance in the regions where agricultural production has suffered to a great extent. This is an indicator of how critical our situation has become. There is no doubt in my mind that this is not happening by chance.

BOEKER: Is Colombia losing ground in its efforts to control drug traffic?

LLERAS: A great effort has been made. Drug traffic has inflicted great damage on our country. Its capital has infiltrated many of our most important economic sectors. It is going to be a difficult clean-up operation; we need to exercise a greater degree of judicial power and be constantly vigilant to bring the guilty to justice. Our first priority must be to restore confidence and faith in our judiciary. Our people are skeptical of the results of the penalties inflicted so far, as they seem to have had no power of deterrence. This is a dangerous frame of mind. The people have to feel that the guilty ones will be brought to justice, but we have lost the validity of this concept because of rampant corruption. Drug dealers enjoy tremendous resources and power, but we'll do whatever it takes to solve this problem which unfortunately seems to have gotten out of hand. We need to involve all the branches of government in this fight. There is no other way.

BOEKER: Is there a particular agenda that you would suggest to the new administration in the United States with respect to Latin America?

LLERAS: There was a time when we had illusions of Pan-Americanism. It was the time of the Alliance for Progress and there were attempts at economic integration. Unfortunately much of that momentum has been lost, and now we have a sentiment which runs almost contrary to those ideas. The Latin American countries which used to seek help from the United States for development purposes are now apprehensive of the restrictions and conditions that might be imposed. We have lost the feeling that we Latin Americans and the United States enjoy a special relationship.

BOEKER: Would it be worthwhile to pursue the revival of that relationship?

LLERAS: In my opinion it is essential. World politics seem to point to the usefulness of such a relationship.

BOEKER: North Americans have lost sight of the economic and political weight which Latin America can represent.

LLERAS: The United States has been totally preoccupied with the Soviet Union to the exclusion of everything else. Perhaps now that there is a more pacific atmosphere on that front, the United States might shift priorities. At the present time the U.S. economy plays a very important role in the world economy, but it has changed from what it once was. Our Latin American markets now have the ability to grow, which can help the U.S. I have always favored Latin American integration and we were hoping for encouragement on the part of the United States; it just didn't happen.

BOEKER: Is there still a possibility that the United States can help in efforts to achieve economic integration in Latin America?

LLERAS: I believe so. We need objective research centers such as the United Nation's Economic Commission for Latin America, even though ECLA's work has been very controversial. When Raúl Prebisch was alive and working in Santiago, the predominant idea was that of close cooperation. I believe we need a research center where work is done continuously by scholars from all the countries involved.

BOEKER: You belong to one of Colombia's most distinguished political families—one which has given to your country many prestigious leaders. Is there some secret which explains why generation after generation of prestigious Colombian families encourage their children to enter politics? Can you pass on the secret to other countries of the hemisphere, some of which are suffering from a missing generation of leadership?

LLERAS: In a family like mine, dedication to politics is hereditary, a product of the family environment. My great-grandfather was a very good friend of General Francisco de Paula Santander who is considered the founder of the Colombian Liberal Party, and a whole tradition was built on that relationship. His children fought in the civil wars. By tradition our family has also been very academically oriented. Most of us have gone into teaching as well. Two traditions have been kept: affiliation to the Liberal Party and dedication to teaching. There are other families with similar traditions. Inheritance of our parties' ideologies has been one of the hallmarks of Colombian politics.

BOEKER: Did that legacy move you to dedicate a lifetime to politics, or was there something more specific?

LLERAS: Actually I began to participate in politics as a student at the university when I advocated reforms for national education. That put me in contact with very prestigious people, so that when Enrique Olaya Herrera led a liberal revival starting in 1930, after forty years of Conservative Party dominance, it seemed natural that I should join the movement. Thereafter, my law practice was constantly interrupted by my appointments to government positions. In 1932, I was responsible, as secretary of government, for the administration of the city of Bogotá. After that I ran for Congress and later I was appointed minister of finance. I was always interested in economic and financial matters and continually taught public finance at several universities. During the whole World War II period, I had the good fortune of combining the teaching of fiscal policy and practicing what I taught, as minister of finance for almost four years.

BOEKER: In this generation of Latin American leaders is there one you particularly admire for his achievements?

LLERAS: The people I most admired have passed away. I was a great admirer of Raúl Prebisch's clear thinking. He knew his objectives and he had much faith in them. There are plenty of people nowadays who are very competent, but somehow without great effect.

ALFREDO POVEDA

Retired Admiral Alfredo Poveda now lives on shore, in an attractive apartment high above Guayaquil's waterfront looking out to the sea. It was on this retirement "bridge" that I was received by the intriguing, key military figure in Ecuador's transition to civilian government in the late Seventies. Poveda's squarish build is fit snugly in a gray suit for which he seems to have grown in retirement one size too large. His round, usually smiling face is topped by flattened gray hair, cut short on the sides. His tall, elegant wife accompanies him on our visit, completing a team of contrasting members. The two prized memorabilia in the apartment are signed photos of Jimmy Carter, with Poveda at the White House at the time of the signing of the Panama Canal Treaties in 1978, and one of Ronald Reagan.

Poveda, head of Ecuador's last military junta, 1976–79, throws light on both the easy entry and difficult exit of the military from civilian politics in Ecuador. Because the military has not been particularly repressive when governing Ecuador, it is not feared by most Ecuadorians. The military enjoys too cozy a relationship with civilian politicians who have often tried to ride to power on the back of this tiger. In the postwar period, the military has thus moved both in and out of power with the collaboration of some civilian groups. The military stepped down in 1980, without being discredited or under great pressure from civilians. Thus, Poveda can comfortably imply that this was not a permanent abrogation of the military's "responsibility."

Because the military do not see themselves as having been rejected, they believe they can easily come back if the civilians cannot handle their affairs in an orderly way. The no-holds-barred style of Ecuadorian civilian politics has also too often tempted politicians to draw the military into the political play as tactical allies—but with the danger of strategic consequences. President

Rodrigo Borja, elected in 1988, intends to give the military no such pretext. He also wants to change the military's cozy relationship with civilian politics by treating the military as a security force, under civilian authority, and not a political player. (Both Borja and Christian Democrat Osvaldo Hurtado criticize Ecuador's President from 1984–88, Leon Febres Cordero, for negotiating some political issues with the military.)

Giving up the fruits of power has been much more difficult for the military. Yet under Poveda's persistent direction, the military managed an orderly, well-conceived transition to civilian rule in 1979–80. Poveda kept that transition doggedly on course despite cold feet in both the military and some civilian sectors.

Poveda is a man obviously satisfied with himself, and he has some reason to be. Ecuador has elected three successive presidents since the transition. Those presidents, not the military, have had to deal with Ecuador's daunting economic and social problems and have suffered an unusual run of bad luck: the El Niño phenomenon which devastated Ecuador's agriculture and fisheries; an earthquake which destroyed the pipeline carrying Ecuador's oil exports; and a collapse in the price of oil to half the level prevalent when Ecuador contracted much of its large foreign debt. Governance of Ecuador is not a very tempting takeover target now. Yet it is a good time to build stronger institutional defenses and traditions of effective civilian management.

Because Ecuador's military does not wish to be rejected by Ecuador's people, it does not want to be "odd man out." The Ecuadorian military is thus more influenced than Poveda admits by the state of civilian government in the countries around it, particularly the large ones. This bi-play is the reason for Borja's strong desire to gain membership in the Group of Eight; so that that association of democratic Latin American leaders can ventilate the thinking of Ecuadorians, particularly the military.

Poveda himself presents a clear image of a military which is out of power by its own choice, but with no sense of having been removed from the political scene.

* * * * *

BOEKER: What were the reasons why you, as head of a military government, decided to turn over power to civilians?

POVEDA: When I finished as minister of government in 1972, the head of the military government, General Rodríguez Lara

(1972–76), asked me to formulate a plan to transform the political system. I wrote that plan, along with representatives of the three branches of the armed forces. On the basis of the conclusions of this working group, a plan for political opening was presented to General Rodríguez Lara. That plan was still under consideration when the armed forces decided to replace General Rodríguez Lara with a government made up of the heads of the three branches of the armed forces, including myself.

The objective was that we should initiate a transition to a civilian government. Thus, the idea was not just mine. As President of the Supreme Council I made clear in my initial public statements the sincere and profound commitment of the armed forces to return the government to civilian authorities within a reasonable period of time. The plan was implemented after contacts were made with the political parties.

BOEKER: The military government that preceded yours was accused of corruption. Did those charges influence your thinking when you decided that it was not in the interest of the military to continue in power?

POVEDA: There were two points of view on this. One charged that there was corruption in the government of General Rodríguez Lara. Others simply wanted a change of government and pressed General Rodríguez Lara to carry out a transition.

All the charges of corruption were investigated by a military commission. To be very honest we found almost no substantiation for the charges. In my opinion what really happened is that there was a division within the army, with a majority siding with General Rodríguez. There could have been some corruption; most governments have some. But I cannot talk in terms of corruption because of the lack of evidence from our investigation.

BOEKER: Throughout the transition period (1976–79), your public declarations were very clear, but there were contradictory statements made by other military figures as well as efforts to manipulate the results of the vote as happened during the first election in July 1978. Did you have to contend with groups who wished the military government to continue?

POVEDA: There were quite a few people who sincerely expressed their desire that the military government continue, but the majority of the officers supported return to constitutional government. Personally I was irrevocably committed to it; I had given my word to turn over power, and to establish another system for a different future. I resisted all pressures and was determined to fulfill our commitment.

Of course in order to ensure a durable democratic system, we faced many substantive difficulties, with respect to the organization of the elections, fundamental legislative reforms, and laws governing political parties. We could not just turn over power and let the chips fall where they may. We needed to undertake fundamental reforms; we were not giving up power because we had to; we wanted to establish a democratic system that would endure, and this took some time.

We had to re-establish all the electoral institutions, electoral courts, electoral legislation, and political parties. Most important of all, we had to put to the people a constitution which would encompass all these changes in a modern concept. With the help of the cabinet, I was involved personally in all this political activity. My sincere hope and desire that the new political system work were expressed clearly and decisively to the public at every possible opportunity.

There are always special circumstances, given our political-military tradition, when the stability of the country must be assured, whatever the political system. When there are serious problems which threaten the dignity and national security of the state, there is no question that a situation may emerge which would be contrary to a democratic system.

What we all worked for and were trying to accomplish was a stable, representative government based on the leadership of the political parties. If that leadership falters, is weak or becomes anarchical, the results are not going to be what the nation either deserves or wants. We had to collaborate to produce a durable system. The rules for the political parties were written by civilians in coordination with the military, which made some suggestions, without exerting pressure. Some of those suggestions were accepted, for example that political parties must have clear platforms and adequate financial support to ensure a certain level of activity; also that they had to represent real currents of opinion and not mere coalitions based on personal interests. The concepts presented were as sincere and patriotic as possible.

In effect I asked political parties to organize themselves not only quantitatively but qualitatively, so that they could become stronger and more decisive and lead the country toward a successful and effective democracy.

BOEKER: Was there at any time opposition to the transition from civilian groups?

POVEDA: I would not say opposition. The transition went more slowly than planned which caused apprehension among the political parties. Despite interest in accomplishing the transition as quickly as possible we never gave in to pressure from one side or the other. We needed to have the appropriate conditions and guarantees to reach the final political objective of transferring power to democratic government which would last.

BOEKER: Was it difficult to carry out the transition plan?

POVEDA: More than difficult. It was a cause of constant concern, as all national problems usually are.

BOEKER: Why did the process drag out so long? Elections were held one year later than planned and the whole process took longer than anticipated.

POVEDA: The causes for the delay had to do with the need to prepare properly for a referendum, to institute a practically new electoral system and to write a constitution which would be accepted by the people. This is fundamentally what took longer than anticipated. Once the preparations were complete, we moved as fast as possible. The proof is the results. We now have a functional democracy.

BOEKER: You chose a favorable moment, a moment when the military was not yet discredited. You managed an orderly transition, calling upon prestigious civilian politicians to create a new constitution. It was a well implemented decision.

POVEDA: I think so because we satisfied both the civilians and the military. It was a challenge, and perhaps my greatest satisfaction was to have left my people, soldiers, and officers content and with their dignity. I sincerely believe that we turned power over at the right moment, before the armed forces discredited themselves. We did not allow the armed forces to lose their dignity and disintegrate. We left with our dignity and the respect the armed forces need to fulfill their obligation to maintain national security.

BOEKER: Are you still satisfied with the decision you made?

POVEDA: Absolutely, we transferred power in an adequate and dignified manner which reflects the armed forces' concern for national security.

Since that time we have had two elected governments, and a third which now is beginning in the midst of disturbing economic conditions at home and abroad. During the Febres Cordero administration the political situation here undoubtedly could have been seen to warrant intervention by the military, but the armed forces have remained solid and resisted many efforts of interested sectors to involve them. This result stems from the well planned actions taken earlier.

BOEKER: During the Febres Cordero administration there was at least one attempt to overthrow him.

POVEDA: I do not believe there was an attempt to overthrow the government. There was a disagreement between the government and a small group within the armed forces. It had nothing to do with the armed forces' support for internal security and constitutional government.

BOEKER: Do you think that the policies of Jimmy Carter, with their emphasis on democracy and human rights, had any influence or impact on the decisions of the military government?

POVEDA: Absolutely not. The situation was rather one of satisfaction on the part of a democratic leader (Jimmy Carter) with a military government which was taking the necessary steps to strengthen a future democracy. The fact that we had his support does not mean there was pressure of any kind. This was confirmed by letters I received from him expressing his satisfaction with our plans, without exerting any pressure. If he had pressured us, the transition might have been, at best, delayed, because we are very independent-minded.

BOEKER: What was the nature of your visit and conversation with Jimmy Carter.

POVEDA: Those of us who were heads of state at the time were invited to attend the ceremony of the signing of the Panama Canal Treaties. President Carter was kind enough to invite each one of us to have a brief but private conversation.

BOEKER: That occurred before the Ecuadorian transition.

POVEDA: Yes.

BOEKER: Were the military influenced in any way by the fact that other countries of the Andean Pact were in a transition period?

POVEDA: No, because we were the first to declare our intention. When you are the first you are not copying anyone. It was our own voice, our own thinking, and our own decision that led us to seek an acceptable political solution here.

BOEKER: What concerns do the armed forces have now about the future of Ecuador? What are they worried about?

POVEDA: The military are citizens in uniform who love their country and are concerned about everything that is happening, but I don't believe this concern is destined to result in their taking over power. I believe it is their hope that the nation develop and grow, and that the states of the region evolve toward a continental integration.

BOEKER: Do you think that military governments are now part of history in Ecuador or do you foresee the possibility of another military government in the future?

POVEDA: The answer is up to civilian authorities. They have to take the reforms needed and find solutions to the real problems, within the limits of actual possibilities of the country. Reform for the sake of reform is useless and you cannot create wealth by decree. The strengthening of democracy through the actions of political parties is a question of taking action, writing laws to deal with our national problems. The military authorities will be as satisfied as the civilians with an effective government.

We don't want our democracy to burn out. For instance, nobody wants one political party maneuvering to destroy another.

We have a very professional army willing to work with the civilian authorities to solve the nation's problems. Furthermore we are trying to integrate the civilian and military sectors of society for the purpose of reaching an interaction and understanding which will permit the democratic system to develop as it should. The military leadership is not expecting civilian government to fail. The civilian government continues to be weak, but it can grow stronger. It just needs encouragement and further continuity to achieve cohesion, firmness and success for our democracy.

OSVALDO HURTADO

Ex-President Osvaldo Hurtado met me at the offices of his own think tank in Quito, the Corporation for Development Studies. The attractive receptionist behind a Formica counter, a maze of tweed-covered low partitions arrayed among walls of bookcases, and young men in shirt sleeves scurrying among them set a scene like that in the many think-tanks around Dupont Circle in Washington. But the president of this one looks more elegant and prosperous. A handsome man, looking younger than his forty-eight years, Osvaldo Hurtado wore a freshly pressed three-piece dark blue suit with deep maroon tie. His sharp, clean features seldom yielded to a smile as he discussed the turbulent world of Ecuadorian politics.

A reflective, serious intellectual of international standing, Osvaldo Hurtado is still trying to bridge his two roles as political science professor and politician. The professor is a consummate gentleman, who is offended by the personal invective of Ecuador's recent election campaigns and what he sees as the "bullying" tactics of Febres Cordero, Ecuador's president from 1984–88. As a politician and leader of Ecuador's Christian Democratic Party, Hurtado has been unable to control the ward politicians who have grown up in the party he founded at age twenty-four. In July 1988, his own party, against his wishes, joined President Rodrigo Borja's Social Democrats in a coalition of the center-left, because jobs and power today are what ward politics are all about. But Professor Hurtado looks down the road and fears that the stern measures needed to break Ecuador's raging inflation will burn all parties in the current government and hand the 1992 elections to the right if no center-left party holds itself in reserve.

Hurtado is quick to point out that he was never elected president. He became president in August 1981, just one year after the transition to civilian rule, when the charismatic Jaime Roldós was killed in a plane crash. As presidential and vice presidential candidate in the 1979 election, Hurtado and Roldós, both then in their thirties, presented an unusually young team. But there the similarity ended.

Hurtado, the bookish, thoughtful political scientist, had played an important role in the transition. He chaired the commission of experts which drafted the new constitution for Ecuador's civilian regimes. This constitution excluded any president from serving more than one term, a provision which ironically later ended Hurtado's presidential career at age forty-four in August 1984, when he finished the term he and Roldós started together.

Hurtado himself believes that the two roles of professor and politician actually did come together in his presidency, when he claims his political science concepts actually helped him understand the rough-and-tumble play of Ecuadorian politics. As president, Hurtado's task was a tough one, trying to confront a series of financial and natural disasters (particularly the El Niño phenomenon) in the face of a strident opposition majority in Congress. Ecuador's young democracy has not yet sired a sense of constructive opposition, which recognizes that ferocious assaults on the government can weaken the democratic system as well as the regime. The tactical quest for jobs and power is as far as some politicians look. Hurtado and his successors have all suffered from such destructive opposition tactics which still leave Ecuador's democracy vulnerable.

However Hurtado may blend the roles of professor and politician in the future, he comes out in this interview as an impressive representative of the fresh talent which has entered politics in Latin America over the last generation.

* * * * *

BOEKER: During the 1978–79 electoral campaign both you and President Roldós were under forty, which is young for politicians in this hemisphere. Do you believe this was important in your electoral victory?

HURTADO: I believe it is one factor among many. Ecuador is a young country. Our campaign was youthful and innovative, conveying an image of change to an electorate ready for something different from the old politics. It was not just the physical appearance, it was how we expressed our thoughts to the Ecuadorian people. At that time television had already reached most homes and I took advantage of it, much more than Roldós did, to address the electorate and discuss some basic substantive problems. However, there were other factors, such as our confrontation of the dictatorship and mobilization of the people, which were instrumental in our electoral victory.

BOEKER: You have said that both you and President Roldós had a political style different from that of Ecuador's traditional politicians. How would you describe that new political style?

HURTADO: Political debate in Latin America and Ecuador in particular has had a strong personal focus, at the expense of discussion of the real problems of society and of the solutions they demand. My political science studies and my experience first as a politician and then as president all taught me to concentrate on Ecuador's basic, specific problems. More substantive, and less personalized, discussion is one characteristic of the new political style we introduced in Ecuador.

A second characteristic is that we tried to put behind us the relentless logic of "friend or foe" which has characterized Ecuadorian politics, and to replace it with the logic of democracy. That logic considers the opposition as both adversaries and potential allies whom one needs to work with, listen to, and consult. That has not been the practice in Ecuadorian politics.

A third characteristic was the introduction of technical discussions into the political debate. Political speeches in Ecuador were largely rhetorical and literary, only alluding to specific economic and social problems. I think I have contributed to rational debate of economic problems.

BOEKER: When you became president did your approach have to change under the pressures of the office you held?

HURTADO: My presidency reaffirmed my view and introduced a new dimension—a great interest in concrete problems of economic policy. When I became president and during the 1978 presidential elections, my vision focused on long-range, structural problems. Yet the crisis we are now facing has made it clear to us Latin American political leaders that the region's fundamental problem is management of the economy. We will be successful in the long term only to the extent that we can find economic policy responses to our present problems.

BOEKER: A political analyst whom you know, Nick Mills, passed an interesting judgment on the Roldós-Hurtado administration: He said, " for Roldós and Hurtado, democracy necessarily involved patience, tolerance, bargaining, negotiation, and compromise, qualities they both exercised to such a degree that they were criticized for not exercising enough authority and for not using a heavy hand..." Are you satisfied with that judgment?

HURTADO: The analysis is correct. It is another way of saying what I did in answer to your second question. The logic of friend or foe, which aims at destroying your adversaries, is characteristic of dictators, and forces the same behavior on political parties trying to destroy the dictatorship. However, this cannot persist under democracy. Even in countries with a dominant majority party, the opposition has a voice. This is especially important now that the media is instrumental in shaping public opinion.

The essence of democratic politics is dialogue, the search for compromises, and the formation of a majority. This is all new to Ecuadorian politics. So much so that when my presidential term ended, the country went back to the practice of a political style which was not at all the one we had tried to establish as one worthy of being called democratic.

I believe I am one of the few politicians in Ecuador who has never, or very seldom, insulted another political leader. You will never find in my speeches or statements anything offensive. However I am one who has suffered more than his share of insults.

During my administration I had almost everyone against me. The extreme left and the extreme right were both radically opposed. Groups representing industry, trade, and agriculture were all united in militant and active opposition. Labor unions declared more general strikes than they did during the dictatorship. The center-left parties were also against me, especially the Democratic Left.

The question is thus: how did I survive during a government of transition, in the midst of a serious economic crisis, in a country without a tradition of stability? Public opinion held that devaluation, which I had to carry out, was tantamount to treason. I was not an elected president: I was sworn in after Roldós' fatal accident. He was the one who had been the popular leader. The answer then would have to be that I had the loyalty of the armed forces and that I was able to reach what I call Ecuador's "Silent Majority." This group supported me and my presidency despite the organized opposition.

BOEKER: Well, I wonder if Rodrigo Borja would agree with your statement that you may have suffered more verbal abuse than other politicians?

HURTADO: He is a beginner. I lived through that starting when I was a vice-presidential candidate.

BOEKER: He feels that he suffered much abuse during the past presidential campaign.

HURTADO: It is even worse when one is president of the country and is still given the same treatment.

BOEKER: With the third democratically elected president since the transition now in office, do you think there is more political stability than at the time of your administration?

HURTADO: There are two ways to analyze the stability of democracy in Latin America. One is by the length of time over which normal democratic succession has occurred. For example, Ecuador in 1988 transferred power from one constitutionally elected president to another for the third consecutive time. However, I believe that the problem is more complex and has to do with the nature of the social, economic, and political structures which support the democratic form of government. From that perspective I think that in general, Latin America has not changed much and in the specific case of Ecuador it has deteriorated.

The fundamental democratic institutions in Ecuador have suffered over the four years of the Ferbres Cordero administration. I will mention just two examples. First, the armed forces have intervened in political decisions on various occasions, acting as deliberative bodies, exercising an arbitrary function in the political life of the country. Second, the president has frequently governed by executive decrees, which have been used to reform laws, to create them and to prevent others from entering into effect. An elected and active legislature is a pillar of the democratic structure, together with recognition of the rights of the opposition, freedom of the press, and respect for human rights. These are areas which have suffered severely during those four years.

From 1984 to 1988 in Ecuador we had an abuse of democratic institutions similar to what happened in Chile under President Salvador Allende. Of course Allende had an ideology totally opposite to the one of our head of government from 1984 to 1988 (Febres Cordero), but some measures taken here were equivalent to those taken in Chile under Allende. Our system of government was in danger since democracy depends on the legitimacy of its origin and of its actions.

BOEKER: Do you believe that President Borja's administration can recoup what you see as the weakened legitimacy of democratic institutions?

HURTADO: I believe so. The electoral outcome was a vote for return to democratic values—clean and honorable. Despite having had dictatorial regimes, Ecuador is a democratic country, and even our dictatorships have had to keep in mind the democratic conviction of our people; thus, our military dictatorships have been "soft" ones. President Borja's administration also represents a political party which stands for democracy, not only in Latin America but throughout the world. I believe that President Borja will govern taking fully into account the Ecuadorian preference for a democratic style and democratic values.

BOEKER: I understand you were opposed to your party participating in the Borja government. Why?

HURTADO: I was opposed when we had the national party convention in May 1988. What has happened since then has proved me right. Within my party, my opinion was that we should support the new administration along with other democratic forces in order to help restore democracy and rebuild the economy. There was no talk of opposition. The only difference of view occurred between those who insisted my party should be represented in the cabinet and my view that this was not at all necessary; all we needed was to support the government in Congress. I believe the new administration will need support throughout the whole presidential term, and the type of bid for offices made by my party does not assure that.

Finally, I feel strongly that a political party should always keep its eye on the long-term horizon when it takes decisions. That horizon is the year 1992, when new presidential elections will take place. If we think about the devastating economic crisis that we are facing today, and the negative impact it will necessarily have on the government, then it is crucial that the Christian Democrats are prepared to hold themselves apart as an alternative in 1992. We must prevent a return of the forces which in the last four years damaged the country's economy and its democracy. We must prevent a basically non-democratic populism from winning the elections, as it was so close to doing in the last months of the 1988 campaign.

BOEKER: Do you believe that the policy of President Carter with its emphasis on support for democracy and respect for human rights played an important role in the 1979 transition to civilian rule?

HURTADO: I have never understood how the United States, a genuinely democratic nation, with the oldest democracy in the hemisphere, could be so disinterested for most of its history in democratic government and values in Latin America. In light of this history, one has to give President Carter credit for having changed this lack of concern into concern for Latin American democracy. What he did in Ecuador is a good example.

I participated directly in the process of return to democracy. I presided over one of the commissions which drafted the laws governing the referendum, the elections and the role of political parties. In these functions as well as later as a vice-presidential candidate, I was very aware of all the conspiracies within the military, but even more so in the civilian sector, to frustrate the transition.

I know of diplomatic messages sent to the military government by President Carter, which had great influence in preventing these anti-democratic forces from succeeding. These forces wanted first to stop the constitutional referendum, then the elections and finally the transmission of power we had legitimately won.

BOEKER: Was there any thing more that Washington could subsequently have done to help you as president consolidate Ecuador's new democracy?

HURTADO: Latin American democracy has more to do with our own actions than with those of the U.S. I am not denying the United States the role it could play in the building of Latin American democracies. In fact, I have just mentioned what President Carter accomplished.

When I visited with President Reagan at the White House I expressed my concern for the future of Latin American democracy in light of the economic crisis. I did not go to the White House to ask specifically for help for Ecuador; I talked about problems that were critical for the region. President Reagan's reply was that Latin America's crisis would be solved by renegotiation of debt, by austerity programs such as I had implemented, and for which he congratulated me, and "the locomotive effect" of a booming U.S. economy on the growth of our economies. I expressed my disagreement with this argument, and I believe that the historical record has proved me right. I might add that during my presidency the U.S. administration, while recognizing our problems, did not take any specific steps to support us in our efforts to overcome the crisis.

BOEKER: Are there any measures or policies which you would like to suggest to a new administration in Washington to help cope with the problems in the hemisphere?

HURTADO: Latin America will overcome its crisis on the basis of a prolonged national effort which extends beyond a particular administration; Latin America needs continuity. By this I mean that I do not share the opinion of some Latin American politicians who argue that all of our problems are somehow foreign-made and that the solutions can be found abroad. Latin America needs to make a tremendous effort to raise the level of savings and investment, and to work with discipline and a sense of organization.

Even with all that, Latin America will not be able to overcome its crisis until we resolve the "bottleneck" of our international accounts which in some years has resulted in an annual transfer of financial resources in the amount of one hundred billion dollars. There has not been a country in the world's economic history which has developed while being a net exporter of capital. All countries which have developed have been net importers of economic resources. It was the case with the Roman Empire and with the United States. Under these circumstances I believe that the best thing the developed countries can do for Latin America is to contain this outflow, and if possible reverse it, although the latter is probably not feasible. Many ways have been suggested as to how to contain the outflow. What matters is the result; namely, to arrest the net export of capital to the United States and other industrialized countries. If we do not find a way to stop this transfer, or at least to decrease it, our economies will remain stagnant.

I would not be surprised if toward the end of century, ECLA (the U.N. Economic Commission for Latin America), could say that in the year 2000 the level of development and the welfare of the Latin American people will correspond to that of the Seventies, which would mean that we would have lost thirty years of development. This is going to happen to a continent with enormous possibilities and one which is very much linked to the hemispheric security which so worries the United States.

During my presidency I was able to lower the public sector deficit to zero. However, the Ecuadorian economy continues to have problems. Why? Because we did not have the resources to invest, to create jobs, to produce capital and thus to achieve some progress. One way to reverse the transfer of resources is by finding a solution to the debt problem. Another possibility would be through increases in the prices of our export commodities. Another would be through increases in the volume of our exports. Such an increase depends on our effort and our investment capacity, but we cannot be successful unless we have access to the markets of the industrialized world.

RODRIGO BORJA

Ecuadorian President Rodrigo Borja—widely considered the "Mr. Clean" of Ecuadorian politics—received me, shortly before his inauguration, in his modest transition office furnished starkly in Scandinavian bargain furniture. Unsmiling and austere in appearance, Borja wore a light gray herringbone suit, blue shirt and slate-blue tie with a thin, faint pattern. A sharp aquiline nose formed by two straight lines meeting at an angle of about 135 degrees, gives Borja's otherwise unexceptional face an appearance of strength. Long, crinkled black hair, curling up behind his head, provides the other small bow to machismo in this plain, unassuming man.

Borja's electoral victory is proof that dull politicians still have a future in democracy. He presents, in fact, a complete contrast to the flamboyant, and tainted politician (according to an Ecuadorian arrest order of July 1988) he defeated in the second-round presidential elections in May 1988. Borja, who once described himself as unsociable, has to work at mixing with people on the campaign trail. He prides himself in his careful, understated style and refused to be provoked into matching the reckless invective characteristic of recent Ecuadorian election campaigns. ("Communist" and "fairy" were among the milder epithets hurled at candidates of the center-left in the 1988 campaign.)

Borja took his time in framing careful answers to my questions, revealing the same cautious style he showed in the campaign—prompting some Ecuadorians to wonder whether he will be indecisive as president. But Rodrigo Borja has had twenty-five years to think about what he would do as president. He is not likely to be at a loss for what to do now that his long drive has reached its goal. "Persistent" is his favorite adjective for himself.

Born to a middle class family in Quito, Borja was elected to Congress at twenty-seven. By the time he was thirty-five, he had

255

formed his own social democratic party. As head of that party, he ran for president, unsuccessfully, in the first two elections after the transition to civilian rule, before reaching the presidency at fifty-three in his third try. His driving ambition, unwillingness to give up in the face of repeated defeats, and private discomfort with people have led some to compare Rodrigo Borja with Richard Nixon, a comparison which makes Borja uncomfortable.

In terms of his goals, Borja sees himself closer to Jesse Jackson, whose book, *Straight From the Heart,* was on the shelf at his side as we spoke. Borja sees his agenda as complementing Ecuador's institutional democracy with social and economic justice for the poor. Ecuador's poor, who used to suffer quietly in the countryside, are now pouring into the towns and cities, particularly the rival cities of Quito in the Andes and the larger Guayaquil on the coast, and making their demands felt.

Borja has a better political base for such a program than his predecessors. He has a popular mandate and a center-left majority in Congress. But the economic resources are not there—not for new social programs nor to pay the service on Ecuador's large debts. While Borja's party includes many adherents of the state-directed growth strategy expounded by the late Argentine economist Raúl Prebisch, Borja has chosen not to put them in charge. His conservative economic team has to concentrate on cost cutting and fund raising rather than new spending.

As you will see from this interview, Borja is aware of the disastrous mistakes made by his left-populist neighbor Alan García in Peru, and does not want to repeat them. But Borja has little international experience and much to learn before the successful politician becomes a successful statesman. His inauguration was a bumpy start. His two-and-one-half hour inauguration speech was filled with the clichés of Third World ideology which left seven Latin presidents in attendance wondering whether this was a leftover campaign speech. But Borja has the savvy to move on from there to address pragmatically the real problems which dominate the lives of his fellow presidents in the region.

*   *   *   *

BOEKER: To begin, I would like to know the reasons why you, as a young man, decided to enter political life and work at it so persistently all these years?

BORJA: I believe the fundamental motivation is that of serving others. Politics for me is an altruistic mission—one of continual struggle to achieve a higher standard of living for our people. I could have been a successful attorney with a high income, but I would not have felt fulfilled with such a selfish attitude. I believe this is the source of the strength that has helped me make my way through the hostile tangle which is politics in Latin America, or anywhere else. I believe I have a drive which needs to apply itself to the struggle for social solidarity.

BOEKER: Electoral campaigns in Ecuador are very harsh. Personal attacks here seem to go beyond the practice in other countries. Why?

BORJA: You should not think it has always been like that. In previous years electoral campaigns were civilized. Political competition prostituted itself because of the presence of elements, atypical of our society, which cannot be considered legitimate representatives of the level of education and culture in Ecuador today. Nobody regrets this more than I, but some people have a savage style of conducting politics.

BOEKER: Is your political style different from that of the leaders of the past generation?

BORJA: I believe there is a difference in style. The leaders of the past generation had a different concept of the subjects appropriate for public discussion. Debates were limited to political, ideological, and historical themes; economic and social problems were never discussed. It was my party, the Democratic Left, which eighteen years ago first pressed social and economic concerns. From that moment on politics in our country entered the modern era, and we began to deal with issues which had been largely ignored by our traditional political leaders.

BOEKER: To what do you attribute your electoral victory?

BORJA: My victory was the victory of a new political ideology which plans to extend the democratic system in its economic and social dimensions. What we have done in our country, up to now, is to struggle for political democracy so that we can express ourselves, enjoy freedom, and make sure differing opinions are respected. Once this political liberty has been obtained, we must strive for economic freedom and social equality for the poor. If we fail to do this, I am afraid we will offer our people only the facade of democracy, not the essence. My victory is in response to a clamor for better economic conditions.

BOEKER: You face an economic crisis. In your opinion, is this solely an economic problem or does it extend to a threat to the democratic system of government.

BORJA: I believe Ecuadorian democracy is deepening its roots. It is a system which is becoming increasingly solid. Despite the serious problems we have faced, the democratic process has survived uninterrupted. I don't see any threat to democracy lurking on the horizon. There are many elements committed to the survival of the system, such as the progressive political parties, the media, labor unions, universities, and even the armed forces. These elements are deeply committed to the survival and strengthening of our constitutional regime. However, democracy is an everyday struggle. Democracy needs to be cultivated with affection and dedication if it is to flourish.

I don't want to give you the impression that I am not worried about the serious economic and social problems we now face. In the social area, there are serious conflicts such as inflation, unemployment and the unjust distribution of income. In the economic field, the foreign debt and the fiscal deficit are suffocating us. All these are serious problems which we have to face. Potentially they are all a threat to the democratic system.

We are determined to create an international public conscience, to make it known that unfavorable trade terms among countries constitute a threat to our new democracies. The same can be said of our foreign debt. If all the fruits of the labor of our people have to be sent out of the country to service the foreign debt, then Latin American democracies will not be able to meet the socio-economic needs of their people. It is in this sense that I see a threat to constitutional governments in Latin America. If we continue to operate in this manner the people will lose faith in the efficacy of democracy, and they will start looking for alternatives. This is what has prompted several of our Latin American leaders to ask for understanding on the part of the industrialized countries in order to create a sense of democratic solidarity which is needed today more than ever.

BOEKER: Do you have a formula in mind to deal with the problem of foreign debt?

BORJA: Some points are perfectly clear. Our debt is disproportionate to our capacity to pay. This has led us up a blind alley; we either pay the debt or take care of the domestic needs of our people. We cannot do both. I am not suggesting that we repudiate our obligation, but that the terms of payment be renegotiated, extended so that we can first grow and develop economically and regain solvency, and then pay what we owe.

We must share responsibilities. We the debtors are responsible for having requested easy credit and for not having adequately invested those resources. The creditors are responsible for exerting pressure through various methods, including corruption, to recycle the excessive liquidity which flowed into their economies. The end result was an uncontrolled growth of Latin America's foreign debt, which is today the most serious problem of our economies. We need much imagination and good will, but what we cannot do is let our people go hungry so that we can service the debt.

BOEKER: During the Febres Cordero administration, there was at least one serious incident which could have led to a coup on the part of the armed forces. Do you foresee any problems in trying to exercise civilian authority over the military?

BORJA: I do not expect to have any problems at all with the armed forces. They have a constitutional duty to accept civilian rule. I have to deal with them within the framework of the law. It's that simple. Our army is very professional, with no political ambitions. They carry out their specific duties and strive to serve their country.

The unfortunate incident to which you refer occurred as a consequence of the behavior of a president who used the barracks as a political platform. This will not happen again.

BOEKER: Up to now, the original Group of Eight democratic countries, growing out of the Contadora Group, has not included other democratic governments such as Ecuador and Bolivia. Are you going to request that Ecuador be a part of this group?

BORJA: We are interested. We want to change the isolationist posture which our country has assumed. We want to become again part of the international system. We want to be a part of the Group of Eight and to collaborate with the other Latin American democracies in our struggle for peace, for economic progress and for good relations among the states of the hemisphere. The Group of Eight is a very important forum for democratic countries.

BOEKER: What would be your advice to a new administration in Washington trying to achieve better relations with other democratic countries in the hemisphere?

BORJA: I believe a new administration in the United States must make an effort to understand better Latin America's complex reality. We are struggling to cope with many problems, and with dire levels of poverty. We need to raise the standard of living and for that it is essential that we can count on the understanding and good will of the United States. I would like the new administration to take a more active role in helping to solve the debt problem. The United States needs to collaborate with the Latin American countries to seek viable long-range solutions which would not mean the asphyxiation of our economies and solutions which would permit us to take care first of our domestic problems, and then to meet the service and amortization of our foreign debt. On this matter the new administration can be of much help to the benefit to all concerned.

BOEKER: Are you ready to offer stabilization programs worked out with international financial agencies as part of a long-term solution?

BORJA: That depends. There would be no problem if we can reach agreement on such programs and provided the measures they suggest will not cause social disorder, increase unemployment or cause a recession.

BOEKER: Unless I am mistaken you are not thinking of unilateral actions such as the ones taken by your neighbor in Peru; you would prefer that the financial institutions renegotiate the debt, recognizing each country's capacity to pay and taking into consideration the fact that there must room for growth so that you can both service the debt and cope with your social problems.

BORJA: We are not interested in confrontations with our creditors; we are interested in a good relationship. We even hope to receive new loans to help revive our economy. However, we are not prepared to condemn our people to go hungry so that we can meet debt obligations. It is not that we don't want to pay; we cannot under the present terms. This is why we are looking for an accommodation with our creditors based on their awareness of our serious dilemmas. I persist in my opinion that U.S. political leaders are in a position to play a key role in seeking a solution.

BOEKER: You and your party are political players not very well known abroad. This is the first time your party will be in power and you have not had the opportunity to make your views known abroad. However, some foreign observers have commented on similarities between you and Alan García.

BORJA: Alan García is a good friend for whom I feel deep affection. He is a strong and imaginative political leader. I knew him before he was president of Peru, but it is obvious that his approach as president has not addressed some of the most serious problems in Peru, which of course are totally different from those in Ecuador.

Each country has a sovereign right to choose its own way. We will choose ours according to our circumstances. I do not believe in following a model. There are no two Latin American countries alike, and thus their policies are necessarily different. Despite the differences, we do share common values such as solidarity, friendship and our common struggle for Latin America's economic independence and more equitable trade and economic conditions.

BOEKER: Are you worried about the stability of your neighbors Colombia and Peru?

BORJA: Colombia's democracy has strong roots. I do not see there any danger of instability. Colombia's economic policies are very effective, including in their management of the debt. The quality of Colombia's political leaders is excellent. I don't think that violence can defeat Colombia's democracy.

As far as Peru is concerned, despite its serious economic and social problems, I think that constitutional government will survive. The present Peruvian administration was the result of a massive mobilization of the people. Alan García is leading his country in the midst of a storm.

BRAZIL

ERNESTO GEISEL

During its first decade, 1964–74, Brazil's tough military regime looked as if it might go on indefinitely. But in 1974 the military regime assumed a new face and a new objective, "abertura" or opening, an image retired General Ernesto Geisel associated with the opening of the heart's valves to pump newly oxygenated blood into the system. Called back by the military to be president from 1974 to 1979, Geisel not only oxygenated Brazilian civic life by progressively ending repression and restoring human rights, but also launched Brazil decisively on a course back to elected, civilian government. Over his five years as president, Geisel restored political party rights, expanded parliament's powers, abolished the military government's blanket decree powers and ran correct parliamentary and regional elections. He then set up a carefully controlled two-stage transition under which Brazil's parliament would elect the first civilian president in 1984, followed by the direct election of his successor five years later. Finally Geisel, over strong military opposition, picked a successor, General Figueiredo, whom he was confident would faithfully carry out the gradual plan, on schedule.

General Geisel's characterization of his transition plan as "slow, gradual, and secure" became the irreverent Brazilian's joking allusion for anything which never quite happens. But it did happen, in Geisel's way and in Geisel's time, to be completed only in 1989 with the first direct election of a Brazilian president in twenty-eight years. To keep this long process on course Geisel had to fight a constant rear-guard fight against military hard-liners who wanted to continue their dirty war against Marxists and perpetuate military rule, a bruising battle still fresh in his mind in his interview with me.

I met with Ernesto Geisel in his stark, modern office at the Rio headquarters of Norquisa-Nordeste, a petrochemical conglomerate of which he is president. A man with a Germanic sense of duty, Geisel is still working at age eighty, and has no wish to ever retire. In fact, the late life sense of mission of this discreet, withdrawn man, reminded me of der Alte, Konrad Adenauer, particularly when Geisel told me in a dead-pan, matter-of-fact way: "When I retire I die." As head of a major corporate empire for the second time, Geisel looks like a Baron of the Ruhr and might have been one today if his father, a German Lutheran school teacher, had not immigrated to southern Brazil before Ernesto was born. He looks the part. His large head is dominated by a high broad forehead, crowned with white hair, brushed back, slightly slavic features, and a massive square jaw.

Despite his circumspect behavior and reluctance to comment publicly on Brazilian political issues, General Geisel remains a formidable figure in Brazil. Military officers still make their way up to his mountain-top home in Teresopolis, near Rio, and his private advice carries great weight. Some Brazilians speculate that a military coup could prevent a mercurial populist such as Lionel Brizola from taking power should he win an election. But Geisel's view is "No," at least for the period of Brazil's first directly elected president since the transition, and that is likely to be the answer, unless a civilian government crosses the watchful military's "red lines." With six military men as cabinet officers in 1989, it would be a reckless president who failed to recognize where those lines are.

General Geisel told me that he considers the continuing participation of numerous military officers in a civilian government as "normal." In fact, the Brazilian military, including Geisel's political advisor and intellectual architect of abertura, the late General Golberi, never foresaw giving up control entirely to the civilian government. Golberi believed retreat from direct responsibility for governance was required to maintain the institutional integrity of the military and its position of respect in Brazilian society. But he planned both a transition guided by the military and its continuing hand in civilian government. Brazil's new constitution foresees five military officers in the cabinet, military participation in a National Defense Council overseeing national security affairs, and the possibility that any branch of the government could call on the military to restore internal order. Thus, the continuing operational participation of the military in civilian government remains a unique Brazilian recipe for managing the still uncertain lines between civilian and military authority.

The influence of General Geisel and the Brazilian military over the entire course of Brazil's transition in the last fifteen years is still clear. When Brazil's Constituent Assembly in the fall of 1988 came to its final decision on whether to hold direct elections for President Sarney's successor a year earlier than foreseen in the military's original plan, most of the Assembly and most Brazilians favored early elections in 1988. But the military ministers gave out the word that the military did not want elections before 1989, and that is the way it came out.

Whether one is partial to Brazil's peculiar formula for civilian-military accommodation or not, one has to be impressed by the stolid, clearheaded persistence of Ernesto Geisel, a man who accomplished exactly what he set out to do, nothing more, nothing less.

* * * * *

BOEKER: The twenty-year period of military government in Brazil was longer than in other countries in the hemisphere. Was there any particular reason why the military government extended its rule so long before holding elections?

GEISEL: We started out from a very complicated situation created by the disgraceful administration of President João Goulart. The March 1964 movement (against him) was not, as purported, a mere military coup. It was a national movement with broad participation of the people, political groups, and industrialists, mobilized by the conviction that the government was leading the country into an untenable position.

The new government under President Castelo Branco was able to restore normal life in the country through reforms, including a new constitution and a serious effort to combat inflation. However, agitation by students and the left in particular grew during the subsequent government of President Costa e Silva. This agitation was then aggravated by the emergence of subversive acts, starting with bank robberies and kidnappings, including that of the U.S. ambassador, followed by other acts of urban guerrillas, and later the formation of rural guerrilla forces. The battle extended over a long period, principally during the subsequent Médici administration, until the guerrillas were totally eliminated.

Later on, during my administration, it was possible gradually to relax these extraordinary security measures, which were still in effect, and to initiate a transition to a more natural, democratic government.

BOEKER: Did such a long period of military government change the character of the Brazilian armed forces, the career aspirations of young military officers? Did it leave any permanent effects on the military?

GEISEL: No, I don't think so. During the revolutionary period the armed forces in general did not display political ambitions. They showed a high degree of unity and hierarchical discipline.

Of course there were a few with political ambitions, but these did not have much influence or success.

I am convinced that the situation has not changed even in the case of younger officers, who are totally dedicated to their military career and without political ambitions.

BOEKER: When you began your program of abertura in 1974, was the objective a return to civilian government or did that objective come later?

GEISEL: No, I believed the country should return to normal life gradually. Subversion had been practically eliminated under Médici. It was the time to attempt to form a more democratic government, not dependent on coercion. But the transition had to develop step by step, to avoid any possibility of setbacks. There was internal resistance from those who wanted to preserve the regime as it was. It was indispensable to neutralize these factions first. This is why we decided on what we called abertura, an open-ended process in which the fundamental step was abolishing Institutional Act No. 5, the principal instrument of rule by coercion. This step was feasible only toward the very end of my administration.

BOEKER: Was this opposition to abertura primarily within the military, or the civilian sector as well?

GEISEL: There was opposition in both sectors, but it was stronger within the military. To overcome that opposition we had to launch a major campaign of explanation and persuasion, in order to reach a consensus and finally clear the major obstacles to abertura.

BOEKER: That's very similar to what General Medina said in

Uruguay, that he found himself spending much of his time trying to persuade other military officers to support him in what he was trying to accomplish.

GEISEL: Without doubt there were some similarities in this respect. However, I must emphasize that my own concept of abertura was synthesized in a sentence that many, especially within the civil opposition, did not want to accept. I said at the time that the process of abertura had to be slow, gradual, and secure.

BOEKER: What were the main considerations which led you to make this process of abertura the centerpiece of your government?

GEISEL: Obviously the rule under which we lived was not the natural way of life for the nation. We had to assure civilian authorities greater political participation so that they would gradually assume responsibility for governing, above all because it is not the mission of the armed forces to rule the country.

Our kind of government could not perpetuate itself indefinitely; this would have been an abnormality. The government necessarily had to evolve into a predominantly civilian administration, which was more democratic and without any extraordinary powers.

BOEKER: The Brazilian military retains an important voice in government, for instance, through several ministers who are also military officers. Would you see this as a stage in a transition yet to be completed or as a necessary part of the political structure of power in Brazil?

GEISEL: I find that to be quite normal in our system of government. In my view those ministers who have traditionally been chosen from the military—though they could also be civilians—have as much right to a voice as the rest. The head of a ministry, regardless of whether or not he is in the military, forms part of the government. He has to give his opinion and can attempt to persuade or advise the president with whom he collaborates. I don't think this is irregular or undue interference.

It would be ridiculous if a minister could not tell the president, of whom he is a direct advisor, his opinion on the situation of the country and its problems in various areas relating to the military. He participates in the government and has to be loyal to the president and tell him what he thinks, making suggestions and proposing solutions. This does not mean that the armed forces want to impose their will. Needless to say there is a difference between a minister advising and giving his opinion to the president and the armed forces telling the government what to do.

BOEKER: As president you met military leaders from many other Latin American countries, and I would be interested in hearing your view about something frequently said with respect to differences between the Brazilian military and other military establishments in Latin America. This may be merely academic, but it is said that Brazilian military officers, either because of their background or because of their education, feel much more comfortable with their civilian counterparts. In other words, the dividing line between civilians and the military is less clear in Brazil and less marked by social distinctions, much less resentments.

GEISEL: The only South American country I know is Uruguay, where I served as military attaché for two years. Their armed forces, especially the army, easily identified with the civilian sector from which they came. It was not a separate caste. They did not live in isolation, and they conducted themselves democratically, like the rest of the people.

I don't know about the relationship between the military and civilians in other countries. I just don't have any information on which I could base a valid judgment.

In Brazil the military has always been linked to the people, which is where we all come from. A majority of our officers have rather humble origins. From the beginnings of the empire and the republic, the Brazilian armed forces have always identified with the sentiments of the people. We have obligatory military service for a period of at least a year, so our soldiers are literally representative of our population.

BOEKER: How do you see the morale of Brazil's armed forces, since they left the government in 1984?

GEISEL: I have not had too much direct contact with the generation which is running the military today. They're a lot younger than I am. Judging from conversations with some of my colleagues, the army is essentially concerned with problems related to its profession, such as modernizing its equipment, and advanced professional training and development. The same goes for the navy and the air force. There do not seem to be significant frustrations, and morale is good.

BOEKER: Have you ever looked back with any regrets at the great work of abertura you launched, or are you satisfied with the transition to an elected government and your role in it?

GEISEL: Neither with regret nor complete satisfaction. I am merely convinced that I fulfilled my duty. I will let the record speak for itself.

When one talks about democracy in Brazil, it is necessary to see the picture as it is. Despite our enormous potential and all of our efforts, Brazil is still an underdeveloped country. The Brazilian people are poor and culturally behind, with a high level of illiteracy. Even among those who are educated, there are not many who have a realistic view of the nation's problems. The people govern in a democracy through their representatives, but unhappily they lack the conditions to make good choices. Thus, the process of selecting the country's leaders at all levels, municipal, state, and federal, suffers the consequences. That is, our democracy is a democracy still learning to crawl; it cannot be compared to democracy in the United States, England, France, or Germany.

Now this picture is made worse by two serious problems, inflation and debt. Inflation hurts and debilitates the population, especially the poor. The external debt complicates the country's life tremendously. With a poor, backward population, high inflation, and a burden of debt accumulated over many years, it is not easy for democracy to work as it should.

I thus say that I am neither full of regret nor very satisfied. I would like to see the country in a different situation. I would like to see the country continue growing, developing. But the country has practically stopped; its development has stagnated because of this inflationary spiral. At the same time our political parties are weak, lacking adequate structure. Today one changes party in Brazil as if one were changing shirts. There are no solid party organizations, which in turn causes the democratic regime to suffer.

Despite this pessimistic picture I am convinced that what we have done has not been in vain, and that with time our nation will develop, attaining the level of democracy to which we all aspire.

BOEKER: Do you think that military government in Brazil is now part of your history, something of the past, or is it still a possibility at some point in the future?

GEISEL: I don't have a crystal ball; I can't predict the future. I hope there won't be another military government. I believe the effort must be made to avoid that from happening, but I can't foresee what may happen in Brazil some day. At this time, I don't see a possibility of the military interfering, at least not in the near future but I cannot assure it could not happen one day.

BOEKER: From all your experience and wisdom, do any suggestions emerge as to what the government of the United States ought to consider in terms of its policies toward Brazil and Latin America, to help in the problems you cited: fragile democracy, poverty, and economic development.

GEISEL: I do not think that the United States could help directly with these internal problems, but I would note the following. I have always considered Brazil and the United States to be friends in the international arena and able collaborators who should continue as such. Yet, I often perceive a somewhat egotistic tendency in the United States, where because of domestic interests it sacrifices relations with countries such as Brazil, particularly with regard to trade. I see trade restrictions by the United States which in my opinion are unjustified. Of course the United States has its domestic interests, but its approach hurts relations with Brazil. I have always thought of Brazil and the United States as good friends and good allies. I had differences of opinion with President Carter, but for reasons other than Brazil's attitude toward the United States.

BOEKER: You have had a very full life, such as few people have had; you've been the leader of your country's military, you've been president, now you are director of an important business enterprise. Which role gave you the most satisfaction?

GEISEL: Each activity has its time. I was a dedicated military officer; I lived my profession and was very fond of it. Being president of the republic was an accident which I never imagined happening in my life, but circumstances arose which led me to the presidency. The best day of my life was the one on which I left the presidency, and became free of the responsibilities of that post. Today I am in business because I think one has to work. Idleness at my age is death; when I retire I die. I am very much of the opinion that Brazil needs to work harder; work is necessary. Living for work as one does in Germany or the United States may be a neurosis in some ways, but here it is essential to work like that to improve the country's economic situation. Therefore, if I propound this view that it is essential to work harder, then I have to set the example myself; I have to work.

My whole life centered on the military. That was the profession I liked and to which I dedicated myself. I believe I was a good military officer, a good professional. What of these other activities? Becoming president was accidental and working in business today is a necessity.

JOSE SARNEY

José Sarney was never meant to be President. He was a lawyer, poet, and provincial politician in Brazil's small and desperately poor state of Marinhao, where he worked closely with the military government and became a member of its favorite political party. For Brazil's first, indirect election of a civilian president after twenty years of military rule, Sarney was put on the ticket of opposition leader Tancredo Neves as vice presidential candidate, to comfort the military and the right. But after his election and just before inauguration, Neves suddenly died and fate thrust José Sarney to the presidency of Latin America's largest nation at a critical point in its long road back to democratic rule.

José Sarney is struggling to fulfill that role with limited assets. He has virtually no civilian political base and was made a member of Neves' MDB party only shortly before his nomination. In governing Brazil after 1985, Sarney had to stay close to his military backers and show them some deference, as he does in this interview. Sarney also had to share substantial authority with the powerful leader of the MDB party in the parliament, Ulysses Guimarães. The process of shared governance among Sarney, Guimarães, and the military was a fitful and ineffective one.

In an environment of power divided three ways, with a weak center, no one lived within his means. The parliament mandated social functions for provincial governments without providing resources to pay for them; Sarney broke his own budget by forgiving the provinces part of their financial obligations; and the military worked to increase its force levels by one hundred thousand men (for what purpose?).

I met with Sarney at his official residence, the Palace of the Dawn, seemingly floating on diamond-shaped arches over a flat penninsula surrounded on three sides by the large artificial lake which spreads its fingers through much of Brasilia. The Palace of the Dawn (Alvoreda in Portuguese) reflects the infatuation of

Brasilia's architect, Oscar Niemeyer, with cold, empty, and unfunctional spaces. One wonders how a president can live in this space-age movie set of echoing marble caverns. (Some have chosen not to.)

The contrast between the cold dawn of Alvoreda and its current occupant could hardly be more complete. José Sarney is a warm and cordial man, as well as a gracious host. When a thunderstorm broke during our conversation he asked a military aide to drive my car into the basement so I would not get wet. Despite the political storms of the day, Sarney appeared relaxed sitting in a large leather easy chair, with only a constantly wagging foot of the leg crossed over revealing the inner tension with which Sarney lives. He wore a trim, European-cut, double breasted suit and a maroon silk tie with a faint cross-hatch brocade pattern. At fifty-eight, Sarney is a dramatically handsome man with thick black eyebrows, bright dark eyes, and a large, brush mustache. He looks like a Latin James Mason at about fifty.

In September 1988, with the help of his military allies, Sarney won a protracted, bitter fight with Brazil's Constituent Assembly to assure himself a fifth year for his term as president. Many Brazilians were hoping he would fight as hard to protect his budget and rein in Brazil's roaring inflation. Sarney recognized, as in his comments to me, that inflation is the main threat to consolidation of Brazil's democracy. He fears accelerating inflation will increase the political allure of radical populism (read Lionel Brizola, former governor of Rio); but Sarney himself failed to brake inflation by matching his government's spending to its means.

Like many Brazilians, José Sarney has an expansive view of the weight and mass of Brazil and its ostensibly ineluctable contribution to stability and prosperity in the hemisphere. But at the same time he expresses to me the same anxiety as many other Latin American presidents that something is deeply wrong. Because of its economic problems, Latin America, he fears, seems to be falling further behind the major economic powers in the world and faltering in its efforts to invest and absorb new technology.

As Sarney was escorting me out of Alvoreda he stopped to give me an eloquent, almost impassioned statement of his view that Brazil and the United States are the two forces which, if they worked more effectively together, could pull Latin America out of its economic stagnation. Brazil and the United States, he believes, have a self-confident relationship, neither patronizing nor defensive on either side, which could cut some new deals in U.S.-Latin American cooperation, if the United States would look up, look south, and take Latin America's potential more seriously. A skillful match of U.S. technology and financial power with Latin America's enormous, underdeveloped market is a natural marriage in the eyes of this eloquent visionary who is still struggling to match cold realities to his comforting vision.

*   *   *   *   *

BOEKER: What would you hope to see as the most significant achievement of your presidential term?

SARNEY: I don't have any doubt that the most important achievement of my government will be that of having presided over the transition to democracy. It was a period characterized by the lack of cohesive political parties, by the work of a constitutional assembly and by our holding four elections in a country where the practice of democracy was new. It is very significant that under those conditions we are close to completing the transition without ever having to call a military alert and without suffering one single act of terrorism or threat to our democratic institutions. Add to that the fact that we have had to live with a serious economic crisis and social upheaval. Completing the transition to constitutional government has required an extremely difficult piece of political engineering.

BOEKER: Is the military's significant participation in government in Brazil to be seen as part of a transitional process, or is this a necessary part of the permanent governing structure in Brazil?

SARNEY: The participation of the military in the transition process has been exclusively on a professional basis. There has been no interference in politics. The armed forces have returned to their professional duties and have consistently supported the transition. I made it clear at the beginning of my term that we were going to accomplish the transition with the military, not against them. The restoration of democracy in Brazil was a broad-based movement which included the military. Alienating the military would have blocked our path to democracy. The conduct of the armed forces has been impeccable and within the context of their constitutional and professional responsibilities, contributing to the consolidation of our democracy.

BOEKER: Is the new constitution which the assembly completed in 1988 a workable framework for long-term consolidation of Brazil's democracy?

SARNEY: The implications, importance, and durability of a law go beyond its text. Only time will tell what consequences the new constitution will have in the life of Brazilians. The political tradition of Brazil is to find solutions through dialogue. Our desire for consensus and our spirit of conciliation is reflected in the constitution. We have passed two hundred and seventy laws and forty-six supplementary ones to try to achieve the changes and goals the constitution set out. The constitution itself foresees that in five years the whole text will be reviewed.

BOEKER: Has the transfer of significant financial resources and functions from the Brazilian federal government to state governments been mainly a financial necessity, or is there some conviction on your part that stronger regional governments are a good thing for Brazil in the long term?

SARNEY: Like most other nations, we have gone through cycles of de-centralization and centralization. We are now in a phase of redistribution of resources and responsibilities. This is not something that can be completed in days or even in months, but it is already having important consequences. The establishment of a new federation can even be seen as the principal feature of the recently approved constitution.

Within that context, the central government is no longer the authoritarian "savior" and the center of power. There is a new sharing of responsibility between the executive and the legislature. The Brazilian Congress will no longer be simply a forum for speeches. It will have to adapt itself to a modern style of administration, commensurate with a country with a very complex economy and even more complex political system, requiring the highest level of competence and management.

BOEKER: What do you see as the main risk Brazil faces in its continuing effort to consolidate democracy.

SARNEY: The great enemy of democracy in Latin America is inflation. Its perverse economic and social consequences are exploited by populists to gain power. Populism does not solve any problems and in the end weakens our institutions. Brazil has suffered epidemics of populism before, so our people are well aware that it offers no way out. The populist myth of the state as an all-purpose savior, omnipotent, and omnipresent, leads to unchecked growth of the state. This unrealistic approach has already exhausted itself. Today more than ever, we know that the state is not in a position to fulfill all the responsibilities prescribed by the populist model.

BOEKER: Can Brazil grow while continuing to service its debt?

SARNEY: We made a great effort to reintegrate Brazil into the international financial community. We cannot succeed by taking unilateral action. There has to be a broad understanding with creditor countries, which goes far beyond what is in any signed agreements. Brazil is an example of the difficulties faced by most of Latin America, where the net outflow of capital has become unsustainable.

The debt problem affects creditors and debtors alike and should be resolved jointly on the basis of financial and political considerations. By seeking only short-term, financial solutions one ignores the structural roots of the problem. The debt needs to be dealt with in global terms. We need to assure regular, financial flows, economic growth and consequently political and social stability. There are indications that this reality has begun to be perceived by creditor countries. We believe that this awareness will continue to grow and that we will arrive at lasting solutions for the debt problem. Brazil has exercised great responsibility and made great sacrifices to meet its commitments. We hope, therefore, that we will now have the understanding and cooperation of our partners.

BOEKER: What would you like to see from the administration in Washington in terms of its policies toward Brazil and Latin America?

SARNEY: The enormous responsibilities of a superpower like the United States, with interests throughout the world, have resulted in its giving low priority in its foreign policy to Latin Amer-

ica. Our region gets attention only when there are immediate security issues, generally ones linked to strategic confrontation
with the other superpower. Somehow this has been the context
within which the conflicts in Central America and the Caribbean
have been viewed.

The United States should look at Latin America from a different angle. It should look at us as a contiguous community which
is as close in political, cultural, and economic terms as it is geographically.

U.S. interest in Latin America could be awakened by the serious economic situation Latin America faces, with serious implications for the future. Latin America is the only continent which
has gradually gone backwards. Some decades ago Argentina had
a per capita income higher than that of Italy, and no country in
Latin America had a GNP lower than that of the less developed
East Asian countries. Today Latin America has fallen behind
these countries. The situation has drastically changed. The Latin
American countries have become net exporters of capital, and we
have serious problems. All this reflects a continent which suffers
from a disease. This situation will make it necessary for the
United States to pay more attention whether it would like to or
not.

With respect to Brazil, we are fifth largest country in the
world, with most of our 8.5 million square kilometers economically exploitable. Toward the end of the century we will represent
half of the population of Latin America. Brazil also enjoys a
healthy industrial structure that places us among the world's largest market economies. Brazil's foreign trade reflects a dynamic
economy despite the difficulties of the present decade. In 1988
our trade surplus was surpassed only by Japan and the Federal
Republic of Germany. We have earned the right to greater participation in management of the international economy, especially
when it comes to science and technology.

Given these considerations we would expect and appreciate a
more positive reaction from the United States with respect to the
many possibilities for collaboration between our countries, instead of creating obstacles to commercial, scientific and technological interchange. These obstacles force us to look for markets
elsewhere when it would be easier, simpler and more logical to
promote stronger ties within our own hemisphere. I have always
said that we need to establish a positive agenda for U.S.-
Brazilian relations. Instead of incessant arguing about our prob-

lems we should explore further the enormous possibilities for co-operation and use them as a powerful tool which can promote better bilateral relations.

BOEKER: Your anxiety about Latin America's stagnation reflects a concern which has been mentioned to me by many chiefs of state in Latin America.

SARNEY: It is natural that we in Latin America share this common concern. This is one of the main reasons for the renewed and generalized interest in integration. From my first day in office I have, therefore, given high priority to issues of Latin American integration. Aware that the era of foreign aid has passed, Brazil has looked for more realistic formulas of cooperation with its partners, especially within the region.

In reality Latin America cannot remain outside the growing movement toward the formation of large economic blocs in today's world. It is essential to promote regional integration with firmness and determination, though obviously following a pace and mode appropriate to the particular situation of each economy.

BOEKER: The Group of Eight democratic chiefs of state represents an exciting, new development in the hemisphere. Do you see this as something permanent, and possibly as a step in the direction of integration?

SARNEY: The Group of Eight in Latin America reflects a worldwide tendency to form groups, to coordinate efforts. We see this in Europe, in Asia, almost everywhere. Latin America has been the only region without a body for top-level coordination. The Group of Eight does not aspire to be a formal mechanism; it seeks to facilitate sharing of information and opinions at the regional level, in a world increasingly interdependent. In that sense, the group will consolidate its structure. The greatest contribution to this consolidation would be increased awareness on the part of participating countries that our destinies are closely linked. We all share common traditions and similar problems, especially in the economic and financial fields. Overcoming these problems will be much easier through cooperative efforts.

ULYSSES GUIMARÃES

Ulysses Guimarães was a central figure throughout Brazil's long transition to elected civilian rule. During twenty years of military government Ulysses and the late Tancredo Neves were the leaders of Brazil's major opposition party and persistent gadflies to the military. Many felt that Ulysses, not Neves, should have been the MDB Party's presidential candidate in 1984. But at that time Ulysses, who was to the left of Neves, would not have been accepted by the military. To his credit, Ulysses the realist accepted this harsh fact and worked with Neves to win the election in parliament and to put together a broad-based cabinet—which became José Sarney's cabinet on Neves' sudden death.

I met Ulysses at his pleasant suburban house, overlooking the southern part of Brasilia's large artificial lake. Ulysses looked at home in a thin white sports shirt and light grey slacks. At seventy-two he is still a commanding presence. He has just a narrow rim of white hair around his bald head and white angular eyebrows over pale blue eyes which tend to be half covered by his eyelids. Large flat ears flank a squarish head with a prominent nose. The whole impression is close to that of a thin Pablo Picasso.

Many other seekers of favors come to his house at any hour, for political power seems to be Ulysses' only activity and in the late Eighties he wielded more of it than just about anybody else in Brazil. Guimarães' staff calls him Mr. President, because of his role as president of the Constituent Assembly which wrote Brazil's new constitution. On a trip to Paris before the Assembly convened, Ulysses quoted Napoleon's dictum that constitutions should be brief and ambiguous, and assured his audience Brazil's would be neither. The final charter has turned out to be an unusually detailed and cumbersome one which tries to fill in a lost generation in social legislation with extensive constitutional provisions on such matters as the working hours and vacation time of domestic employees. But an agreed constitution had to be hammered out with Brazil's more than thirty political parties before direct elections of the next president could go forward. Most Brazilian politicians concede that only Ulysses could have done this. He is the master broker, one in fact who sees the essence of the democratic process as bringing everybody in, and working out their demands.

As leader of the MDB Party, with the power base President Sarney lacked, Ulysses was a major power during the Sarney government, filling any vacuums which Sarney was unable to fill. Ministers were picked or fired by Ulysses. Despite the unusual nature of this power sharing, Ulysses and President Sarney managed to work continually, if uneasily, together.

Ulysses, MDB candidate in 1989, still feels he deserves to be president himself, despite his age and some health problems. But his party's strength, as he himself recognizes in this interview, has been sapped by Brazil's soaring inflation. Ulysses fears that Brazil is on the verge of a self perpetuating cycle of hyperinflation, with ugly economic and social consequences. He talks of the Sarney government's program to reduce inflation as too gradual and too weak. But the Parliament and Constituent Assembly, and Ulysses' approach to brokering all the demands, have made their own contribution to the deficit spending which fuels Brazil's inflation.

Ulysses does not claim to be an economic expert. His contribution is rather as the power broker who has bashed together the key compromises to keep Brazil's democracy on track. In that realm he has some deep political concerns for the future. Brazil's political parties are weak and largely regional in their bases of support. The larger ones, including most prominently Ulysses' own MDB, have shown a tendency to fragment. In the constitution-drafting Ulysses was not successful in trying to winnow the array of small parties by creating a high threshold of popular votes for representation of a party in parliament. Effective exercise of the Parliament's extensive powers under the new constitution by a body comprised of over thirty parties could be a stormy and ineffective process.

Nevertheless, consolidation of Brazil's democracy progresses on schedule, in significant part because of the persistent efforts of talented politicians like the one speaking in this interview.

*   *   *   *   *

BOEKER: Do you see the constitution adopted in 1988, as a long-lasting one or as a transitional one which will require continuous amendments as Brazil's revived democracy matures?

GUIMARÃES: It will change. Brazil is a dynamic, changing society. The country is virtually an archipelago in social, economic and political terms. Aware of this I persevered in pressing for two ways to amend the constitution. First, the Parliament can amend the constitution by a three-fifths majority, instead of two-thirds. Second, in five years a constitutional reform can be decided by a simple majority. A plebiscite will then decide on a parliamentary or presidential system of government.

BOEKER: President Sarney is concerned that the economic and social provisions of the constitution will require large expenditures that the state cannot yet afford. Will the constitution hinder the government's efforts to reduce its budget deficits?

GUIMARÃES: There were two problems: First, the fiscal structure of the state was in tension with the country's geography. Our geography requires a regionalized, federal system, but the central government receives the tax revenue. We thus provided that the central government must give economic support to the states, and through them the municipalities. Second, we established a modern concept of social welfare which goes beyond what one would call social security. It is a very advanced plan providing major improvements in public health and social welfare programs, which very few constitutions include. There was a great debate as to whether Brazil has the resources for such a program. In the Constituent Assembly we felt that even if the resources were not there, we had to get them. We have a social debt to thirty million illiterates. Brazil may rank eighth among the world's economies (in GNP) but it is sixty-third when it comes to social programs. We also have the lowest per capita income on the South American continent, even lower than Paraguay or Bolivia. It is obvious this situation has to change. The constitution was aimed at correcting social injustices, not only with respect to social issues and workers' rights, but concerning "indirect" benefits such as education, health and transportation. This is why it has been called a "Citizens' Constitution." A citizen is not only a person who has political rights and votes on election day. A citizen is someone who has to eat, dress, and sleep, needs medical care and transportation.

This philosophy of mine is reflected in two facts. First, this new constitution begins with the rights of the citizens, while Brazil's previous seven constitutions began with the structure and powers of the state. Second, we established a participatory and representative democracy where the people can present their own proposals for consideration at the federal, state or municipal level. The people also have the power, through a referendum, to declare null and void a law approved by either the national congress, the state legislature or a municipal assembly.

BOEKER: Under the new constitution the military retain some participation in government, for example as heads of several ministries. Do you see this as a stage in the transition from military to civilian rule, or is some participation of the military in government a necessary part of Brazil's governing structure for the long term?

GUIMARÃES: The military play two important roles: defense of the country's sovereignty in the event of foreign aggression, and maintenance of internal order. However, they act only under the orders of the president, who is a civilian, or the national congress. They do not operate on their own. For instance if a state is experiencing a serious crisis and the governor is unable to restore order, he may appeal to the army but only through the president or the national congress. The military have played an extremely important and supportive role during this transition period. They haven't made high-handed pronouncements or shown any lack of discipline, as occurred in the past. This has been very important for the evolution of our democratic system.

BOEKER: Has Brazil's transition to democracy overcome the vacuum created by the death of Tancredo Neves?

GUIMARÃES: Yes, it has. Even though he was a superb statesman, no one is irreplaceable. He belonged to the same party I do, where there are no domineering or charismatic figures. The MDB has very good teams at both the state and national levels. This was evident throughout the process of elaborating the very difficult and complex text of the Brazilian constitution. There is no question that he was an outstanding figure, but we were able to carry on.

BOEKER: Instead of moving toward a system of two or three large political parties, Brazil seems to be going in the opposite direction, with fragmentation of the large parties and a proliferation of smaller ones. Can this trend be reversed?

GUIMARÃES: This tendency is a mistake and it worries me a lot. In a way it is a consequence of proportional representation which tends to reflect each small interest group at election time. That system tends to pulverize our parties. The other system, that of voting for one representative per district, encourages the emergence of fewer, larger parties.

We have an even a worse problem: we apply proportional representation with a distortion. In an orthodox system of proportional representation, the so-called remainders go to the party that wins the plurality in order to give it more strength. But in Brazil's proportional representation, these seats are divided among all parties, which creates serious difficulties at all levels, municipal, state and national. We tried to remedy this situation by adopting the German system (in which a party has to receive a minimum five percent of the popular vote to get any parliamentary representation), but this was not approved. And we did establish a minimum number of votes in various states for a group to qualify as a party. Still we have a serious problem that needs to be corrected. We now have thirty parties. This is no longer democratic pluralism; this is a multy-party system.

BOEKER: At the same time that the number of parties is increasing, the constitution gives some administrative powers to Congress, such as its right to approve international financial agreements. Isn't this a recipe for problems, even instability: a fragmented Congress trying to exercise administrative powers?

GUIMARÃES: We will try to establish an orderly system through the parliament's internal rules. The idea is to encourage the smaller parties to form blocs by giving blocs a certain role in parliamentary leadership, even if they have somewhat fewer deputies than the larger ones. Therefore, instead of having thirty party leaders we might have eight or nine leaders of blocs— opposition blocs and a government bloc. We still do not have all the necessary elements in place to reach this objective, but the smaller parties have to get together somehow in blocs to function in a more coherent fashion.

BOEKER: What would you see as the main objective of your government if you are elected president of Brazil?

GUIMARÃES: The main objective of whoever does become president must be to restore the country's economic health. Our economic situation is dangerously fragile. The rate of inflation is a challenge to governmental authority; either the government defeats inflation or inflation will defeat the government. We must solve the problem of the government's deficit, which President Sarney has tried to do. There is the long-standing problem of the foreign debt.

Brazil must face its problem of social injustice. In my opinion the two most serious problems which Brazil has at the moment are inequality and injustice among the people and among the regions. We have problems in the northeast, the north and the south, which threaten the unity of the country. We have to deal with poverty so extreme that it just cannot go on. Our generation then has the task of integrating the impoverished masses into Brazilian civilization. The worst part is that we have the money; the money is there, but it is poorly distributed. Some countries just don't have anything to divide up, but we do.

BOEKER: As a Brazilian politician, what would you like to see from the U.S. administration in terms of its actions and policies toward Brazil and Latin America?

GUIMARÃES: I would like to see more closeness between the United States and Latin America. I did not see any effort on the part of the Reagan administration toward this goal. What I do see is lack of understanding, not to use stronger words, with respect to major events in Latin America. The U.S. could have behaved as a helpful neighbor, but did not do so. It would seem that as the United States acquires more power in global terms, its ability to deal with problems within its own hemisphere diminishes.

I would think that the new U.S. administration is going to have to focus on the foreign debt problem. If Latin American economies are strengthened, their purchasing power will increase and we will obviously buy more from the United States. As more jobs are created, our industry will be stronger and we will be in a much better position to meet our debt obligations. So far the policy has been one of procrastination, of rolling over unpayable debts. The debt problem is suffocating Latin American nations beginning with my own. A solution can be found only through cooperation between the banks and the debtor countries. Repaying some debts in kind might be a smart thing to do.

Finally, I can give you an example of the unfortunate distancing of the United States from Latin America. I was president of the Latin American Parliament for a period of three years, and in that capacity I went to the United States. I asked the U.S. Congress to send some observers as the French were doing. It did not do so. As a result what happened was the following. The European Parliament has joined the Latin American Parliament. We have an annual meeting sometimes in Latin America, sometimes in Europe. We exchange ideas and discuss problems as equal partners. I proposed the same to the U.S. Congress. They did not even give us the courtesy of a reply. This is lamentable and incomprehensible.

DOMINICAN REPUBLIC

JOAQUIN BALAGUER

In the Dominican Republic the passage to democratic practice has ironically been marked not by the surge of a new generation but by the new moves of an old man—one whose personal history chronicles his country's crossing from brutal dictatorship to elected, civilian government.

Dominican President Joaquín Balaguer received us in the Spanish colonial palace built by his former boss, Rafael Trujillo, dictator of the Dominican Republic until his murder in 1961. Balaguer stood in his customary spot behind a marble table with his hand extended, moving it in my direction only when the sound of my voice revealed the direction of my approach, for Balaguer is blind from glaucoma—the first head of state elected with such a handicap. While his eyes move continuously, they see only patches of light and darkness but nothing else, including his favorite pictures of earlier days, now all hanging askew, since the staff knows this no longer matters.

Balaguer wore a plain, light gray suit, with pants cinched up high, and a dark blue tie, reflecting the austere, introverted man he is, a life-long bachelor and scholar with few possessions but his books and no taste for the high life. He spoke with us alone, and he governs alone, with no personal advisors other than his ministers. He is a man, as one Dominican put it, who has no one with whom to have a drink. The political slogan of the day for Balaguer's party is, "Balaguer is not alone," but he is—in a personal, if not a political, sense.

As if he did not want his countrymen to forget his service to the dictator Trujillo, Balaguer has published his memoirs under the stunning title, *The Memoirs of a Courtesan in the Era of Trujillo*. So why did the Dominicans, in elections all sides consider legitimate, return this eighty-year-old, blind ex-henchman of the hated Trujillo for a fifth term in 1986 (after eight years in the opposition)? The answer is much clearer to Dominicans than foreigners.

In the Dominican Republic there is widespread, if sometimes grudging, respect for Balaguer because he brought the country safely from the wreckage of a brutal dictatorship to a stable society today. In that society some of the basic elements of democracy are well established—particularly legitimate regular elections and a succession of peaceful transitions from losers to winners. In the Dominican Republic there is broad recognition that probably no one else could have managed this passage, particularly in the critical years just after Trujillo's assassination, when the society could have disintegrated in civil war.

Balaguer is seen as tough—a man of personal courage who resigned from a dictatorship. He once apparently had a machine gun held to his throat by one of Trujillo's brothers, in a confrontation during the chaotic period after the assassination when Balaguer was deftly maneuvering the rest of the late dictator's family out of the country.

Balaguer has an unromantic, but sympathetic view of his people's weaknesses and economic backwardness, and he talks to them better than his political rivals. He is the unrivaled master of the murky medium of Dominican politics. He makes no apologies for the combination of strongman and democratic politician which blend in his political style. But because of that mix Dominicans seem to feel they can count on him to do the necessary to avoid disasters. Even many who do not like him considered him the least bad choice in 1986, to succeed a regime plagued by charges of corruption. But as one talks to this soft-spoken man, who offers a faint smile at intrusive questions, he is hard to dislike.

The question many Dominicans are asking themselves today is, has Balaguer overstayed his time? Yet Balaguer seems not to ask this question of himself. Balaguer told us in 1988 that he wanted to step down because of his health at the end of his term in 1990. But in 1989 the wily Balaguer was once more a candidate campaigning in the dark, to succeed himself. Whether he does or not, he will go down as the consummate pragmatist, a politician who has successfully done the needful to hold his country together. Some would say he has merely done the needful to stay in power—a characterization he passionately rejects, as you will see in this interview with one of the most intriguing strong figures of Latin politics.

* * * * *

BOEKER: Your role in the political life of the Dominican Republic spans a period of dramatic changes—from Trujillo's dictatorship through the difficult period thereafter when your administrations took some tough measures, to a very different era today. In that era power has peacefully passed from your party to the opposition and vice versa, and the roles of both governing and opposition party have become routine. My question is: how have you personally adapted to these changes? Have you changed your way of thinking and governing as the political system has developed?

BALAGUER: Yes and no. What hasn't changed are my objectives. Our policy, which we initiated in 1966 and even in 1961, after Trujillo's dictatorship, is geared toward raising the standard of living of the Dominican people. In pursuing that goal, we have given special emphasis to agrarian reform. For the most part, our lands had been usurped by Trujillo, who used them for his personal gain. After the fall of the dictatorship, ownership passed to the people, not one individual but to the government itself. However the old system of landholding still existed. The campesino remained a slave in his own country in the sense that he lacked the land to earn a livelihood for his family.

After Trujillo's death in 1961, my administration changed the system of landholding through agrarian reform. Through this reform we parceled out most of these lands to the campesinos working the land. I consider this the first substantive step taken toward the democratization of the country.

Other measures opened a new political chapter. Within a few days after Trujillo's death there was total freedom of expression, which was the second major step toward Dominican democratization. A series of other measures created a base for the country's economic, political, and social development, including the execution of developmental projects, many with the help of international organizations. This led to the creation of small industries, to incentives for industrial investments, and to the opening of the economy to foreign investment.

The economy has diversified considerably; a country which imported most of the goods it consumed gradually became an exporter to neighboring countries. From being a country exclusively dependent on foreign industries and economies, we became self-sufficient in many of our economic activities.

BOEKER: Are there any specific qualities which are essential to be successful in the Dominican Republic's political life?

BALAGUER: I believe the most important is to know the milieu of Dominican politics. To know the psychology of the Dominican common people, to understand the country's problems—some similar to those in other Latin American countries, some our own. This is essential to be successful in politics in an underdeveloped country such as ours. I also believe those are the reasons for the relative success which I have been able to achieve over a public service career which spans almost fifty years. I was born in the country and lived there among the people until adolescence; I am practically a campesino. That gave me my grasp of the milieu.

We were until very recently essentially a rural people. As we have grown, like most Latin American countries, most of our rural population has been attracted to the urban centers and has agglomerated around the country's largest cities. One of our most serious problems is that the countryside is being abandoned. As the level of education increases, the younger generation tends to settle in the cities. There has also been an economic decline due to the decrease in the production of sugar. The presence in the country of large numbers of Haitian laborers has also substituted for Dominican labor in the countryside.

FISHER[13]: To observers of Dominican politics you continue to be a paradox. Sometimes you surprise them, sometimes you disappoint them. Would you say that there has been a direction, an objective or a philosophy that has endured through the years and which has eluded political observers?

BALAGUER: I am neither a conservative nor a revolutionary. I am not a conservative precisely because the social revolution in this country for the most part was initiated by us. As many here recognize we are the parents of agrarian reform in the Dominican Republic. I am not a revolutionary in the sense that we

---

[13]I was joined in this interview by Richard W. Fisher of Dallas, Texas, a long-time student of the Dominican Republic and chairman of the board of the Institute of the Americas.

recognize the need for stability in our government if we are to develop and promote economic growth. To the degree that it was possible with our people, we have developed the revolutionary ideas, in a Dominican sense.

Our population for the most part has not gone beyond elementary education. There is a high rate of illiteracy. But our people are innately intelligent and have assimilated many modern ideas through radio and television. Our culture is the product of the media. There isn't anybody in this country, regardless of how isolated the region where he lives, who does not own a radio and know what is going on in the world. In this manner the Dominican middle class has achieved a worldly education, despite the lack of schools.

This has been a tremendous help to our country, and has compensated for the lack of education. Our population has the capacity to assimilate any type of economic, social or political reform and can become an instrument for its promotion.

BOEKER: You said that you are neither a conservative nor a revolutionary. But do you have a political philosophy, an ideology, or do you see yourself as strictly a pragmatic leader?

BALAGUER: Mostly pragmatic. The style that I have developed in the sixteen years at the helm of public affairs is purely pragmatic. We are a country in the process of development, a country which was born to democracy only after 1961. We cannot introduce in the Dominican Republic methods or theories which work in other countries but may not work for us. Out of necessity a politician here needs to be pragmatic, adapting his ideas and his principles to the national climate, to the needs of the country. Any politician who is not totally pragmatic would not succeed in the Dominican Republic. The same is true in most of Latin America's underdeveloped countries.

BOEKER: Are there important differences between the Balaguer now and the Balaguer of twenty or twenty-five years ago?

BALAGUER: No, I don't believe so. I have always been faithful to the same ideas and to the same principles. However, as circumstances changed I have had the flexibility to adapt pragmatically to the new situations in order to address the problems we faced at a particular time. Certainly circumstances have changed;

the country today is not at all as it was in 1961. There have been fundamental changes in the ideas and in the education of the people. As these changes occurred politics had to adjust. The changes in policy are the result of changes in the Dominican reality; they do not stem from personal transformation.

BOEKER: One of the reasons why you seem to be an enigma to observers is that your personal style can be at times that of a strongman, yet you are a democratically elected president under a system with impressive continuity. Is there a mixture of these two personal styles in the real Balaguer?

BALAGUER: There is a mixture of both traits in my personality; the country demands it. It is not a country that can be governed by a pure democracy; neither is it a country that can be ruled by force. Dominican politicians have to adapt themselves to the environment. If a politician is to be successful in the Dominican Republic he cannot act according to his own beliefs if they are not in harmony with the country's climate, with the demands of the milieu. I have had to adapt throughout all my public life. Sometimes I appear to be democratic and sometimes I appear to be a strongman as circumstances may require. In all sincerity, however, my ideas have always been the same; essentially I believe only in democracy. A country should be governed in freedom. As Churchill said, "Democracy may not be the best system, but there isn't a better one."[14]

FISHER: Speaking of adapting to circumstances, is there some missed opportunity, disappointment, or frustration which still bothers you in looking back at your administrations?

BALAGUER: The circumstances now are not favorable for us or any developing country. The economic situation has changed drastically. It is very contradictory. In reality this is both a prosperous and a poor, even backward country. We are a prosperous nation because we have a dynamic population, very intelligent, easily adaptable to change, and a very aggressive business sector which has developed in recent years. The labor force has also made a great contribution to economic development in the Do-

---

[14]Churchill's famous axiom was precisely: "Democracy is the worst form of government, except all those other forms that have been tried from time to time."

minican Republic. However, both the country and its citizens have lived through difficult circumstances caused by foreign economic measures. For instance, recent years have brought a drastic fall in the production of sugar which has always been our main source of foreign exchange, and economic progress.

The country once had a sugar quota in the U. S. of approximately seven hundred thousand to eight hundred thousand tons. Now it has been reduced to a minimal portion of that amount. To that degree an essential factor in our growth has changed, and with it the economic situation of our country. I repeat, it is a country rich in resources, but very poor in the sense that we are dependent on an agricultural sector now going through a crisis because of foreign developments.

BOEKER: Looking to the future, how certain are you personally that the present system of elected civilian government, which your country has achieved with such a great effort over the last decades, will endure?

BALAGUER: I am an optimist. I believe the country has already assimilated democracy and would not easily accept a government established by force. Any attempt at establishing a dictatorship here would run up against great difficulties. Though ignorant in some areas our people are very intelligent in others; they have experienced the good feeling of life in a democracy, and I do not believe they will accept regimes opposed to their democratic institutions. Any attempt to change the present system will encounter serious opposition by a large majority of the population.

FISHER: What will be the legacy of Balaguer's years? Some experts expect fundamental changes. Others see you as the patriarch of the country's modern political system which will continue more or less in its current form. What is the future for Dominican democracy after you leave power?

BALAGUER: Democracy has already left its mark in the Dominican Republic; it would not be easy to change the political system. During most of our years of independence we have lived under totalitarian regimes of force, and finally Trujillo's dictatorship. The country has now totally changed, and has internalized—to the extent that they are part of its psychology—the value of democracy and the advantages of elected leaders. I do not believe there is anything that anybody could do to change this course which is the result of what we have lived through in the Dominican Republic.

BOEKER: Personally, I believe that one of the fundamental accomplishments here is having diminished the role of the military in the country's political life. Does your previous answer mean that there is nowhere on the horizon the possibility of a military government?

BALAGUER: I don't think there is. If there were for any reason, it would be terrible. Democracy has already grown roots in our country; it reflects the feelings of the common people; it reflects the ideology of the majority of our population, and I just do not believe that de facto government can be imposed. We live in a democracy and we will have to continue within that system.

BOEKER: In 1978 you seemed unsure as to whether someone else could replace you and keep the country stable. How do you feel now about the new generation of Dominican leaders? Are they ready to govern?

BALAGUER: The country has developed a lot since that time. There are many capable leaders in the different parties. The leadership crisis in the Dominican Republic is not the same as exists in many Latin American countries. Potentially there are many leaders with brilliant futures who have not had the opportunity to develop fully. The next elections in the Dominican Republic will be the freest ever, because the electoral laws have been modified based on past experiences. That election will contribute further to stabilization of the democratic system in our country.

BOEKER: And in your own party? Are there opportunities for young leaders?

BALAGUER: Absolutely, I am now in my last term of office. It is my intention to get out of politics after 1990. Because of my health and because of my age, I have no choice. I am doing my best to give complete freedom to the young leadership within my party to campaign and to compete for leadership during the next election.

FISHER: During your speech on Independence Day you stated, "Corruption is not a blot exclusively on Dominicans: it exists in most Latin American nations." Did you mean that corruption is a particularly serious problem in Latin America, and if so, what are its main causes?

BALAGUER: In the first place, corruption is rampant all over the world. The world's values have changed. Education has changed. Illicit enrichment and greed are characteristics of the present status of civilization. In developing countries, such as the Latin American nations, corruption has surged more dramatically. In the Caribbean region it has reached alarming proportions. In our country corruption was unknown until some time ago. I would say it was unknown until Trujillo. For instance President Morales Languaso, upon leaving office, had to earn a living selling tickets while living in a neighboring island, Saint Thomas. He had absolutely no personal wealth to meet his living expenses. This is just one instance, and not an isolated one by any means. Dominicans were poor when they left government. However, Trujillo brought rule by force and he concentrated all public wealth in his hands. After that the situation changed.

At present the idea of ill-gotten gains is in the minds of the majority of Dominicans, especially those engaged in politics. It is one of the worst maladies we have to fight. I have given the Justice Department carte blanche to proceed on its own to eradicate corruption.

BOEKER: What do you consider the most serious threat to continuation of democratic government in the Dominican Republic?

BALAGUER: Poverty: the absence of economic development, unemployment, and all the economic, social and cultural ills they bring. Among other ills corruption in this country has its principal source in poverty.

BOEKER: The United States has tried to influence politics in your country in various periods. In 1966, President Johnson sent U. S. Marines to the Dominican Republic, and in 1978 President Carter pressured your government to continue the counting of votes which was suspended in the tense aftermath of a close election. In hindsight, how would you now judge these actions on the part of Washington?

BALAGUER: I would say that there have been no such pressures. I will refer to the case in the 1978 elections in which I was involved. President Carter did not influence in any way the decisions made by my administration, nor the outcome of the election. I did receive a call from the secretary of state (Cyrus Vance) which was restricted to his inquiry as to the reasons why the counting of votes had been interrupted. He was informed that the count had been interrupted because a group within the military had made a show of force, which alarmed the judges of the Central Electoral Committee, forcing them to abandon their posts and interrupt the electoral count.

The commission from the Organization of American States which I had requested and which included Galo Plaza from Ecuador, Misael Pastrana Borrero from Colombia and Julio Méndes Montenegro from Guatemala, visited me and informed me of the interruption. I immediately ordered that the partial results be annulled, and called the president of the electoral committee to whom we gave full guarantees. That same evening I went on national television to make clear to the country that there would be no fraud, that the will of the people would be respected. Calm was restored immediately and the next day the counting resumed, and Antonio Guzmán of the opposition Dominican Revolutionary Party (PRD) was declared the winner. Thus there was no pressure from President Carter, who was always most respectful.

FISHER: What changes would you like to see in the foreign policy of the United States during the new administration? What actions would you suggest with respect to Latin America?

BALAGUER: The most important would be a change of attitude regarding Latin America's debt. That debt is the result of lack of foresight by our governments. In those years the facilities extended by international lenders were abused and our countries were overwhelmed with debt which was not well administered or necessarily used for anything useful for our development. The debt is a commitment we have to honor. But the creditor countries need to recognize reality and adopt a more liberal attitude regarding mode and timing of repayment.

BOEKER: Do you have a specific mode in mind?

BALAGUER: We need to figure out a formula which would permit countries to pay according to the volume of their exports. It need not be ten percent as the Peruvian government maintains, but it should be something similar which would allow debtor countries to meet the required payments without jeopardizing their chances for growth. If the debtor countries cannot grow, the creditors face the reality that the debt becomes unpayable. But if you look for adjustments which reflect the capacity of each individual country, we can do both, pay the debt and grow.

FISHER: A personal question. Is there a figure in the history of Latin America who has been a model for you?

BALAGUER: There have been many. For instance in the Dominican Republic we have had leaders such as retired General Horacio Vázquez, who was the only civilian ruler after the 1916 intervention. He was a man with sound ideas, a product of the circumstances and of the environment in which he lived. He rose to the occasion. He passed into history as a great democrat, despite his having been a man of arms.

JOSE FRANCISCO
PEÑA-GOMEZ

José Francisco Peña-Gómez, leader of the Dominican Revolutionary Party, provides an opposition perspective on the enigmatic Joaquín Balaguer. But Peña-Gómez is also a force of his own in Dominican politics. A large man, he dominates an ample stuffed chair in his living room, and a continual flow of political associates and petitioners passes by. I met him there at his home, a pleasant small villa in Santo Domingo. His favorite chair was surrounded by photos, but not of himself with the political greats of this world, but rather of personal friends.

This articulate spokesman for a younger generation and the opposition to Balaguer may yet be a broker in the succession to the octogenarian old guard of Dominican politics—Balaguer and the quixotic Juan Bosch, Peña-Gomez's mentor. (Bosch bolted the Dominican Revolutionary Party which he helped form in exile during Trujillo's time and is now heading his own splinter party.) Despite his talents, Peña-Gómez faces a high hurdle in the way of any presidential aspirations—his Haitian origins, which evoke still strong prejudice in the Dominican Republic. The Republic was invaded by the Haitian army in the nineteenth century and by low-wage Haitian laborers ever since, inspiring the usual resentments among unemployed Dominicans.

Peña-Gómez appears resigned to the still significant role open to him. He is, in fact, not a driven politician, like Balaguer or Bosch, determined to fight for power regardless of odds or age. Unlike Bosch, Peña-Gómez holds no personal grudge against Balaguer and can thus present a balanced perspective of Balaguer.

Peña-Gómez respects Balaguer for his dismantling of Trujillo's apparatus of repression, his refusal to let the military take the 1978 presidential election victory from the Dominican Revolutionary Party, and his latter-day democratic vocation, as Peña-Gómez sees it. But the younger politician faults Balaguer for his authoritarian style, particularly within his own party, and his economic management. Peña-Gómez believes that Balaguer's engineering approach to development (acridly called here a "Pharaonic" one) has emphasized construction of public works over the development of institutions and a policy environment which might generate more private activity. Despite his respect for his elders—Juan Bosch and Joaquín Balaguer—this Dominican politician of the next generation makes clear in this interview his belief that both have over-stayed their time and should give way to a new generation.

*   *   *   *   *

BOEKER: The Dominican Republic has a formal democracy with a good track record—free elections, long continuity of civilian government, and active political parties, such as yours. Yet some thoughtful observers see Balaguer as an elected dictator. Have the fundamental elements of a democratic system been implanted in this society?

PEÑA-GOMEZ: My answer would be a qualified "yes." The Dominican Republic has had one of the most stable democratic regimes in the hemisphere. It is now unthinkable to imagine a coup, an assassination of a president, or disruption of that nature. In the past events such as these were common in Dominican politics. The democratic process has now been totally consolidated, and I would say that most of the political demands have been satisfied. The problem we have is that the success of our political system has not been duplicated in our economy, even less in the social field. We need to enhance Dominican democracy with economic success.

BOEKER: Do you believe that these economic problems are so serious as to affect the stability of the democratic regime?

PEÑA-GOMEZ: Yes. It would have already done so if the political parties in our country had not reached the degree of maturity they have. If this crisis had come up in the Sixties or the Seventies democratic governments probably would not have survived. But the crisis hit in the Eighties when rule by force would go against the nature of the country. No one wants to see in power an abusive military regime, contrary to the popular will. Everyone is conscious of the need to preserve the system. If Balaguer has to be removed from power, it has to be through the electoral process.

BOEKER: Do you believe that your own political party has overcome the limitations of personalism? Is it now a political party which can get popular support under different leaders and candidates?

PEÑA-GOMEZ: The Dominican Revolutionary Party—the country's first, really—is an institution with roots in the national consciousness. It has forty-nine years of existence, twenty-seven of them in this country (after its life in exile under Trujillo). We already have in our party two generations—the parents in their sixties and their children in their thirties. Whatever strength we have lost over the years, we have recouped.

Our party was weakened during Jorge Blanco's last administration, particularly because of the measures it had to take to comply with agreements with the International Monetary Fund. However, we have recovered, despite the split in our party.

BOEKER: What would be your answer to the same question with respect to the party in power?

PEÑA GOMEZ: Balaguer's party is dominated by the personality of its leader. It is active during electoral periods and it has deep popular roots. However, it is a totally conformist party; it does not function on an organic base, but rather on the basis of Balaguer's personality. When Balaguer steps down there is going to be fierce competition for control. His party will survive but most probably it will split. The party is twenty-five years old, and those who have been with it all along will stick with it, assuring that it remains a major party, but some will leave.

BOEKER: How do you explain the paradox of Juan Bosch? How is it possible that a figure so important in the origin of democracy in your country could lose popularity for so long, before his recent revival?

PEÑA-GOMEZ: Bosch lost popularity because he made the serious mistake of radicalizing like a student. He thought that the old democracy had accomplished its historical mission, that the American intervention would not permit the establishment of a democratic government, and thus he turned more radical. He got ahead of his people. At present he has rectified his position; he has placed himself at the center-left, and therefore has regained popularity. His faction has increased its parliamentary strength from seven to seventeen representatives, but his real weakness is that he does not have the votes of the rural population, nor of the poor in the cities.

BOEKER: Do you expect the 1990 elections to be fair?

PEÑA-GOMEZ: I have great doubts that there could be elections without fraud, especially if Balaguer is a candidate, not so much because of Balaguer—he is a civilized man—but because of the military. Many of them were fired by our party when we were in power.

FISHER: Do you believe that Balaguer for certain is going to be a candidate?

PEÑA-GOMEZ: Dr. Balaguer loves power so much that everybody believes he would like to remain in power until he dies. Also in 1992 we will be celebrating the five hundredth anniversary of Columbus's landing in America, a celebration which will take place both here and in Spain. The prospect of presiding over this grandiose celebration with the King of Spain must be causing Balaguer many sleepless nights. My impression is that Balaguer is going to run. There is also of course the question of his age and the fact that he has lost a lot of popular support.

BOEKER: Balaguer presents a paradox. On the one extreme he is a "boss" (caudillo) and a strongman who has used some force in power, and on the other extreme he is a democratically elected president.

PEÑA-GOMEZ: He used to be a strongman, not any more. We had to take power from Balaguer (in 1978) and even then the military tried to remain in control. At that juncture he reacted very well; he did not back the military. But he took away our majority in Congress and in this manner he retained control of the Senate and the judiciary. (Judges are appointed by the Senate.) Nevertheless, the Dominican Revolutionary Party set a new standard (after 1978) by legalizing all the political parties, allowing the return of those in exile and releasing political prisoners. The governments of our party created an environment such that when Balaguer returned to power he could not go back to his old style of government. For the country as it is today, that would have been unacceptable. He has had to change.

BOEKER: Do you now consider that Balaguer is a democratic politician?

PEÑA-GOMEZ: He is acting as a democratic politician; within his own party he continues to be an autocrat. In general terms I have to admit with sincerity that he has presided over a democratic administration.

BOEKER: Since Trujillo's death civilian governments have consistently weakened the armed forces in the Dominican Republic. Who is responsible for this phenomenon?

PEÑA-GOMEZ: This weakening of the military was not Balaguer's doing. It was President Antonio Guzmán Fernández who removed from office all high-ranking military personnel who were involved in politics. When Balaguer came to power there wasn't that much left for him to do. He is now reintegrating some people previously removed from office. There is now actually a shortage of police. Nobody wants to be in the police force because the pay is so poor.

BOEKER: Are the armed forces now totally outside the political arena?

PEÑA-GOMEZ: For the time being, yes. We need to keep in mind, however, that if Balaguer runs for reelection and does not have enough support, he will resort to his traditional scheme of turning the army into an official political party.

BOEKER: Is there anything the administration in Washington could have done during the past five years to help the Dominican Republic deal with its political and economic difficulties?

PEÑA-GOMEZ: Balaguer does not have a foreign policy, not with the United States nor with Europe. He doesn't have a program. In reality it cannot be said that he has made any recommendations to the U.S. administration. Nobody knows him. Balaguer is a ruler who operates strictly on a personalistic basis. He does not meet with any economic team; he sends for a minister to talk to him and then does not see him for three months. He does not plan anything. However, it must be recognized that he is a resourceful man.

BOEKER: So you respect him?

PEÑA-GOMEZ: Balaguer is a great figure in the Dominican Republic, who has been president five times. He is one of the most solid intellectuals in the country. But his vision of economic policy is a backward one. He believes that development comes through the construction of great pharaonic projects.

FISHER: In historical terms, has Balaguer been a positive force for democracy?

PEÑA-GOMEZ: Now he is, but this had not always been the case in the past. But it must be recognized that upon Trujillo's death, Balaguer quickly dismantled the organizations which had been Trujillo's instruments of terror.

BOEKER: Here in the Dominican Republic people talk about a potential leadership crisis. What is going to happen after Joaquín Balaguer and Juan Bosch abandon politics? How do you feel about the next generation?

PEÑA-GOMEZ: The analysis is only partially correct. My mentor is Juan Bosch who together with Dr. Balaguer represents the statesmen of this generation. The mistakes made by Bosch took him out of the political game. His role was a marginal one after 1973, when he left the Dominican Revolutionary Party, to the point that in 1978 he obtained only eighteen thousand votes. This did not entitle his group to congressional representation. Thus it was our party (the Dominican Revolutionary Party) and Balaguer, who dominated the government for ten years. It is only recently that Bosch's group has achieved the status of a third political party and obtained seventeen representatives in the same election in which our party won forty-eight seats.

The premise of the question—what is going to happen when Juan Bosch and Joaquín Balaguer are no longer in politics—does not take into account the success of our party. After Bosch left us, he was no longer a national leader. We have already filled the political vacuum. When we had less experience than Bosch, we gained power and governed democratically for four years. I don't see why people are pessimistic. Their analysis is very superficial. Bosch has recouped some of his leadership, but he has not influenced Dominican politics for the past ten years. What is difficult to predict is what will happen to Balaguer's Reformist Party.

BOEKER: Do you believe your party can overcome the temptation to split again rather than presenting a unified front?

PEÑA-GOMEZ: Of course, our party has been divided three times in the past, with the largest division at the time Bosch left to form his own party. But we have overcome these divisions.

BOEKER: So you are ready for 1990?

PEÑA-GOMEZ: We are ready to compete. That is what we have always done.

BOEKER: The new administration in Washington, like all incoming administrations, will rethink policy toward Latin America. Do you have any recommendations?

PEÑA-GOMEZ: The first thing to be done is to get closer to the leaders of Latin America. Make them its partners. Second, implement policy designed to protect Latin American exports and resume economic and technological aid for development. Finally, we need help in reaching a solution to the debt problem; otherwise, there is not going to be further development in Latin America. I am opposed to a moratorium, but I do think that the lenders have to reach some agreement to write off a considerable part of the debt.

The administration in the United States is going to be more liberal than Ronald Reagan's. Yet the Reagan administration was a great surprise in many respects, particularly in its closer relations with the Soviet Union. This is very positive for Latin America because it will contribute to less rigidity in the communist parties of Latin America, as Gorbachev is striving for a democratic communism and liquidating the authoritarianism of the past.

The United States and Latin American Democracy

I have never understood how the United States, a genuinely democratic nation, with the oldest democracy in the hemisphere, could be so disinterested for most of its history in democratic government and values in Latin America.

Osvaldo Hurtado—July 1988

The whole culture of anti-Americanism as it has existed in Latin America since the early decades of this century has fortunately receded, opening the doors of our countries and our people to authentic cooperation. The moment has come to initiate this new kind of relationship between the United States and Latin America.

Carlos Andrés Pérez—September 1988

Americans tend to think that support for the spread of democracy has been one of the cornerstones of U.S. foreign policy since 1776, when the Declaration of Independence proclaimed to all people their inalienable political rights. They can be shocked by Latin Americans' perceptions, reflected in Osvaldo Hurtado's harsh judgment above, that U.S. foreign policy in Latin America has not looked that way to Latins. Until recently Latins' perception was that the U.S. got along quite well with Latin American dictators and was indeed virtually a patron of some of them, like General Somoza in Nicaragua.

Latin Americans sensed a new direction in U.S. policy when former President Jimmy Carter gave a dramatic, high profile in U.S. foreign policy to two of the guiding principles of American governance, democracy and human rights (the "rights of man" as Thomas Jefferson called them two hundred years earlier). "One has to give President Carter credit," says Hurtado, "for having changed (the U.S.'s) lack of concern into concern for Latin American democracy." (p. 251) Carlos Andrés Pérez also perceives a clear shift in U.S. policy. "There has also been a change of attitude in the industrialized countries. Before, the attitude of the U.S. was suspect by virtue of its support for some dictatorships. Today the attitude of U.S. governments is one of frank opposition to military coups and strong defense of democracy in Latin America." (p. 132)

The Latin civilian leaders speaking through this book all believe that the unambiguous and energetic U.S. support for democracy in Latin America under Jimmy Carter and Ronald Reagan—after a fitful start—contributed to the decline of military dictatorship and the renaissance of democracy in Latin America.

Jimmy Carter's thrust of human rights to the top of a moral agenda for U.S. foreign policy created a changed perception of U.S. policy in Latin America. Latin Americans perceived a withdrawal of U.S. support for the military dictatorships whose human rights violations Carter protested. The effect in Latin American eyes was to discredit military government and to sap its legitimacy.

U.S. policy thus contributed to an environment in which military governors themselves felt pressure to define their mission as completed and to generate their own plans for withdrawal from power. Civilian politicians were encouraged to press their demands and protesters of military governments' abuses were emboldened by a new sense of patronage and protection from abroad. Even the former military rulers grudgingly recognize Carter's contribution to the atmosphere in which military government lost its ability to renew its license on power.

Much more controversial was the impact of Jimmy Carter's specific diplomatic pressures on critical decisions in the political transition in particular countries. The civilians struggling to get into power, including those represented in this book, are virtually unanimous in their view that U.S. policy contributed to some key successes in their struggle. The proud military governors who were the object of Carter's diplomatic pressures, including the four military ex-presidents represented in this book, are equally unanimous that U.S. pressures were not helpful and may, they say, have complicated their tasks in dragging their military colleagues out of government. Most American diplomats trying to carry out Carter's policies on the ground, as I did in Bolivia, will agree with the Latin civilian politicians on this point. U.S. policy had its effect on some specific decisions in Latin America's passage to democracy as well as on the general environment in which the military lost its license on power to civilians. Carter's policy also saved lives as it focused intense international scrutiny on the cases of specific individuals under detention by military governments.

Yet as Jimmy Carter finished his four years in the White House, the political results of his thrust for rights and democracy appeared meager, and the evidence for the powerful trend just getting under way was limited. During Carter's term the specific tactical successes for democracy were most apparent in the smaller states—the ones more easily pushed around, one could have judged cynically at the time, as some in the U.S. did.

In Bolivia, the military government of General Hugo Banzer decided to step down in 1978 and call elections, in part because of U.S. censure of its human rights abuses. The most specific effect of U.S. pressures, however, was probably in preventing the military from canceling a scheduled 1978 election because it feared this brusque reversal of its own ostensible democratic opening would bring a cut in needed U.S. aid. But as Carter left office a fledgling civilian regime in Bolivia could not be stabilized in the face of the rise within the military of a dangerous clique up to its ears in the drug business.

In Ecuador a successful transition to elected civilian government was achieved in 1980, and the key surviving civilian leader in that transition, ex-President Osvaldo Hurtado, gives Carter's policy and diplomacy significant credit for keeping the transition on course. Hurtado describes the Ecuadoran transition from 1978 to 1980 as plagued by continual pressures and conspiracies within the military, and even more so, civilian groups. These groups tried to drag out, and eventually cancel, the protracted schedule for return to civilian rule via a constitutional reform and a national referendum, elections and a delayed transmission of power to an elected president. Hurtado says, "diplomatic messages sent to the military government by President Carter had great influence in preventing these anti-democratic forces from succeeding. These forces wanted first to stop the constitutional referendum, then the elections and finally the transmission of power we had legitimately won." (p. 251)

The key figure in Uruguay's transition to civilian rule, Julio Sanguinetti, also gives Carter's diplomacy credit for influencing significant decisions made by the military. Sanguinetti believes that the military's basic decision on a timetable for return to civilian rule was made under the pressure of high level criticism of the military's human rights abuses by Carter's administration. Carter's diplomacy, says Sanguinetti,

> . . . without doubt . . . had a positive impact. I can highlight one event. The timetable for the transition was set the day before Terence Todman, the U. S. assistant secretary of state for Latin American affairs under President Carter, arrived as an envoy to discuss human rights and a political solution for Uruguay. The military leadership met and set the timetable. Nothing was announced at the time. But much later the date of that meeting became known and we were able to determine without any question that the military's decision was made under the pressure of Todman's visit." (p. 93)

With Latin America's perception that Jimmy Carter's support for human rights and democracy was a new and perhaps personal cause, it is not surprising that Latin American leaders feared a conservative U.S. president, Ronald Reagan, would bring a change in that policy. During the first two years of Reagan's first term there appeared to be real cause for such concern. Reagan's first secretary of state, former general Al Haig, enthusiastically embraced Jeane Kirkpatrick's dichotomy of "authoritarian" (i.e., military) and "totalitarian" (i.e., Marxist) dictatorship as an apparent apology for military dictators in Latin America. Haig dispatched high-ranking U.S. emissaries to signal U.S. goodwill to military regimes in Argentina, Brazil, and Uruguay, just at the point when these regimes were on their way out, under the build-up of popular pressures.

Senator Jesse Helms and some other conservative Republicans were apparently looking for some dramatic signals of a clear change in policy on Latin American dictators. Helms pushed hard in 1981 for the Reagan administration to send a new ambassador to Bolivia to take up a dialogue with the corrupt and drug-tainted military clique which had some months earlier overthrown Bolivia's civilian government. The U.S. ambassador in La Paz had been withdrawn in 1980 by Carter, largely because of threats against the ambassador's life from sources close to the same military clique. Sending a U.S. ambassador back after a period of more than six months inevitably became associated in Latin American and U.S. eyes with some element of endorsement for, and willingness to work with, a corrupt military government.

The Reagan team's vocal admiration for General Pinochet's Chicago school economic policies and the efforts of Reagan's first ambassador in Santiago to work with Pinochet also left the Chilean opposition concerned. Gabriel Valdés calls Reagan's first ambassador in Santiago "a Pinochet sympathizer." (p. 32)

For the first half of Reagan's first term, U.S. policy on Latin American democracy and dictatorship was a muddle. A confusing and acrimonious debate raged in which a few conservatives sympathetic to some of Latin America's remaining military dictators seemed at least to have the loudest voices. But they did not have the last word. After 1982 the gradual assertion of George Shultz's role as secretary of state made a difference. Shultz, a careful man suspicious of ideologues, correctly perceived that Latin America was turning broadly against dictatorship in any form. He quietly dropped Kirkpatrick's concept of bad and not-so-bad dictatorships. Reagan himself was actually a strong, if not always consistent, proponent of democratic values in U.S. foreign policy, as indicated most clearly in his moving May 1982 speech to the British Parliament. Reagan's views on the role of democratic values in U.S. foreign policy were much closer to Shultz's than Haig's. But Reagan's and Shultz's own views on democracy took longer to find their logical role in Latin American policy than elsewhere. By the end of the last year of his first term, Reagan, Shultz, and their key appointees on Latin American affairs had established a clear line regarding Latin American democracy. Reagan settled on a policy which basically followed the same lines established by Carter, despite some differences in rhetoric.

Haig's Assistant Secretary of State for Latin American Affairs, Thomas Enders, was able to take some clarifying steps as early as 1981. Despite enormous pressures from Senator Helms, Enders managed to delay for a year sending a new U.S. ambassador to Bolivia. Enders correctly wanted to send a clear message of disapproval to the military regime there. By the end of 1981 the key figures in Bolivia's military regime were on their way to indictment in the U.S. on drug-related charges. At that point even Senator Helms had to recognize that General García-Mesa's regime had nothing to offer the U.S. on any issues which mattered, of which drugs was the most important.

In Chile, Reagan's policy during his second term dropped its ambivalence and established a clear pattern of actions supporting human rights and encouraging the democratic opposition to

Pinochet. In August 1985, the administration supported negotiations between Pinochet's government and its opposition. In February 1986, the Reagan Administration pressed anew for extradition of those responsible for the murder of Orlando Letelier and his American colleague Ronni Moffitt in Washington. In July 1986, the administration protested bloody suppression of demonstrators in Chile and proposed in the U.N. Human Rights Commission a resolution very critical of Pinochet's regime. Such actions established that U.S. support for human rights and democracy was more important than regard for Pinochet's economics or his anti-communism.

Reagan's own escalation of the military pressure on the Sandinista regime in Nicaragua ironically brought home a necessary corollary to even those like Senator Helms who were most reluctant to put pressure on "friendly" military regimes. The administration's own policy to resort to force to press for "democratization" in Nicaragua would appear hypocritical unless paired with diplomatic pressures in support of democracy elsewhere in Latin America.

The abrupt and humiliating collapse of military rule in Argentina and General Figueiredo's faithful implementation of Geisel's plan for 1984 presidential elections in Brazil made it clear that the trend to elected civilian governments was a tide that would sweep all of South America. The Reagan administration not only welcomed the trend but continually listed in its recountings of favorable developments to which the administration had contributed the fact that "over ninety percent of Latin Americans now live under democratic government."

The leaders of Argentina and Brazil represented in this book make clear that the transitions to democracy in these two largest South American countries progressed under their own political dynamic, not foreign pressures. But Reagan's reaffirmation of Carter's strong support for democracy and his and George Shultz's continual talk of elected civilian rule as the normal status to which all of Latin America should be headed, contributed to an environment, developed under Carter, of increasing illegitimacy surrounding military government and dictatorship in any form.

The Reagan administration's policy of diplomatic pressures also had some of the same kind of tactical successes for which Latin American leaders credit Carter. In Chile, for example, leaders of the opposition to Pinochet cite diplomatic pressure from the Reagan administration as having influenced important tactical points in the transition similar to Hurtado's and Sanguinetti's judgment of the role of Carter's diplomacy. In December 1987 Reagan and Shultz issued a statement on the conditions which would make it possible to accept the validity of the Chilean plebiscite, including access by the opposition to television. Such access proved critical to the opposition's victory and its leaders believe that U.S. pressure on this point was an important factor.

Gabriel Valdés also sees this kind of tactical success for U.S. diplomacy in the days just before the Chilean plebiscite in October 1988. In the week before the plebiscite the deputy secretary of state called in Pinochet's ambassador to express strong concern about any interruption of the plebiscite. The State Department issued twenty-four hours later a public statement of concern and strong support for a fair plebiscite vote. As some military leaders and civilian supporters of Pinochet absorbed during that fateful week the increasing evidence that Pinochet would lose the plebiscite, "there were people close to him," says Valdés, "who advised that he either cancel or postpone the plebiscite. At that juncture the U.S. Department of State made a statement to the effect that there were some worrisome rumors about the Chilean plebiscite which were a cause of concern to the U.S. government. That was a timely and effective declaration because there was a risk of canceling the plebiscite and of launching another coup." (p. 27)

What do the Carter and Reagan years tell us about the future? In particular what U.S. policies and pressures will be most effective in helping Latin Americans themselves gain democratic control of their own government in the remaining cases of dictatorship—Haiti, Panama, Cuba, and Sandinista Nicaragua? In Chile measured but steady U.S. pressures have played a modest but constructive role in keeping the country's transition on track. U.S. pressures were effective in Chile because they were based on U.S. support for human rights and democracy, enjoyed broad bi-partisan support in the U.S. and could thus be consistently applied. In Panama, however, even massive U.S. economic pressure in the last year of the Reagan administration could not shake the hold of the military leader over the country. In one case, Chile, an increasingly assertive Reagan policy is credited with strengthening the hand of civilian politicians and is welcomed by people long allergic, as all Latins are, to U.S. intervention in their internal politics. In another case, Panama, U.S. trade and financial pressure produced popular resentment and allowed a dictator to wrap himself in the flag of nationalism and play the victim of foreign intervention.

The Latin American leaders themselves find that the critical differences in U.S. policy in the two cases concern both strategy and tactics. At the strategic level the most thoughtful Latin veterans of the passage to democracy believe the effectiveness of the U.S.'s role in pressing for democratic change depends on scrupulous maintenance of the important linkage between human rights and democracy, the one providing the essential credibility for the U.S. role on the other. It is the continual protest of human rights violations which most effectively discredits a dictatorship. It is the argument that only democracy can guarantee human rights which makes pressure for a change in regime appear more than that in the eyes of Latin American peoples. When linked to peoples' universal desire to carry on their lives without arbitrary denial of their rights, U.S. policy carries an unassailable moral force, which cannot be diminished by charges of intervention. Julio Sanguinetti makes this point eloquently, but pointedly:.

> The United States' role on questions of basic human rights is very important because here it has the capacity to exercise a moral influence, with significant political force. It is not so influential in other areas where its policies are either weak or unclear. But in the area of human rights, the U.S.'s own political system provides in its strong guarantees of those rights, a solid base for its role. Why does the U.S. continually raise the flag of human rights when negotiating with the Soviet Union? Because on this issue the U.S. has credibility which strengthens its negotiating leverage, and I think it is a smart approach. The same holds true in our part of the world. When the U.S. carries the flag for human rights, it does so with political credibility and thus its influence is great. (p. 94)

Where U.S. policy has not been effective in exerting pressure on dictatorial regimes, as in Panama, Latin leaders tend to cite the failure to put human rights up front and the quick resort to heavy sanctions, such as trade embargoes. Both tend to leave the U.S. vulnerable to the charge its objective is simply overturning a regime, thus sapping U.S. policy of the strength it derives from broad popular support in Latin America for human rights and democracy and creating an opening for a nationalistic appeal by the dictator. The U.S. was particularly vulnerable to this line of attack in Panama, where important U.S. strategic interests and

U.S. intervention in Panama earlier in this century left Panamanians suspicious of U.S. motives.

Gabriel Valdés makes the same point in explaining why a different U.S. policy of human rights and steady diplomatic pressure worked in the case of Chile:

> I believe that the Chilean experience has proved one thing: foreign intervention generally does not work, and economic boycotts do not produce the expected result, but rather the contrary one, unity against foreign intervention. At the same time we are seeing how in the Chilean case the universalization of the concept of human rights, not just in the sense of torture, but of liberty, is something that the country has accepted and needs and that we have greeted with much enthusiasm. (p. 32)

Mario Vargas Llosa argues that the U.S. should not limit itself to countering the few remaining dictatorships, especially those which affect U.S. security interests, but should aggressively take broader initiatives to strengthen democracy in Latin America and to create a sense of a community of democracies in which all dictatorships are alien bodies. "It is important," Vargas Llosa believes, "that the U.S. take initiatives that give it the image of a country continually promoting democracy in Latin America, rather than just defending its security. It is bad that the image of the U.S. in Latin America is that of a country which seems to react only when its interests are at stake, and not out of conviction, in the spirit of good neighborliness among democracies." (p. 190)

Oscar Arias faults U.S. policy toward the Sandinista regime in Nicaragua on similar grounds—not enough emphasis on human rights as the basis of demands for democracy and use of force and unilateral boycotts in ways which make U.S. strategic interests and foreign intervention the battleground, not democracy and human rights for Nicaraguans. Arias does not see an incompetent and impoverished Marxist regime in Nicaragua as immune to erosion from the same kind of internal and diplomatic pressures which have humbled military regimes throughout Latin America. Arias talks of "the failure of the Communist experience in their country (Nicaragua)." (p. 109) He sees both the disastrous economic management of the Sandinistas and continuing strong internal dissent and resentment of their political and human rights abuses as providing the sparks which can be provided continual oxygen by diplomatic pressures for democratization within the context of the Central American peace process.

Arias considers the Nicaraguans' agreement in the Central American peace accords to parallel pursuit of peace negotiations and internal democratic reforms as both his greatest personal achievement and the lever the Latin Americans and the U.S. can use to apply continual pressure for internal change. Arias is sharply critical of U.S. and Latin American failure to hammer the Sandinistas publicly for every abuse of human rights and every instance of abridgment of political freedoms. "I am only sorry that I seem to be the only one called upon to raise a voice every time a step backwards is taken." (p. 107) Arias believes any fatigue in protesting the Sandinistas human rights abuses saps the call for democratization of its greatest source of strength and resonance inside Nicaragua.

Arias vigorously opposes any proposal to unlink democracy and security in Central America. It would be tempting but foolish, he believes, to concentrate on international security accords in Central America while leaving internal democratic reforms for a later stage. "I do not believe that there will be real peace in Nicaragua unless it moves toward pluralism and democracy. One cannot exempt any signatory from being democratic because the essence of the plan I presented to my colleagues is precisely the democratization of the whole region." (p. 108)

In Central America or elsewhere, diplomatic pressures for human rights and democracy are most effective when the Latin American democracies join the U.S., which some have not always been willing to do. The collaborative and deliberate approach is clearly the one Latin America's current democratic leadership would like to pursue with the U.S. Their model is the approach the European countries and the U.S. pursued in nurturing democracy in Portugal, Spain, and Greece, an approach based not on sanctions but on continual diplomatic pressures on dictatorships and the prospect of political and economic carrots, if they adopt democratic reforms. The Latin Americans judge that the U.S. acting on its own reaches for quick success through forceful measures, such as trade embargoes, when the tide of Latin American history opens the way to steady, if gradual change through more subtle, collaborative pressures. As Raúl Alfonsín puts it: "If we are going to live in a developing continent, clearly defined as democratic, why the unilateral action? And why not talk about our problem? I believe that through dialogue and by getting to know each other, we will find fruitful solutions for all the parties involved." (p. 61)

Obviously one of the reasons the Reagan administration could not work out a coordinated approach with the Latin Americans in Nicaragua or Panama, was that the Latins were unwilling to take the forceful actions favored by the Reagan administration. The Latins are generally unwilling to support armed intervention or trade sanctions against other Latin American states, even when they are errant military or Marxist dictatorships. Much of this is due to the instinctive fear of small states that such intervention, if generally sanctioned, will be aimed at them some day. But there is also increasingly a political judgment behind their preferred diplomatic strategy—the political judgment reflected in Alfonsín's confidence that the hemisphere is increasingly being defined as democratic. Latin America's leaders believe that history in Latin America is not on the side of either Marxism or military dictatorship. The remaining dictatorships are seen as isolated and vulnerable to erosion through the slow pressures of internal dissent, encouraged by diplomatic action from democratic neighbors. The Latin Americans see the trends as ones in which patient diplomacy will have its rewards without paying the price of armed intervention and trade boycotts.

Behind this conclusion of the Latin leaders represented in this book is their judgment that Marxism is a spent force in Latin America. In Chile, the Marxists' power in the beleaguered government of Salvador Allende was seen by many Chileans in 1973 as the justification for Pinochet's coup. Today, however, the Chilean Communist party, the oldest and most powerful in South America, is not seen as a significant threat. Gabriel Valdés sees "a party that is suffering all the crises of international communism caused by 'perestroika' and internal divisions. We don't think it will survive here, as it did not in Argentina and Uruguay where it is almost non-existent. In Chile we think that with democracy the Communist party is going to disappear, because it no longer has ideological force." (p. 31) Arias talks of communism in Nicaragua as "a failure."

Castro's Cuba, once a source of fascination for Latin intellectuals, is today ignored in most of Latin America (except Central America, where Castro supports insurgents in El Salvador and the Sandinistas in Nicaragua). Peru is perhaps the one country in South America where Marxist ideologies still play a significant role, both in the United Left Coalition and the Maoist Shining Path guerrilla movement.

Over the longer term Latin America's leaders expect their region's identity as a community of democracies to take some definite, if still not well defined, political form. The model that many of the leaders I talked to have in mind is the European Community. Without quite intending to be so, the European Community became an association of democratic states which created a powerful pole of attraction for others, such as Greece, Spain, Turkey, and Portugal, whom the Community would not admit so long as they were non-democratic. For political and economic reasons many Latin American leaders long for such a dynamic in Latin America. The formation of the informal Group of Eight democratic countries in Latin America is a first effort to create this kind of dynamic, which the group put in practice by suspending Panama from participation after General Noriega deposed its civilian president. Several of the smaller democratic governments, such as Ecuador's, are pressing to join the Group of Eight so that they can hold up to their military that the country will be suspended from a prestigious organization if the military takes over.

Gabriel Valdés explicitly looks for this dynamic in a community of Latin American democracies. "The Greek colonels did not participate in the European Economic Community and neither did Franco. The EEC is defined in terms of human rights. Here in the Americas we still need to consecrate the principle of human rights as the basis for our relations. Once this concept is promulgated the conclusion follows that the hemisphere is an association of democracies and that dictatorship is a foreign body which arises by virtue of violating certain rights." (p. 33) Others talk of giving still greater content to a community of democracies. Rafael Caldera suggests non-recognition of governments resulting from coups, which Venezuela tried on its own after 1958 under Rómulo Betancourt, its first president after the fall of the dictator Pérez Jiménez. If all states of the hemisphere adopted a common policy of non-recognition of regimes imposing themselves by force, it would give decisive effect to the existence of a community of Latin American democracies, Caldera argues.

The Organization of American States, for which several of the Latin leaders in this book express low regard, is clearly not the political base for the new community of democracies Latin America's leaders seek. The Organization of American States is still seen as basically a structure, if little used, for Latin America to deal with the U.S. Latin Americans' desire for a political community of democracies may more logically take the form of a Latin American organization, with a friendly U.S. on the outside. The Group of Eight is an initial response to this desire for closer collaboration and reinforcement among Latin America's democratic leaders. This Group could grow into the community of democracies many Latins seek if it expands its membership to include the smaller democratic states. If the Group of Eight remains a clique of eight, now seven, and concentrates on international coordination of these countries' external diplomacy, it will leave Latins looking elsewhere to realize the dream of a political structure for Latin America's democracies.

The model Latins most often mention, the European Community, had its origins in a far-reaching economic accord creating a common market. Political cooperation followed later. Without a similarly far-reaching economic dimension, a Latin community of democracies may remain a mirage on the far horizon. Given Latin America's frustration over a generation in trying to give real life to a Latin American Free Trade Area, one is tempted to judge Latin American economic integration even more of a comforting, but utopian vision than a political community. In fact, however, the psychological perceptions pushing Latin America toward economic integration are much stronger than the U.S. has yet perceived.

Many of the Latin leaders in this book express a sense of desperation at Latin America being left behind economically and technologically in a rapidly developing world of powerful trade blocs—the European Community, the U.S.-Canadian Free Trade Area, and Japan, a bloc unto itself. And all of these leaders draw the conclusion that economic integration is an essential part of Latin America's prospects for reversing this widely perceived decline. To President José Sarney in Brazil:

> Latin America is the only continent which has gradually gone backwards. Some decades ago, Argentina had a per capita income higher than that of Italy, and no country in Latin America had a per capita GNP lower that that of the less developed East Asian countries. Today, Latin America has fallen behind these countries; the situation has drastically changed. We have serious problems. All this reflects a continent which suffers from a disease. . . . From my first day in office I have, therefore, given high priority to Latin American integration. (p. 280)

Carlos Andrés Pérez talks in similarly sharp terms of a Latin American malaise or trap and integration as the only way out. He sees a long path for getting there but also a new "consciousness of the necessity of integration." (p. 135)

The leader of Colombia's conservative party, Misael Pastrana, puts it even more strongly:

> With the consolidation of the European Common Market, possible renovation of the Soviet economy, Japan an economic super-power, and the United States and Canada more closely tied, if Latin America does not do something to become part of this inter-dependent world, it will be off the map. If Latin America does not integrate it will remain a foreign body within a world of integrated economies. (p. 217)

There is strong economic logic for the integration these leaders seek. The dynamic trade creation resulting from a lowering of regional trade barriers, especially if combined with a common external tariff, could provide a burst of energy to Latin American growth some day. Oscar Arias reminds us that in his region the "Central American Common Market was the most dynamic factor for growth in the last thirty years," (p. 105) until Central American wars cut short its life. At the sub-regional level significant integration is taking place, particularly between Argentina and Brazil and among the Andean countries.

Latin America's leaders do not see a role for the U.S. in their own problem of giving some real content to their dream for integration. U.S. leaders will, however, need to recognize that this drive, and the logic behind it, are quite strong. Latin America will revive its drive for integration in coming years and the U.S. need not see this as in any sense a move away from cooperation with the U.S. Carlos Andrés Pérez believes an impetus for revival of Latin American integration could come as soon as the debt crisis eases. He believes Latin America's economic and debt crises have sapped the force of earlier drives for integration as hard-pressed leaders have been forced to turn inward and concentrate on their overwhelming national problems.

As Latin America's democratic leaders each struggle with the problems they see as threatening their young democracies they are not happy with the state of the U.S.'s understanding of and response to their plight. They all approach the Bush years with a desire for a greater appreciation in Washington and a more supportive response.

Since 1982, Latin America's leaders have seen their economic crisis as the principal threat to the consolidation of democracy. That crisis steeped for six years as a slow-brewing one of stagnation and gradually declining standards of living. In 1988 and 1989, however, a surge of hyperinflation in Argentina, Brazil, and Peru threatened to blow the top off these societies' social stability by causing a rapid erosion of assets and incomes and a depression in some of these important countries. Yet throughout the Eighties several of the leaders of newly restored democratic regimes sensed little concern, even interest, in the White House for their overriding preoccupation. Peru's president from 1980 to 1985, Fernando Belaúnde Terry, says he left a 1984 meeting with Ronald Reagan at the White House feeling "there never was a serious desire in Washington to help." (p. 175) Ecuador's president from 1981 to 1984, Osvaldo Hurtado, expresses similar disillusionment after a meeting with Reagan in Washington:

> I did not go to the White House to ask specifically for help for Ecuador; I talked about problems that were critical for the region. President Reagan's reply was that Latin America's crisis would be solved by renegotiation of debt, by austerity programs and the 'locomotive effect' of a booming U.S. economy on the growth of our economies. During my presidency the U.S. Administration, while recognizing our problems, did not take any specific steps to support us in our efforts to overcome the crisis. (p. 252)

These two presidents of countries which had just emerged from military dictatorships obviously expected a different U. S. reaction to their countries' deep economic crisis.

In 1989 the lack of a directed U.S. response to Latin America's persistent economic stagnation remained Latin leaders' principal indictment of U.S. policy. There is an element of incomprehension and some bitterness in Latin leaders' perception of U.S. lack of interest in their major economic crisis since the Great Depression.

Raúl Alfonsín laments,

> The United States uses a different criterion when looking south. Just as it is true that we have advanced greatly in regard to democracy,...so it needs to be understood that the burden of the

foreign debt is generating tremendous problems in our continent—stagnation, misery, drug traffic, guerrillas. We are clearly seeing people who desperately look for alternatives—still within the system for now, but who knows what can happen. . . . Something is very wrong. People are looking for alternatives, seeking changes; they are desperate with things as they are. After World War II, the Allied countries acted with creativity, imagination, and generosity—the Marshall Plan—and democracies were thus consolidated. Today in Latin America the democracies are being reborn within an economic framework similar to the post war era. Even though there has been no war, our economies are devastated. Yet we are being subjected to a [n economic] Treaty of Versailles. 'This cannot be.' (p. 60)

"I would not be surprised," says Osvaldo Hurtado, "if in the year 2000 the level of development and the welfare of the Latin American people will correspond to that of the Seventies, which would mean that we would have lost thirty years of development. This is going to happen to a continent with enormous possibilities and one which is very much linked to the hemispheric security which so worries the United States." (p. 253)

Thoughtful Latin American leaders like President Julio Sanguinetti in Uruguay see a constructive U.S. response to Latin America's economic crisis as more than the debt issue, as important as that issue is. Sanguinetti gives equal weight to U.S. trade policies, particularly in gaining significant concessions for Latin America's products in multilateral GATT negotiations and avoiding new protectionist barriers in the U.S. against Latin American goods.

Despite the more histrionic views of some U.S. commentators, none of the leaders I talked to said democracy in their country would fail without debt relief. Latin American leaders do not see their democracy as that fragile. Debt relief is seen rather as a necessary step to give them leeway to invest more at home and thus contribute to reviving growth. Debt relief is part of the solution to a long-term economic problem, not a political panacea for Latin America. Latin leaders' attitude is more reflective of the mature realism of Latin democracy today than the hysteria of one-issue politics. Debt relief is needed, but so are other tough actions by the Latins themselves to gain the return of enormous amounts of Latin American capital which have left their countries.

But many Latin American leaders believe they have now reached the point where they cannot service their debt and meet their minimum needs at home. "Our debt," says Ecuador's President Rodrigo Borja, "is disproportionate to our capacity to pay. This has led us up a blind alley; we either pay the debt or take care of the domestic needs of our people. We cannot do both." (p. 259)

Mexico's new President Carlos Salinas de Gortari began his administration determined to press for a significant reduction of Mexico's debt, believing, as other Latin leaders do, that the U.S. administration had to play a role if he were to succeed. In July 1989, Mexico and its foreign bank creditors did reach a precedent-setting agreement, with pressure from the Bush administration, involving significant reduction in debt and, more important, financial payments by Mexico to service its debt. Salinas was able to succeed in achieving a path-breaking debt reduction in part because Mexico's claim on U.S. attention exceeds that of any other Latin American country. The effects on the U.S. of protracted economic stagnation in Mexico are very clear, most dramatically in the increased flows of illegal immigrants to the U. S. The Bush administration, thus, had more political room to help make a deal between Mexico and U.S. banks. Many other Latin American countries hope to achieve relief comparable to that obtained by Mexico.

The second major issue where Latin America's democratic leaders are looking for major new approaches from President Bush is drugs. The threat of drugs to their own societies is starkly apparent to Latin America's leaders. Drugs are "the cancer of modern society," says Carlos Salinas; "the most formidable threat humanity has faced," says Carlos Andrés Pérez. To Colombia's President Virgilio Barco, the drug trade is "the worst threat that confronts Colombian democracy." The current Latin American presidents with whom I met all expressed a determination to take strong action to fight drug production and use in their countries. But they also expressed a clear sense that cooperation with the U.S. in fighting drugs is not going well, starting with the overall framework of political understanding among governments.

Latin America and the U.S. "are engaged in a dangerous and useless controversy," says Carlos Andrés Pérez. The U.S. throws blame at Latin American countries as producers of drugs. "Latin Americans are seeking to avoid responsibility by saying that drug production is driven by consumption and financing in the United States." (p. 136) The political tone of some of this effort to lodge blame elsewhere has gotten quite ugly. In particular, the effort in the U.S. Congress to brand Mexico's anti-drug efforts as unworthy of U.S. "certification" has raised Mexican national sensibilities to a point which could give drug cooperation with the U.S. a bad name in Mexico.

Carlos Salinas bristles at the perceived breach of Mexico's sovereignty: "What happens in Mexico is the exclusive responsibility of the Mexican people and the Mexican government," he says. Virgilio Barco is equally prickly in reacting to criticism by Amnesty International and some U.S. congressional voices of rights abuses allegedly involved in Colombian armed forces' treatment of captured guerrillas and narcotics producers. This backbiting over failings in respective national drug efforts is in danger of being blown out of proportion without a stronger framework of political cooperation at the highest level to fight drugs throughout the hemisphere.

Latin American leaders are looking to President Bush to join them in creating such a framework. They want, in effect, a healthier inter-American political environment for everyone's fight against drugs. Carlos Andrés Pérez and less specifically several Latin leaders have suggested a high-level agreement which commits all participants to take major new action in their countries, thus strengthening everyone's political hand at home, and to adopt specific new international measures. Carlos Andrés Pérez reasons that drug traffic, "is a major international crime and if we do not forge a common effort to fight it, we will never resolve this problem. The U.S. could help a lot by prosecuting consumers, and by cooperating with Latin American authorities within a well thought out inter-American plan that would include intelligence, technical cooperation and economic assistance. It might require a major Latin American conference to take some joint actions against drugs. We at least have to prevent the charade of drug traffickers hiding behind the protection of national sovereignty. An international police, whose effectiveness does not stop at borders, should be established. There has to be an all-fronts attack on the drug problem." (p. 136)

The leaders of the countries most threatened by the drug problem are clear that one of the benefits they seek from a new agreement on fighting drugs is major new action by the U.S. itself to limit its massive consumption of drugs. Virgilio Barco and other Colombians express a sense of desperation that their own efforts to fight the pernicious spread of drug money and power in Colombia can never succeed as long as the huge U.S. market for drugs offers such ready profits to producers and traffickers of cocaine. "The worst threats to Colombia's democracy," says Barco, "are the tolerance which cocaine consumption enjoys in the U.S. and other countries, as well as the tolerance for growth and transportation of raw materials to processing centers and for laundering the profits generated from all these illegal activities." (p. 203)

In Peru and Bolivia there is a similar sense of despair that the present powerful attraction of the drug market in the U.S. is too forceful for their own national efforts to succeed. Meanwhile their democratic institutions are being eroded, particularly the court system. "The power of drug traffic is terrible," says Mario Vargas Llosa in Peru. "It creates a source of power which conspires against democratic authority. Drug traffickers acquire such great economic power that they can defeat institutions responsible for enforcement by corrupting the military, police, judges and politicians. All that is already happening in Peru." (p. 191)

Latin America's democratic leaders all express a grim determination to fight drug production, financial power, and consumption in their own countries. But they believe they will not succeed unless drug use, particularly in the U.S., declines parallel with their own efforts. New U.S. programs against drug consumption are thus vital to their own prospects.

Beyond the specific areas of cooperation between the U.S. and Latin America's democracies, there is a strong desire for a new quality in the relationship between the U.S. and Latin America's democratic leadership. One after another, Latin America's leaders speaking out in this book have expressed their desires and hopes for a closer relationship with the U.S. and its leader. Yet almost in puzzlement they wonder why the United States is not more interested in them. Raúl Alfonsín laments, "the people of the United States just don't think of Latin America as very important in their foreign policy. While there is of course concern for the situation in countries such as Cuba, Nicaragua or Panama, the general problems of Latin America are just not portrayed to the American people as a subject of importance."(p. 60)

There was an expectation that U.S. lack of interest would change with the dawn of democratic government throughout Latin America, and there is great frustration that it has not. After all, Latin America and the Caribbean represent today the greatest concentration of democratic states outside Europe—four hundred million people, led by modern, reform-minded democratic leaders representing the political and economic ideals the U.S. sought to foster, mostly in frustration, at the time of the Alliance for Progress.

Why the neglect? Quite simply, the U.S. has been busy elsewhere. In its diplomatic approach to the south, U.S. energies for most of the last decade have been absorbed in Central America, where U.S. security interests have been affected by a Marxist takeover in Nicaragua, insurgency in El Salvador, and a drug-tainted military leadership in Panama. Latin America's democratic leaders are convinced that U.S. priorities should change to devote more attention to the other ninety-five percent of Latin America which is ultimately more important to the U.S. than Central America.

Latin America's democratic leaders also feel keenly that they deserve the same credibility in American eyes as the democratic leadership of Western European countries. The Latin American democrats believe more could be achieved for U.S. and Latin American policies if the president of the U.S. dealt with them as he does his counterparts in the European Community. They would like to be consulted. They would like to receive some of the phone calls the president of the U.S. exchanges with European leaders. Oscar Arias' plain advice to President Bush is that he "should listen more to those (in Latin America) who have been elected by our people to direct the destiny of our countries." (p. 111)

If President Bush seeks such a new relationship based on respect among fellow democratic leaders of the hemisphere, he will find doors open to him in a way they have not been for the U.S. in a generation. He will be dealing with pragmatic, flexible, and problem-solving politicians who are more his "kind of guy" than U.S. Presidents have ever found in Latin America. And they are prepared to deal with the U.S. largely without the psychological and defensive baggage of the anti-Yankee past of Latin American populism.

The spread of democracy under realistic and pragmatic leaders has created an opportunity ready to be realized by the leadership of the U.S. and of Latin America's democracies. Carlos Andrés Pérez has said it aptly: "The whole culture of anti-Americanism ...as it has existed since the early decades of this century has fortunately receded, opening the doors of our countries and our people to authentic cooperation. The moment has come to initiate this new kind of relationship between the United States and Latin America."

That kind of relationship, says Raúl Alfonsín, "consists fundamentally in recognizing both our mutual interests and our differences—what I call maturity between friends."

Paul H. Boeker
President, Institute of the Americas

Paul Boeker, a veteran career diplomat of twenty-seven years experience, served in key policy posts under both Democratic and Republican Administrations. He was appointed Ambassador by both President Carter, 1977 to Bolivia, and President Reagan, 1984 to Jordan. Long considered one of the U.S. Foreign Service's top strategic planners, Boeker served on Henry Kissinger's policy planning staff in 1974 and again as a member of Secretary of State George Shultz's Policy Planning Council, 1983 to 1984. From 1980 to 1981, Boeker was Director of the prestigious Foreign Service Institute in Washington.

In 1988, Paul Boeker left the U.S. diplomatic service to take over the presidency of the Institute of the Americas, an independent, non-partisan institute for research, analysis and dialogue on the major challenges facing the countries of the America's—challenges such as consolidating democracy, reviving economic growth and development, countering narcotics abuse and traffic, and protecting the environment.

From July to October 1988, Paul Boeker carried out the interviews with twenty-six key leaders of Latin America's democratic revival represented in his book, "Lost Illusions." He benefitted from the help of two Latin American colleagues, Carlos Pino of Chile who recorded and transcribed the interviews, and Sula Sragovicz of Colombia who assisted in translating them.